Counter-radicalisation policy a
the securing of British identity

Manchester University Press

Counter-radicalisation policy and the securing of British identity

The politics of Prevent

Thomas Martin

Manchester University Press

The right of Thomas Martin to be identified as the author of this work has been asserted by him in accordance with the Copyright, Designs and Patents Act 1988.

Published by Manchester University Press
Altrincham Street, Manchester M1 7JA
www.manchesteruniversitypress.co.uk

British Library Cataloguing-in-Publication Data
A catalogue record for this book is available from the British Library

ISBN 978 1 5261 4008 1 hardback
ISBN 978 1 5261 5611 2 paperback

First published 2019

The publisher has no responsibility for the persistence or accuracy of URLs for any external or third-party internet websites referred to in this book, and does not guarantee that any content on such websites is, or will remain, accurate or appropriate.

Typeset by Newgen Publishing UK

Contents

Tables

Acknowledgements

This research would not have been possible without the generous support provided by the Economic and Social Research Council. I am thankful that it is still possible to acquire research funding for critical inquiry such as this.

This research benefitted greatly from the interviews that I was able to undertake with many of those responsible for the Prevent policy. While I did not cite them all directly in the text, they were of incomparable help, shaping my thinking on the policy. I am deeply grateful to all of those who gave up their time to talk with me on this subject.

Special thanks are due to Stefan Elbe and Shane Brighton for their assistance with the research. Without their insight and generosity, this would have been a much weaker piece of work.

I would like to thank all the staff at Manchester University Press, and especially my editor, Robert Byron, for their expertise and assistance, and for making the publication of this book a real pleasure.

Finally, none of this would have been remotely possible without the love and support of my family and friends. My eternal thanks to my parents, Caroline and Clive, and my brother, Luke. I have been immensely fortunate to have such kind and generous parents. Thanks are also due to Leo and Dave for putting up with me for so many years.

Lastly, my darling Rebecca. You continue to amaze and inspire me.

Interviewees

During the course of this research, I was fortunate enough to interview many key figures who played a part in the making of the Prevent policy. I am extremely grateful for their time.

Many of those interviewed have held a number of different roles. I have noted here only those positions that were of direct relevance to this book. Some interviewees preferred for their contributions to the research to be anonymised. I have included here the term by which they will be referred in the text, to give an indication of the scope of the research.

Hazel Blears	Minister of State for Policing, Security and Community Safety (2003–6); Secretary of State for Communities and Local Government (2007–9)
Professor Ted Cantle	Author of the 'Cantle Report' for the Home Office in 2001 and Founder of the Institute of Community Cohesion
Lord Carlile of Berriew	Independent Reviewer of Terrorism Legislation (2001–11) and provided independent oversight of the 2011 Prevent Review
Charlie Edwards	Deputy Director for Strategy and Planning in the Office for Security and Counter Terrorism (2009–11), responsible for the development of CONTEST 2011 and for independent oversight of the Prevent Review
Sir Peter Fahy	Chief Constable of Greater Manchester Police (2008–15) and Prevent Lead for the Association of Chief Police Officers (2012–15)

Robert Lambert	Head of Muslim Contact Unit within the Metropolitan Police (2002–7)
Tony McNulty	Minister of State for Security, Counter Terrorism and Policing (2006–8)
Baroness Pauline Neville-Jones	Minister of State for Security and Counter Terrorism (2010–11)
Jacqui Smith	Home Secretary (2007–9)
John Wright	National Coordinator for Prevent within UK Police Service (2007–13)

Official within the Muslim Council of Britain
Senior Civil Servant
Senior Council Official with responsibility for Prevent delivery
Senior Official at the Office for Security and Counter Terrorism
Senior Researcher in a Public Policy Think Tank

Abbreviations

ACPO	Association of Chief Police Officers*
DCLG	Department for Communities and Local Government**
DCSF	Department for Children, Schools and Families†
DfE	Department for Education†
MHCLG	Ministry of Housing, Communities and Local Government**
MCB	Muslim Council of Britain
MCU	Muslim Contact Unit
NPCC	National Police Chiefs' Council*
Ofsted	Office for Standards in Education, Children's Services and Skills
OSCT	Office for Security and Counter-Terrorism
PVE	Preventing Violent Extremism
WRAP	Workshop to Raise Awareness of Prevent

* The National Police Chiefs' Council was established on 1 April 2015, replacing the Association of Chief Police Officers.
** The Department for Communities and Local Government was renamed and made a ministry on the 8 January 2018, becoming the Ministry of Housing, Communities and Local Government.
† The Department for Education was formed on 12 May 2010, replacing the Department for Children, Schools and Families.

Introduction

The 'Trojan Horse' scandal

On 27 November 2013, a letter was allegedly discovered in a school in Birmingham. The concerned member of staff sent it to the Leader of Birmingham City Council, Sir Albert Bore. While of questionable authenticity, it contained the details of a plot termed by those involved as 'Trojan Horse'. The alleged plotters stated in it, '[w]e have an obligation to our children to fulfil our roles and ensure these schools are run on Islamic principals [sic]' (Clarke, 2014: 109; the letter is reproduced in Clarke, 2014: 107–112). The letter outlines a five-step approach to taking over a school, claiming that: 'We have caused a great amount of organised disruption in Birmingham and as a result now have our own Academies and are on the way to getting rid of more head teachers and taking over their schools' (Clarke, 2014: 109). Over the next month, the letter was sent to local council staff, the police and the Department for Education (DfE). It was leaked to the media in February 2014 (Adams, 2014). While the original letter is widely considered to be a hoax due to factual inaccuracies, it was understood to reflect practices that had been seen in some Birmingham schools, detailing how to install new governors sympathetic to the Islamic faith, and how to undermine uncooperative head teachers. Later it became apparent that the DfE had been previously warned in 2010, by a senior Birmingham head teacher, that issues of the nature reported in the Trojan Horse letter were a concern to some in the city.

Upon being leaked to the press, the story prompted numerous headlines and a flurry of activity. Over the course of the next two years, a number of investigations were launched to ascertain whether the activities cited in the letter had credibility, and what lessons needed to be learnt. The Office for Standards in Education, Children's Services and Skills (Ofsted) inspected twenty-one schools, fifteen of which were at the express behest

1

of the DfE. The Education Funding Agency, responsible for funding and monitoring academies, undertook its own, separate investigations. Official inquiries were launched by Birmingham City Council, the DfE and the House of Commons Education Select Committee.[1]

The reason for this activity is a set of concerns, drawn from the original Trojan Horse letter, that these schools were promoting a conservative, Islamic ethos and were distancing themselves from mainstream 'British' society. At one level, this is a question of how much leeway state-maintained schools should have in their curricula, and how schools servicing ethnic minority students should support the cultural and religious beliefs of those communities. Yet these investigations go far beyond mere questions of pedagogy.[2] At stake within the Trojan Horse scandal is a novel question: has this promotion of an Islamic culture, and this distance from 'British values', engendered within these children a vulnerability to radicalisation? This question links security and identity in important and novel ways. 'Trojan Horse' was not a scandal because of the identification of terrorists or the promotion of terrorism. It was a scandal because the conservative Islamic environment allegedly fostered within these schools, and the distance this created from mainstream 'British values', was understood to *generate potential vulnerabilities* among the students towards *becoming* terrorists in the future.

As this book will demonstrate, this interpretation is one that could not have been made prior to the 'Prevent' strategy. Prevent, one of the four pillars of British counter-terrorism strategy instituted in the aftermath of the 9/11 attacks on the United States in 2001, represents an innovative approach to tackling terrorism, one that has been copied and implemented around the world. It seeks to identify and act upon vulnerabilities to radicalisation: the potential that some individuals are seen to display towards becoming violent extremists. The intent of this book is to analyse how British security policy understands this potential for radicalisation as a threat, a potential that therefore requires some form of intervention. It is thus to ask, how can this potential towards radicalisation be identified in the present and made knowable? Once identified, how can these vulnerabilities be acted upon such that their potential for violence is minimised? In so doing, the book argues that Prevent makes this threat of radicalisation knowable through identifying certain identities as secure and others as risky, containing vulnerabilities to radicalisation. The book argues that this analysis of threat, and the institutional responses that have developed to act on it, have produced a novel and important power and means of governing potential threats and, in doing so, a radical new role for the state. In order to secure the United Kingdom from those who may become terrorists, the Prevent policy seeks to generate 'secure' 'British' identities, transforming those identities it understands to be outside this 'Britishness' and, therefore, threatening.

This analysis of vulnerability to radicalisation is what makes possible both the questions asked and the analysis given within the Trojan Horse scandal. On 9 June 2014, Ofsted and the Education Funding Agency made the results of their inspections public. As a result of the twenty-one inspections carried out by Ofsted in response to the Trojan Horse affair, five of the schools were judged inadequate and put into special measures.[3] Within a year, schools that had been judged to be 'outstanding' were now 'inadequate'.[4] Of the five schools judged inadequate, common concerns can be read from the reports. The reasons for these damning judgements varied by school, but taken together, they encompassed: failures to raise awareness of the risks of extremism; failure to vet external speakers; lack of Prevent training; failures of equalities policies; inadequate teaching regarding other beliefs or cultures, or in the tuition of sex and relationship education; inadequate governance; a small group of governors promoting a narrow, faith-based ideology and a failure to prepare pupils for life in modern Britain (Ofsted, n.d.). These beliefs and cultures, and this faith-based ideology, refer to a focus within the schools on Islam.

Alongside the findings of Ofsted, Sir Michael Wilshaw (2014), Ofsted's Chief Inspector, released a widely reported statement summarising the claims. It concluded that, in some of these schools, a 'culture of fear and intimidation' had rapidly taken root, leading to problematic governance procedures, including a failure to enact sufficient procedures for safeguarding students from radicalisation (Wilshaw, 2014). He stated that leaders may not have adequately addressed the specific risks to their community, such as vulnerability to extremist influences. Wilshaw also hinted at the rumours of conspiracy detailed in the Trojan Horse letter. He claimed head teachers had identified governors influential across several schools who acted inappropriately, trying to organise education in line with their personal views, through promoting a conservative, Islamic education. He further alleged Birmingham City Council had failed to do enough work with local schools to raise awareness of the dangers of extremism, and the potential risks of radicalisation, despite receiving Prevent funding. Ultimately, he judged that, in several of the schools inspected, children were being badly prepared for life in modern Britain. The 'active promotion of a narrow set of values and beliefs' was making children 'vulnerable to segregation and emotional dislocation from wider society', with children 'not being encouraged to develop tolerant attitudes towards all faiths and cultures' (Wilshaw, 2014). Wilshaw concluded by stating that, in 'culturally homogenous communities', schools are a space to learn of other faiths and cultures; schools have a responsibility to promote British values, and if this does not happen, 'the principles that are fundamental to the well-being of our society will not be transmitted to the next generation' (Wilshaw, 2014). When giving evidence to the Education Select Committee, Wilshaw argued that, while the issue of extremism was outside their remit, Ofsted had seen the potential for problems to develop: 'What we did see was the promotion of a culture that would, if that culture continued, have made the children in those schools vulnerable to extremism because of, as I said, the disconnection from wider society and cultural isolation' (Education Committee, 2014).

The problem of Trojan Horse is *not* that, by the government's own definitions, extremists were involved in the radicalisation of children at these schools (see Morgan, 2014). Nor, indeed, was any 'evidence' of 'extremism' found. The problem is that the environments being produced in these schools is seen to have left these children more *vulnerable* to the possibility of radicalisation in the future. This point is eloquently summarised by Lorna Fitzjohn (Ofsted's Regional Director for the West Midlands) who stated to the House of Commons Education Committee:

> It is difficult to predict what they might do. What we are looking at is the *potential*, really. What we want children protected against are any potential influences they might have. We want children to have a broad and balanced view and to have British values instilled in them in schools so that they are better able to deal with any pressures they might have as they go through life, whether it be within their community, whether it be on the internet or any other way that they may well be influenced. It is that strength that they come out of the education system with that we are most interested in. (Education Committee, 2014, emphasis added)

By promoting Islam as a part of their education, and in being seen to not actively promote 'British values', the children in these schools are left more open to pernicious, potentially violent, extremist influences.

Charting the same terrain, the Clarke Report (commissioned by the DfE) concluded that there had been a 'co-ordinated, deliberate and sustained action' to introduce an 'intolerant and aggressive Islamic ethos' into some of the schools in question (Clarke, 2014: 14). The report clearly identifies areas of poor practice, including problematic relationships between governors and head teachers, irregular employment practices, the poor treatment of female members of staff, and inappropriate use of funding for a trip to Mecca. Moreover, some of the individuals involved in the schools held views that would be inappropriate were they taught in schools. Members of staff had, for instance, claimed that the bombing of the Boston marathon and the murder of Lee Rigby were hoaxes and had made homophobic statements (Clarke, 2014: 62–66). These views were discussed on a private forum and not expressed at school (or at least it cannot be said in the report that this occurred). However, the broader problem identified by Clarke, in line with the Ofsted reports, is that many of the schools in question reinforced a Muslim identity to the exclusion of other identities. Clarke specifically refers to, for instance, attempts to ban celebration at school of non-Muslim religious festivals such as Christmas

(Clarke, 2014: 42–43). While listed as separate areas of concern, the following can also be understood within this framing: increasing faith components within the curriculum; segregated sex and relationship education, tuition of which may have strayed from the curriculum;[5] Islamic posters (some in Arabic) being displayed in schools; pressure to teach Arabic at the expense of other lessons; conservative Islamic practices being introduced such as prohibitions on music and ensuring art tuition was in line with Islamic practice; 'anti-Western' assemblies;[6] and gender segregation (Clarke, 2014: 33–47).

The headline conclusions directly link these identity practices with an increased vulnerability to radicalisation. Clarke articulates three primary concerns deriving from witness evidence given to the investigation. First, a fear that 'children are learning to be intolerant of difference and diversity'; second, that, 'young people, instead of enjoying a broadening and enriching experience in school, are having their horizons narrowed. They are not being equipped to flourish in the inevitably diverse environments of further education, the workplace or indeed any environment outside predominantly Muslim communities. They are thus potentially denied the opportunity to enjoy and exploit to the full the opportunities of a modern multi-cultural Britain'; and third, that the 'very clear evidence that young people are being encouraged to accept unquestioningly a particular hardline strand of Sunni Islam raises concerns about their vulnerability to radicalisation in the future. I have heard evidence to the effect that there are real fears that their current experiences will make it harder for them to question or challenge radical influences' (Clarke, 2014: 13). The report concluded that, regardless of the motivations of those involved in this coordinated plot, 'the effect has been to limit the life chances of the young people in their care and to render them more vulnerable to pernicious influences in the future' (Clarke, 2014: 14).

The schools at the heart of these allegations may have questions to answer regarding their governance practices. Discussion regarding the extent to which schools can and should cater to particular faith communities is legitimate (although, so far, this has predominantly been a question of Islamic faith communities). The scandal has received much academic scrutiny. Miah (2017a) has argued it represents a racial governmentality that equated specifically Muslim cultural conservativism with extremism, and he details the problematic and hypocritical approach taken by Ofsted inspectors in their investigations (see also Miah, 2017b). Holmwood and O'Toole (2018) have convincingly argued the affair represents a serious miscarriage of justice, wherein no evidence of extremism or religious conservatism was present, and exemplary teachers and governors were vilified in service to a wider populism that scapegoats Muslim citizens in the UK.

Yet, what has been less remarked upon, and what is crucial to the core claims of this study, is that what emerges as central within Trojan Horse is a particular – and crucially important – *analysis of threat*. Both the Ofsted and the Clarke reports go beyond a critique of governance practices. At their heart lies an *analysis of threat* that belies a deeper claim about the contemporary relation between identity and security. The analysis is that the promotion of an Islamic ethos, and the distance from mainstream 'British values', is seen to constitute a failure in safeguarding these children from becoming vulnerable to radicalisation. The Islamic identities being promoted, and the 'British' identities being marginalised, are seen to represent an increased potential for these children to one day become involved in violent extremism. These Islamic identities being promoted are rendered threatening. As such, what is at stake within the Trojan Horse scandal are fundamental questions of national security.

Four claims

The intention of this book is to articulate this analysis of threat that makes the questions raised by the Trojan Horse scandal possible. It will be argued that Prevent produces and acts upon the threat of radicalisation through ordering identities in the present as risky or secure, by virtue of the potential they are understood to contain. The identities that are seen to carry a risk, those that are produced as potentially vulnerable to radicalisation and violent extremism, are those that are understood to be alienated from mainstream 'Britishness', not sharing 'British values'. Although these performances of identity are not illegal, the threat of radicalisation they pose requires intervention. Prevent is the institutional space in which this problematisation of security and identity, and the interventions that are required to minimise the risk of vulnerability to radicalisation, is located. Prevent has been the object of much political debate in recent years. Engaging with, and reframing, these debates, this book situates the policy as playing a key role in producing and then policing contemporary 'British' identities. The book demonstrates this through articulating the form of power that Prevent mobilises, and the assumptions upon which this power relies. It is a power that generates security in the present by producing certain identities as threatening for the future, and then acting to transform these identities in the present. In order to make this argument, the book develops four claims.

The first claim of the book is that the predominant readings of the Prevent policy, found in both the political debates and the academic literature, establish the core question of Prevent to be that of the relation between, on the one hand, its security focus, and on the other, broader concerns regarding identity and values. Thus, the policy debates establish Prevent as containing two strands: a security-focused strand that emphasises targeted interventions into those vulnerable to radicalisation; and an identity-focused strand, which argues the policy must also engage with the identities and values of the Muslim community, as these can create an environment conducive to radicalisation. The political debates that have informed the development of the policy, encompassing its internal negotiations and self-critiques, that are evident in policy documents, committee reports and the interviews carried out with those who developed Prevent, concern how these two strands can and should relate. At times the two strands are brought together. At times it is their separation that is advocated. This analysis is reproduced in much of the academic literature, wherein the 'problem' of Prevent is often framed as the institutional relationship between these two strands, with the charge often being that they are too close.

The second claim of the book is that this analysis is inadequate. In focusing on the institutional and practical relationship of the security and identity strands, what is occluded is a reading of the policy that sees the two to be intimately and conceptually related. *Both* strands, it will be shown, are built upon an analysis of the *problem of vulnerability to radicalisation*. The book challenges these existing accounts through demonstrating the importance of temporality to understanding Prevent, and, in doing so, seeks to contribute to, and extend, emerging work in critical security studies that foregrounds the analytical centrality of the relationship between security and temporality. It argues Prevent represents an important and novel temporal ambition to intervene early into these newly problematised vulnerabilities, identifying potential to radicalisation prior to its actual emergence. Central to Prevent is, therefore, the question of how this potential future threat can be made knowable, and, therefore, actionable, in the present. The analysis of this book demonstrates that, in crossing this temporal gap – the space between the present and the future violence one seeks to avoid – it is the performances of certain identities that become intelligible as signs of potential future violence.

This claim is made through providing a second reading of the Prevent policy. The first reading, detailed in the first claim, provides a history of the institutional transformations of Prevent, focusing on the internal debates that have informed the development of the strategy. This history is mirrored in the academic literature, which narrates Prevent in its disjunctures and transformations over time. The second reading, through focusing on the problem at the heart of Prevent – vulnerability to radicalisation and violent extremism – shows its continuities. Through a close, textual reading of the Prevent documents, it can be demonstrated that the discursive production of vulnerability to radicalisation and violent extremism constructs an account of those identities which are deemed risky as those that are alienated from a conception of 'Britishness' and 'British values'. It is through recognising these risky identities in the present, and then acting upon them, that the threat of radicalisation in the future is minimised. Prevent, therefore, conceptually links questions of identity and security, transforming identities in the present in order to preclude the potential emergence of threats in the future.

In reading these discursive ascriptions through a post-structuralist frame, Prevent can be understood as a set of productive practices. Thus, it is argued that the concept of identity, within Prevent, does not represent an extant and pre-existent riskiness. But rather, it is *through* the security act of Prevent that this riskiness and alienation, these identities outside of mainstream 'Britishness', are produced and rendered intelligible. Those identities that are understood as threatening are, therefore, also *produced* as external to 'Britishness' and 'British values'. 'Britishness' is thus constituted as secure and securing; it is normalised. While that which is produced as external is rendered threatening. Through ordering identities in the present as risky and secure on account of their coherence with, or alienation from, 'Britishness', intervention is made possible into those now understood as threatening. In this way, Prevent brings together questions of temporality, security and identity, producing and then securing the threat of the future, through an analysis of performances of identity in the present. It therefore establishes its own boundary between a secure 'Britishness' and a risky outside.

The third claim is that, on the basis of this analysis, it can be shown that Prevent operates as a form of power that produces, and then acts upon, identities. By analysing the practices of Prevent, it is possible to locate the concrete identities Prevent renders as threatening, and the particular forms of power that are mobilised in order to act upon and govern them. It is these identities that are produced *as* alienated and outside of 'Britishness' and 'British values'. The book establishes that both the identity and security strands of the Prevent policy order and act upon identities in the present, in order to manage the threat they are seen to hold for the future. First, the policy demands a focus on the environments that are seen to be productive of potential towards radicalisation. At one level, this has resulted in a focus on the ideas and identities that circulate within communities, notably concentrating on Muslim communities within the UK, and is most clearly evident within the community cohesion framework. At more localised levels, there is a clear emphasis on problematic institutional spaces, such as prisons, schools and universities. In regards to both, action within the Prevent framework is taken to encourage and generate 'secure', 'British' identities while minimising threatening, 'extremist' identities. Second, at the level of the individual, there is the need to identify those who are vulnerable to radicalisation, which then allows for targeted interventions. This occurs primarily through the development of the 'Channel' project. These vulnerabilities, it will be shown, are made knowable through making intelligible certain identity practices as risky, which, concretely, have often been ascribed to expressions of Muslim politics and religiosity. These then require mediation, transforming them, in order to bring them back in line with a mainstream 'Britishness'.

What is thus identified is a form of power that is mobilised through the production of identities that are deemed secure. In this regard, the book reads Prevent as a function of power, a way of thinking about and acting on those who may go on to engage in terrorism, that both is, and potentially could be, applied to any particular identity seen to signify a potential future threat. The argument of the book is thus in tension with an analysis that would locate Prevent as embedded within specific histories of Islamophobic and racist state security practices. This is not to deny that Muslim communities and individuals have been *the* key subjects of Prevent, that the implementation of Prevent is categorically uneven, and that there have been very real violences suffered by British Muslims within British counter-terrorism practice. Nevertheless, the concern of this book is with the form of power that Prevent produces, and in this context, it is argued that Prevent cannot be reduced to its predominant focus on Muslim subjects. The strength of this approach is that it allows the book to make a wider claim regarding the conceptualisation of the relationship between violence and identity in Prevent. Moreover, it situates the power Prevent produces as translatable and malleable, applicable to other forms of violence such as far-right extremism. But it does so at the cost of minimising the specific, racialised histories of the policing of minority ethnic communities in the UK and broader questions of Islamophobia. It is hoped that in so doing, this reading illuminates more than it obscures.

Finally, the fourth claim the book makes is that, having outlined the form of power that Prevent mobilises, it is possible to demonstrate the consequences of this power for politics and political expression within the UK. In targeting vulnerability to radicalisation, Prevent targets the potential that life may develop into; it does not target illegality, but the spaces that may produce violent extremism, and the individuals who may become terrorists. These identities, both communally and individually, that are produced as vulnerable are those that cannot be allowed on the basis of the potential threat they are seen to contain. Thus, the expression of these identities becomes the object of preclusive security interventions. This power, the book argues, contains important and intrinsic consequences for the possibility of political expression in the UK. These consequences will be examined, showing how they radicalise the relation of security and identity, redefining and extending the scope of those who are subject to security intervention, and those who must maintain vigilance for signs of threat. This reading of Prevent, therefore, situates it as having played a central role in contemporary British identity politics, and foresees its continued, increasing importance.

Prevent has been the subject of intense, and often critical, debate in recent years, in policy circles, the media and the academy. Now a statutory duty for many specified authorities, academic inquiry seeking to understand the policy has extended beyond critical security and critical terrorism studies, and now encompasses a range of disciplinary perspectives, situating Prevent within education (Davies, 2016; Durodié, 2016; McGlynn and McDaid, 2016; O'Donnell, 2016; Saeed and Johnson, 2016; Hill, 2017), healthcare (Goldberg *et al.*, 2017; Rizq, 2017) and social work (Stanley and Guru, 2015; Stanley *et al.*, 2017). It is hoped that the reading of Prevent given in this book provides a holistic and compelling account of the analysis of threat produced by Prevent, and the forms of power that have then been mobilised in response to it. In doing so, this study seeks to make a significant contribution to the Prevent literature, providing a coherent account of the conceptual intimacy found between security and identity in Prevent. And it is hoped this provides a framework for understanding the core analysis and function of Prevent, and a lens through which to comprehend its mediation across institutions and spheres of social relations. Prevent, here, is read as a logic – a way of thinking about the relationship between security, identity and temporality in public life and British social relations – that has informed, and now governs, many facets of British life. Ultimately, this inquiry demonstrates that what is at stake within Prevent is a novel problematisation of threat leading to a new role for the state. A role, which, it is argued, should be of concern to us all.

Methodology: understanding Prevent as a diagram of power

In order to make these claims, the book employs a post-structuralist framework, drawing particularly on the work of Michel Foucault. Rather than understanding the world to exist as independent and objectively knowable, a Foucauldian approach insists there is no underlying truth that can be known; it is only possible to analyse the discursive practices of knowledge and their co-constitution with regimes of power. Through analysing these practices of knowledge/power, the assumptions that Prevent makes regarding threat and identity are brought to the fore.

Utilising this approach allows the book to tell a very different history of Prevent, providing a genealogical analysis of the subject of vulnerability to radicalisation that animates the policy. This methodological approach insists on the importance of relations of power in both the constitution of knowledge and of the subject. It is to insist on the historicisation of subject, knowledge and power. As Foucault states, '[o]ne has to dispense with the constituent subject, to get rid of the subject itself, that's to say, to arrive at an analysis which can account for the constitution of the subject within a historical framework' (Foucault, 1991a: 59). In destabilising the continuities of relations of knowledge and relations to the self, it asks new questions of historical analysis and specifically demands a move away from any conception of origin, or a linear, progressive history. Rather, history becomes a means through which concepts and realities can be destabilised. As Bartelson (1995: 4) states, a key task is in locating points of self-evidence and to set them in 'motion, expose them to contingency and deprive them of their unproblematic status'. It reveals that concepts do not contain 'a timeless and essential secret, but the secret that they have no essence or that their essence was fabricated in a piecemeal fashion from alien forms' (Foucault, 1991b: 78). Thus, relations of knowledge/power are productive of social relations and are generative of the very possibility of interpreting the world and all that exists within it. This approach aims to expose the contingency of particular functions and relations of power; the means through which power operates and the form it takes is not given *a priori*. In so doing, it opens up space for critique and for destabilising the seeming objectivity of these relations. In applying this approach to Prevent, the book asks: how has vulnerability to radicalisation as an object of threat come to be constituted? What discursive practices render problematic environments and individuals as knowable? And how is power mobilised in order to act on these problems?

Problematisation: how is the 'problem' of Prevent constituted?

In order to challenge the conventional history of Prevent, narrated in chapter 1, and the basis of the first claim, the analysis here tells a different story through bringing to the fore the *problematic* of Prevent. The idea of the 'problematic' derives from the work of Bachelard, a French scholar writing on the philosophies of science in the mid-twentieth century who, while not readily translated into English, has been influential on contemporary French philosophy. The core idea of problematisation for Bachelard is that it is not possible to assign a primacy to objects, subjects, things or minds, but that there are problems. As Maniglier (2012) relates, in ascribing ontological primacy to the recognition of problematics, the subject–object relation breaks down, the world cannot be ascribed a material reality that can be read; rather, it is through the process of problematisation that both the subject who thinks, and the object that is being thought, are simultaneously constituted. Following Maniglier, this is to outline the basis of an ontology that sees problematisation as the basis for the constitution and reconstitution of a reality that is always in the making.

The idea of problematisation attains a centrality to Foucault's thought in his later years, and in reflections upon his previous works. In an interview with Paul Rabinow shortly before his death, he argues that his broad methodological approach has been one of problematisation: 'to ask politics what it had to say about the problems with which it was confronted' (Foucault, 2000: 115). In response to questions that are posed, analysis is then able to locate the development of practices in response to such questions. Problematisation can, therefore, be seen as a key starting point within a non-foundational ontology. Foucault articulates it thus:

> Problematization doesn't mean representation of a pre-existing object, nor the creation by discourse of an object that doesn't exist. It is the totality of discursive or non-discursive practices that introduces something into the play of true and false, and constitutes it as an object for thought (whether in the form of moral reflection, scientific knowledge, political analysis, etc.). (Foucault, 1990: 258)

The problematic is thus the act of thought folding back upon itself (Foucault, 2000). In so doing, problematisations reveal new possibilities and convey existing entities in a new light. This is not to say that the act of making problematic has no other context than itself; any specific problematisation may be triggered by all manner of external causes, such as social, economic or political transformations. Nor is it to say that a particular problematic will result in a particular outcome; there are many responses available.

Deacon (2000: 139) identifies within Foucault's concept of problematisation three elements: a 'historical process of producing an object of thought'; the 'mechanisms involved in this production'; and the 'manner in which human beings [...] find themselves engaged objectively, communicatively and governmentally with both process and product'. Problematisation can, therefore, be understood as an oscillating process of thought, moving between the constitution of that which is designated a problem, and the constitution of a response to it. As Warner summarises, problematics represent 'the practical horizon of intelligibility [...] both the conditions that make thinking possible and for the way thinking, under certain circumstances, can reflect back on its own conditions' (Warner, 2002: 154). The play of problematisations and responses is co-constitutive and open to reflexive change. Problems and the responses to them are not static and continuously make themselves anew. It is within this play of problems across an array of connected sites that there is, therefore, space for agency, wherein reflection might prompt new, cascading problematisations. Veyne describes it thus (albeit using the term 'objectivizations'):

> A practice gives rise to the objectivizations that correspond to it, and it is anchored in the realities of the moment, that is, in the objectivizations

of neighbouring practices. Or, to be more precise, a practice actively fills the void left by neighbouring practices; it *actualizes* the potentialities that these neighbouring practices prefigure in hollow form. If these practices are transformed, if the periphery of the hollow shifts [...] the practice will actualize these new potentialities, and it will no longer be the same practice as before. (Veyne, 1997: 162, emphasis in original)

This approach thus enables an articulation of a relational ontology of the problem in which, through iterative problematisations, new ways of thinking, new objects of thought or new practices open up space within which new questions reveal themselves.

These iterative problematisations can be understood as transforming the very grids of intelligibility through which interpretation and understanding is possible, the schemas through which social order is constituted as knowable (Foucault, 1978: 93). Linking this discussion of problematics to Deleuze's reading of Foucault, it is through problematisation that social reality becomes articulable and visible. For Deleuze (2006), it is through regimes of knowledge that the sayable and the visible are constituted. What is thus at stake within processes of problematisation is the fabric of social order, how it can be articulated, and how it can be experientially interpreted. Thus, and harking back to Foucault's work, in the process of problematisation what is often produced is a particular site of intelligibility that is *made* articulable and visible and then illuminated, demanding attention and action. The madman, the vagrant, flows of population – it is through their designation as problem spaces that they attain an intelligibility and visibility. Particular behaviours, identifications, spaces or flows are illuminated. Comprehension cannot be reduced to objective interpretation, but it is rather the complex play of economies of intelligibility that render certain elements of social reality as meaningful, understandable and significant. The book thus shows how Prevent, in its novel problematisation of threat, discloses the world as knowable and visible, and produces novel sites of intelligibility. This allows the book to position the problematic of vulnerability to radicalisation as central to the formation and evolution of Prevent (chapters 3 and 4), and enables the analysis given here to move beyond the established literature (addressed in chapter 2).

The assemblage and power: how is the 'problem' of Prevent acted on?

Through analysing the problematisation of British counter-radicalisation policy, the book asks how the concept of *radicalisation*, and those spaces and subjects that are deemed to be *vulnerable to* radicalisation, come to attain a problematic status.[7] The book then demonstrates how Prevent functions as a response to this particular problematisation. It is in these processes of response, that cohere around a particular problematised object, that the book inserts the concept of the 'assemblage'. By assemblage, following Deleuze and Guattari, the book understands the term to refer to a complex and heterogenous constellation of actions, statements and bodies that come together around a particular function (Deleuze and Guattari, 1987 [2002]: 88). An assemblage is a productive entity that enacts a diagram of power; it seeks to combine its elements towards a particular mobilisation of power in order to transform, in some fashion, the problematised object to which it aims. It is thus the constellation of knowledges and power that is brought to bear on, and seeks to articulate, make intelligible and govern, a problematisation. Drawing again on Deleuze's reading of Foucault, the concept of power is understood in terms of forces; forces can affect and forces can be affected, power becomes a 'physics of abstract action' that passes through the mastered no less than the master (Deleuze, 2006: 60; see also Deleuze, 1986). It is not something that can be possessed, rather it is practised. The question that must be asked is thus that of how it is being practised and to what function it is being mobilised.

This question of function is central. The typologies of power that Foucault identifies all contain within them a particular function that marks out their operation, their actions of force upon force. Foucault variously calls these 'technologies of power' or 'diagrams'. Deleuze opts for the latter term and this book follows his lead. A diagram can be defined as 'the presentation of the relations between forces unique to a particular formation; it is the distribution of the power to affect and the power to be affected' and 'a transmission or distribution of particular features' (Deleuze, 2006: 61, 62). The diagram thus represents an abstract way of thinking about how particular functions within a space of social relations might be produced; or in other words, how mobilisations of power might produce particular outcomes in particular ways. The assemblage is, therefore, that which translates this abstract function into a series of concrete practices, that act as forces upon forces, towards particular outcomes.

A useful way of thinking about the form the diagram takes – and its relation to concrete practices – is in Foucault's exposition of the panopticon. Foucault states that 'the Panopticon must not be understood as a dream building: it is the diagram of a mechanism of power reduced to its ideal form' (Foucault, 1995: 205). He goes on to state that:

> it is a type of location of bodies in space, of distribution of individuals in relation to one another, of hierarchical organization, of disposition of centres and channels of power, of definition of the instruments and modes of intervention of power, which can be implemented in Hospitals, workshops, schools, prisons. Whenever one is dealing

with a multiplicity of individuals on whom a task or a particular form of behaviour must be imposed, the panoptic schema may be used. (Foucault, 1995: 205)

It thus represents an abstract set of functions which can be concretely implemented as an assemblage across an array of domains of social relations. The diagram thus represents the condition of possibility for power to be mobilised and enact particular functions. In the case of the panoptic diagram, its function is to instil and internalise particular behaviours through seeing without being seen, and this is achieved through distributing bodies hierarchically along lines of sight and lines of invisibility (Deleuze, 2006: 29–30). To take another example, the disciplinary diagram functions towards the optimal production of particular bodies (such as the soldier) or completion of particular tasks (such as the factory) through the distribution of bodies in time and space (Foucault, 1995). Likewise, governmentality can be understood as a particular function that aims to normalise population metrics through the regulation of flows (Foucault, 2007).

These diagrams thus provide the function through which concrete assemblages – those that exist within the world – act upon the world. As Deleuze (2006: 32) states:

The diagram or abstract machine is the map of relations between forces, *a map of destiny* [...] the diagram acts as a non-unifying immanent cause that is coextensive with the whole social field: the abstract machine is like the cause of the concrete assemblages that execute its relations; and these relations between forces take place 'not above' but within the very tissue of the assemblages they produce.

Concrete assemblages can thus be understood as those knowledges and practices that, through drawing upon particular operations of power, mobilise a particular function; together, these coalesce around an objectivised site of problematisation in order to act upon it. The concrete assemblage is thus both the knowledges that respond to a particular problematic and the practices that function to transform it. In utilising this methodological approach in regard to Prevent, this book goes beyond the current literature and academic debates, demonstrating that Prevent *produces* vulnerability to radicalisation as intelligible. In making this argument, it then becomes possible to outline the function of power Prevent mobilises, demonstrating that through this problematisation of vulnerability to radicalisation, Prevent productively orders identities as risky and as secure. This, the book will argue, can be understood as the diagram of counter-radicalisation, and it is mobilised through an assemblage of practices, including community cohesion (chapter 5) and targeted interventions into those deemed to be 'at risk' (chapter 6).

Conducting interviews and building the corpus of
documents for analysis

The methodological work of the book is, at its root, textual. The explicit aim is to articulate the problematisation at the heart of Prevent and then to demonstrate how a range of practices enact a diagram of power that functions to act upon this problem. It does so through the analysis of policy documents. The book is thus interested in policy articulations and is concerned with how the problem of Prevent, and the power deemed necessary to manage it, are conceptualised. These articulations of policy take many forms, but for the purpose of the book have largely been drawn from policy papers, statutes, speeches, select committee reports, think tank reports, policy guidance and a number of interviews with those involved in the constitution of the policy. These were then assembled into a corpus that was discursively analysed in order to identify how questions of problem and response were understood. Following Deleuze, this reading was not based upon the statements that are most common or most privileged, but rather on account of the function that they carry out in relation to the problem at hand (Deleuze, 2006: 16). Thus, these documents were read and then brought into alignment based upon the function the book sees them as playing in the constitution of the policy.

This corpus of documents was substantively enriched through the addition of fifteen interviews that were undertaken with key figures who played a part in creating the Prevent policy. The purpose of conducting interviews was twofold. First, the interviews sought to go beyond the policy articulations of Prevent in providing factual information not pub-licly available. For instance, they were useful in detailing the behind-the-scenes discussions that informed the policy, and the negotiations and dissensions that are occluded in published policy documents. Second, they sought to highlight the key themes of the research project. The interviews thus sought to provide the research with a robust articula-tion of the Prevent policy from those responsible for its design. They were able to provide information not readily accessible from public data sources and, through the dialogical encounters with interviewees, were able to shape the reading of the Prevent policy given in this book. Some interviewees agreed to be named in the research, and some asked for their contribution to be anonymised. Where participants opted for anonymisation, a descriptive term of their position has been agreed by mutual consent and will be used within the text.

A deliberate and explicitly Foucauldian choice has been made to withdraw the author from the text. However, in this space, it is worth briefly recognising and reflecting on the positionality of the author, and the effects this might have had regarding the chosen methodology of interviews. That I am a white, male, British citizen, with a name and appearance that would likely be read in this way, speaking with a southern English, middle-class accent, may well have affected the research process. Prevent is a politically charged and contested space, and while one cannot be certain, it might be the case that possessing a name that reads as Muslim, visually appearing to practice Islam, or being read as not ethnically white and British, could have impacted on the research. Being clearly legible as white, male and British quite possibly resulted in an increased ability to gain access for interviews, and it may also have affected the responses given in the interviews, putting interviewees (who were almost all white and non-Muslim) at ease, where my own whiteness did not confront them with the racial and religious politics of Prevent. Answers to my questions might have been more open, with the micro-geographies of power in the interview space more collegiate than for a researcher who was read as of Muslim background or faith. While I have no doubt as to the integrity, honesty and openness of those who gave their time to be interviewed, a researcher who was read as Muslim may have encountered an interview space wherein interviewees might have pre-empted particular critiques of the policy, and attributed a particular politics to the interviewer, pre-judging and potentially shaping the content and tone of the interview. The research benefitted greatly from the interviews. It is thus important to recognise that this process, and the data that it generated, will have been shaped by such factors.

Structure

The structure of this book overlaps with both the four claims the book seeks to make and the methodology outlined above. Chapters 1 and 2 correspond to the first claim, providing an analysis of the conventional understanding of Prevent given by the policy documents, those responsible for the policy and the academic literature. Chapter 1 outlines this within the political debates and the policy documents themselves, while at the same time providing an historical overview of the strategy and its development. This chapter, therefore, provides the first reading of the Prevent policy. Outlining the development of the policy from its origins in the response to the attacks of 9/11, it argues that the primary focus of these political debates has concerned the 'proper' relationship between Prevent's identity and security strands. At times, the strands are brought together, and at times, it is their separation that is advocated. Chapter 2 demonstrates that this analysis has, historically, been reproduced across much of the academic literature on Prevent. This literature, it will be argued, often sees the 'solution' to Prevent as the *separation* of its security and identity strands. It therefore positions the two strands as 'separable', failing to go beyond the questions that the policy itself asks. This chapter then analyses two theorisations of Prevent that provide a means of moving beyond this position: first, an approach that argues Prevent has produced Muslims in the UK as a 'suspect community', and second, an approach that argues Prevent represents a strategy of counter-insurgency.

The next two chapters outline the problematic of Prevent, which allows the book to substantiate its second claim. Chapters 3 and 4 provide a second, discursive reading of the policy, that combined, outline the problematic of vulnerability to radicalisation that is at the heart of Prevent. This analysis challenges the first reading, showing that, rather than being separable policy strands, the security and identity strands of Prevent represent a coherent response to a shared problematisation of threat. Chapter 3 establishes and delineates the central relation within Prevent of security and temporality. It argues that Prevent represents a novel ambition, in that it seeks early intervention into processes of becoming violent, acting prior to an individual being radicalised. It thus intervenes within conditions of uncertainty, in that it is not certain whether such an individual would go on to participate in violence or any other illegal act. Engaging with the emerging critical security studies literature on this subject, the book argues that all acts of securing under conditions of uncertainty require the traversal of a *temporal gap*: the space between the present and the conceptualisation of a threat to come. This in turn requires discursive and institutional mechanisms that make such a threat knowable and actionable. The term *preclusive* is introduced here as a general term that emphasises this relation between security and temporality, making clear that all acts of securing are necessarily productive of a future threat they then preclusively act on to mediate. The chapter then outlines how the concept of radicalisation fulfils this function for Prevent, allowing processes of becoming violent to be identified in the present and then acted upon.

This then allows the analysis of chapter 4, which demonstrates that Prevent traverses the temporal gap by discursively producing certain performances of identity as vulnerable to radicalisation and therefore risky, and that this vulnerability is due to their alienation from a conception of 'Britishness' and 'British values'. It is therefore through understanding and ordering identities in the present that processes of becoming violent in the future can be conceptualised and intervened into. However, in approaching this problematic within a post-structuralist framework, this discursive positioning can be understood as a set of productive practices; it is through the security act that alienation from 'Britishness' is constituted. These productive practices represent the 'preclusive identity politics' of Prevent. 'Britishness' and 'British values' are thus produced as secure and securing; they are normalised, while that which is produced as external is rendered threatening and, therefore, in need of intervention, lest this potential manifest itself. Prevent, therefore, establishes a boundary between those identities deemed secure, those that are contained within a 'normalised Britishness', and those deemed threatening, on account of the potential they may contain. The problematic of Prevent therefore brings together questions of temporality, security and identity, producing and then securing the threat of the future through an analysis of performances of identity in the present.

Having outlined the problematic of Prevent, the book then demonstrates how the counter-radicalisation strategy has responded to this reading of threat, enacting specific applications of power that seek to transform those identities produced as threatening. Chapters 5 and 6 thus articulate the assemblage of Prevent, and the knowledges, practices and institutions it mobilises in order to stop people from becoming violent extremists. They substantiate the third claim of the book, demonstrating how Prevent renders certain identities as risky in the present, thus producing them as alienated from 'Britishness' and 'British values', and then acts upon them. Two clear approaches are visible within this.

Chapter 5 develops an account of how Prevent approaches problematic spaces. Notably, this represents the conflation of community cohesion work and Prevent. While community cohesion develops separately to Prevent, a discursive reading of cohesion and Prevent texts show how the two become conjoined as a way of thinking about, and governing, threatening communal environments. Prevent also contains a focus on problematic institutions such as schools and prisons wherein extremism could take hold. Both rely on an analysis that understands an alienation from 'Britishness' and 'British values' to represent a threat which can be managed by intervening in the spaces in which radicalisation occurs. These spaces may therefore represent communities, or more specific institutional locations. In order to manage these spaces, a governmental approach is invoked, wherein through intervening in the circulation of identities, it is presumed that less threatening identities can be generated. Yet it also pushes beyond Foucault's articulation of this modality of power, seeking not just to regulate flows, but to actively intervene to promote 'British' identifications.

Chapter 6 provides a reading of Prevent's approach to individuals who are deemed vulnerable to radicalisation. It articulates Prevent as a targeted, counter-radicalisation programme, most clearly expressed through the Channel project. Here, the idea is that individuals can be identified as vulnerable to becoming violent, through identifying the 'vulnerability indicators' they display in the present. Channel thus acts as an institutional space to make visible and then intervene in performances of identity that are read as constituting a potential threat. In so doing, it will be argued, it invokes and reworks a pastoral power of care. This power seeks to produce the truth of the individual through interpreting the signs they display in the present. Once identified, intervention is mandated in order to manage these potential processes of becoming violent.

Chapter 7 starts by drawing the analysis of Prevent's assemblage together, showing how these preclusive security interventions represent the mobilisation of a coherent diagram of counter-radicalisation, a diagram that ties security, identity and temporality together. It therefore outlines the core contribution of the book, establishing that Prevent represents a form of power that has played a key role in producing and policing contemporary British identities, and in doing so, has carved out a novel role for the state. It argues that this diagram enacts its own political geography, producing an account of identities as secure or risky based upon their coherence, or not, with a 'British' identity, and then seeking to act on those identities produced as alienated from, or outside of, this 'normalised Britishness'. While this has concretely acted to produce Muslimness as that which, in its alienation, represents a threat, the argument is made that, read as an abstract diagram, the power Prevent mobilises need not be reduced to a focus on Muslim identity, and is translatable beyond its specific genesis.

It then makes the fourth claim of the book, arguing that this function of power has consequences for the expression of politics in the UK. It enacts its own boundary between those identities allowed free expression, and those that, by virtue of their potential, are not. It is a power that thus intrinsically constricts the expression of those deemed vulnerable. It therefore radicalises the relation of security and identity in the UK. Through Prevent's temporal ambitions, it extends the scope of who is subject to Prevent's security imperative and who is responsible for enacting it. The concluding chapter returns to the 'Trojan Horse' affair, demonstrating how it epitomises the mobilisation of this power and the relations it draws between security, identity and temporality.

Notes

1 The DfE investigation was led by Peter Clarke, who, from June 2002 until his retirement in 2008, had been in charge of the Counter Terrorism Command within the Metropolitan Police.

2 While Muslim pupils composed significant majorities in the schools, these were nevertheless state schools, and thus not afforded the room that would be allowed for faith schools or free schools in terms of curriculum design and religious allowance.

3 The inspections themselves did not escape controversy. Days prior to the release of the reports, a group of leading educationalists and Muslim leaders (including Sir Tim Brighouse, a former chief education officer in Birmingham) criticised Ofsted, stating that first-hand accounts of the inspection 'suggest that inspectors were poorly prepared and had an agenda that calls into question Ofsted's claim to be objective and professional in its appraisal of standards in schools serving predominantly Muslim pupils' (*Guardian*, 2014).

4 Albeit both of the two schools previously judged 'outstanding' (others had been judged 'good') had undergone significant leadership changes during the interval between inspections, allegedly due to senior members of staff and heads of both institutions being marginalised and driven out (Gilligan, 2014).

5 In one example, boys were taught that wives could not refuse to have sex with their husbands. This was clarified in an assembly to address this point wherein students were informed that this was true in Islam, but that British society saw it differently (Clarke, 2014: 38).

6 Issues raised here include being told that students will not be employed in this country due to their skin colour, that it is Muslim teachers, not white ones, who have their best interests at heart, and that an external speaker discussed the war in Afghanistan (Clarke, 2014: 41).

7 The book follows Butler's use of the word 'deemed'. She uses the term to refer to the bureaucratic and administrative decisions that might lead to an individual being detained; that this is based not upon juridical evidence, but on the basis that they are 'deemed' dangerous. It is the 'deeming' that is therefore sufficient to ascribe threat, justifying the detention (Butler, 2006: 59).

1

The (problematic) history of Prevent

The attacks of 9/11 constitute one of those moments in history that divides before and after. They led to a declaration of a 'War on Terror' from George W. Bush, President of the United States, on 20 September 2001, a call to arms that would be answered by many European states, the UK included. The threat was understood as an 'Islamist' terrorism, a perverse reading of the Muslim faith whose proponents spanned the world.[1] Soon after the attacks, the United States, with the aid of key allies, invaded Afghanistan on the basis that the Taliban, who ruled the country, had given shelter to Osama bin Laden, who was held ultimately responsible for the attacks. This would be followed in 2003 by the invasion of Iraq by the United States and other members of the 'coalition of the willing'. Over the next decade, the War on Terror would span much of the globe, resulting in a plethora of local, national and transnational conflicts between the forces of Islamist insurgency and terrorism and those opposed to them. The War on Terror was not limited to conflicts abroad. In the aftermath of 9/11, concerns were being raised in the UK's security establishment that this particular reading of Islam would also be a domestic concern. The attacks of 9/11 had shown that this emerging, global, Islamist violence was willing to target 'Western' countries. The fear was that the UK was at risk. This global, networked terrorism rooted in religious conviction and displaying devastating ambition required fresh thinking. The UK would introduce a new counter-terrorism strategy and new legislation in order to tackle Islamist terrorism at home and abroad. Prevent, and the idea that the government should try to stop people becoming terrorists in the first place, represents a key, and increasingly central, element of this response.

This chapter tells the history of the UK's Prevent policy. First presented to Cabinet in 2003, this chapter details the increasing importance of the policy and its institutional and practical developments. In seeking to stop people becoming radicalised, the Prevent policy represents an ambition that has asked novel questions of the capabilities and role of the state. Yet these questions have proved controversial, and both the purpose and delivery of the policy have been contested within government. Central to these political debates has been the extent to which questions of identity *matter* for a counter-radicalisation strategy. The purpose of Prevent is to intervene into processes of radicalisation, but does this entail the state should only intervene when people are actively becoming radicalised? Or should the state also try to intervene into the spaces in which ideas that might lead to radicalisation have taken hold? Should the state focus on a narrow security agenda? Or should the focus extend to Muslim communities, and the identities and ideologies they contain?

The Prevent strategy can thus be read as containing two strands: a security-focused strand that emphasises targeted interventions into those vulnerable to radicalisation; and an identity-focused strand that argues the policy must also engage with the identities and values in Muslim communities that may provide a platform for radicalisation. The political debates that have informed the development of the policy, its internal negotiations and self-critiques, that are evident in policy documents, committee reports and the statements made by those developing Prevent, concern how these two strands can and should relate. At times they are brought together. At times it is their separation that is advocated. These different approaches have led to transformations of Prevent's objectives and implementation. This chapter narrates the story of these debates as told by those responsible for the policy and the policy documents themselves.

In doing so, this chapter provides the first of two different discursive readings of Prevent given in this book. Here, the book is concerned with the political debates regarding the policy, and policymaker narratives regarding what the policy can and should do. This first reading of Prevent is important as it establishes the key assumption that has informed understanding of the Prevent policy. The assumption running throughout the policy is that these two strands are separable; there is a political decision to be made between whether Prevent should be security-focused or identity-focused. The story that emerges from policymakers and the policy documents is of the renegotiations of these strands. Often, critics have argued that for Prevent to work, it needs to focus on security and not questions of identity. Moreover, as will be shown in chapter 2, the academic literature reproduces these debates. Therefore, as the book will demonstrate, understandings of the Prevent policy often fail to go beyond an analysis that sees the key political question to be one of whether the policy should focus on a tight security remit, or intervene more broadly into the identities and values of the Muslim community.

Yet, as this book will argue, this analysis is inadequate. In understanding Prevent as a negotiation between these security and identity strands, it is an analysis that fails to recognise the ways in which the security actions of Prevent are *productive* of identity. The second reading of Prevent will go on to show, though an analysis of Prevent's problematisation of threat in chapters 3 and 4, that to distinguish between Prevent's security and identity interventions is illusory. That, in fact, the problematic of Prevent produces a series of interventions that are productive of *both* security and identity.

In order to narrate and demonstrate these political debates, this chapter tells the history of Prevent. The policy has gone through three major transformations, which broadly cohere with the first three versions of the UK's post-9/11 counter-terrorism strategy, 'CONTEST', published in 2006, 2009 and 2011. The latest iteration of CONTEST, published in June 2018, builds on the 2011 policy and will be discussed, but it does not represent a significant shift in policy. Using these iterations as a framework, the chapter periodises the development of Prevent, and the relations drawn between its security and identity strands, into three distinct phases. The first covers the initial development of the strategy from 2001 to 2006. In this period, mobilising discourses of community cohesion, Prevent is created as a community relations approach to counter-radicalisation. This approach emphasises the need to work with and through the Muslim community, focusing on the ideologies and values of Muslim communities in the UK. The second period covers the consolidation of the policy in 2007–10. First, it maintains the community relations approach, now clearly located within the Department for Communities and Local Government (DCLG). Yet it also establishes a targeted, security strand of Prevent, locating within the Home Office a police-led responsibility to identify and act on those vulnerable to radicalisation. The final period is from 2011 to 2018. This iteration separated Prevent's identity and security elements, claiming that there was no place for broader community initiatives within the policy. Prevent would now be purely focused on individuals vulnerable to radicalisation. Yet, with the renewed focus on extremism through the Extremism Task Force in 2013, the Counter-Extremism strategy in 2015, and the positioning of extremism as a key strategic priority in the 2018 CONTEST strategy, this clear separation of identity and security within the policy is troubled. It represents a recognition that separating a focus on the perceived causes of violent extremism from action to tackle radicalisation was problematic, bringing questions of identity back into the Home Office, alongside Prevent's explicit security interventions.

2001–6

CONTEST: the strategic response to 9/11

The story of CONTEST starts with the appointment of Sir David Omand to the position of first Permanent Secretary and Security and Intelligence Co-ordinator at the Cabinet Office in September 2002. The government had spent the last year responding to the shock of 9/11. While that had entailed a new legal apparatus through the Counter-Terrorism Act 2001, it had yet to translate into a fundamental shift in policy. From the vantage point of the Cabinet Office, Omand drew together a team of officials from across government and the intelligence agencies to work on developing a coherent policy approach to counter-terrorism in a post-9/11 world. This group became formalised as an official Cabinet sub-committee (chaired by Omand and reporting to a Ministerial Cabinet Committee chaired by the Home Secretary), and developed the first iteration of CONTEST (interview with Senior Civil Servant).

The CONTEST strategy, from this first iteration, has been formed of four pillars: Protect, Prepare, Pursue and Prevent. Protect is 'concerned with reducing the vulnerability of the UK and UK interests overseas to a terrorist attack', which focuses on protecting 'borders, the critical national infrastructure, and crowded places' (Home Office, 2006: 22). Prepare seeks to ensure 'the UK is as ready as it can be for the consequences of a terrorist attack' through identifying risks and 'building the capabilities to respond to them' (Home Office, 2006: 25). Pursue is 'concerned with reducing the terrorist threat to the UK and to UK interests overseas by disrupting terrorists and their operations' (Home Office, 2006: 16). This is achieved by making Britain a hostile environment for terrorists, ideally taking the form of prosecution, but also utilising deportation, asset freezing, control orders and the proscription of organisations (Home Office, 2006: 17). Prevent is concerned with 'tackling the radicalisation of individuals, both in the UK and elsewhere' (Home Office, 2006: 9). It seeks to understand '[t]he processes whereby certain experiences and events in a person's life cause them to become radicalised, to the extent of turning to violence to resolve perceived grievances' (Home Office, 2006: 9). Pushing beyond the criminal justice framework of Pursue, the intention of the Prevent strand is to identify individuals that represent a *potential* risk of radicalisation, those who are vulnerable to radicalisation, in order to then act on and minimise the threat they pose.

The central concern of Prevent is therefore stopping people from *becoming* terrorists. From the beginning, the intelligence community understood that this aspect of the new counter-terrorism strategy would require a focus on British citizens. The concept of 'homegrown' terrorism developed in the aftermath of the attacks on the London transport network on 7 July 2005 – the 7/7 attacks. Yet that British citizens might engage in political violence in the name of Islam pre-dates the shock of 7/7, informing the earliest discussions of the new policy. By the late 1990s there was a lot of security activity focused on those in the UK sympathetic to the ideals of groups such as al-Qaeda, and who were demonstrably organising volunteers and money to send overseas (interview with Senior Civil Servant).[2] With 9/11, it became evident that the possibility of al-Qaeda targeting the 'West' was a legitimate concern. By 2003–4, it was demonstrable that attacks on UK soil by UK citizens were being contemplated. This was made abundantly clear with a number of arrests made in March 2004 as a result of Operation Crevice. The plot resulted in the imprisonment of five British citizens, who were found guilty of conspiring to make a fertiliser bomb and had planned to attack targets such as a shopping centre, a nightclub and a gas network. Members of the group had travelled to Pakistan for training and had links to al-Qaeda (see *BBC News*, 2007). By the time of the 7/7 attacks, the idea of 'homegrown' terrorists targeting the UK was 'completely accepted inside the security community' (interview with Senior Civil Servant). The question that therefore emerges is why British-born citizens of Islamic faith are willing to engage in this violence? And is it possible to prevent these individuals from going down this path?

Counter-radicalisation as a community relations strategy

While the attacks of 9/11 bring to the fore the threat posed by Islamist terrorists to the UK, the question of Muslim communities and their place within the UK had already been raised by a number of riots in northern mill towns in the summer of 2001.[3] Seen to be rooted in inter-cultural tensions between white populations and second- and third-generation Muslim communities, the disturbances led to a critique of the current state of British multiculturalism. It was argued, most notably in a Home Office report led by Professor Ted Cantle, that different ethnic communities had become 'segregated', lacking any common identity, with the authors 'particularly struck by the depth of polarisation of our towns and cities' (Home Office, 2001a: 9). Different communities living in the same city were, it was claimed, living 'parallel lives', lives that 'do not seem to touch at any point, let alone overlap and promote any meaningful interchanges', with the report concluding there was 'little wonder that the ignorance about each other's communities can easily grow into fear, especially where this is exploited by extremist groups determined to undermine community harmony and foster divisions' (Home Office, 2001a: 9). The policy recommendation is to develop a communities policy based upon an idea of cohesion, bridging the divide between segregated communities in the UK, and that this will require establishing 'a greater sense of citizenship based on (a few) common principles which are shared and observed by all sections of the community' (Home Office, 2001a: 10). What emerges is a set of policy discourses that question the alienation and segregation of communities in the UK, with a particular focus on Muslim communities. It is feared that such segregation leads to a lack of common values and the generation of extremism, which in turn may lead to violence. It is this analysis that forms the basis for the argument that Prevent, to be effective, needs to intervene into these broader questions of identity and values. The discourses of community cohesion will be explored more fully in chapter 5.

In this period of Prevent's development, the importance of this emerging discourse of cohesion is that it starts to influence policymakers who are now concerned about the possibility of homegrown terrorism emerging from Muslim communities in the UK. This analysis of community relations in general, and the Muslim community in particular, is mobilised by the Home Office Select Affairs Committee who, in publishing an influential report – *Terrorism and Community Relations* – would set the framework for the early years of the Prevent strategy. The report, set up to examine how terrorism had affected community relations in the UK post-9/11, argues that 'the need to overcome segregation [...] and the need for clarity over what it means to be British, are central to the problems discussed in this inquiry' (Home Affairs Committee, 2005: 61). The concern regarding minority groups, and particularly Muslim communities in the UK, is that when 'alienation from the wider society is too great, a small number of people will be drawn to extremist interpretations of their faith' (Home Affairs Committee, 2005: 51). The report states that '[q]uestions of identity may be inextricably linked with the reasons which may lead a small number of well-educated and apparently integrated young British people to turn to terrorism' (Home Affairs Committee, 2005: 52).

Preventing people from becoming terrorists is therefore positioned within the wider question of the place of Muslim communities in the UK. It is segregation and alienation from the mainstream of 'British' society that represents a concern, generating extremism, that might then lead to terrorism. The report argues that the response to the terrorist threat must not simply be 'a set of police and judicial powers', but must also 'explicitly and specifically set out how British Muslim leaders will be supported in assisting British Muslims in resisting extremist views' (Home Affairs Committee, 2005: 49). Noting that the Home Office did not reference community cohesion in their submission to the committee, the report suggests that they did 'not yet appreciate that the implementation of its community cohesion strategy is central to its ability to deal with the community impact of international terrorism', recommending that links between cohesion and counter-terrorism work be reviewed (Home Affairs Committee, 2005: 33). The report concludes that 'the Government must engage British Muslims in its anti-terrorist strategy' (Home Affairs Committee, 2005: 60).

Responding to the report, the Home Office endorses this reading of the relation between questions of Muslim identity and belonging, and concerns regarding extremism and security. As the response argues, the government's recently published communities policy document, *Improving Opportunity, Strengthening Society* (Home Office, 2005a), had already 'heralded the intention to give greater emphasis to promoting a sense of common belonging and cohesion among all groups' (Home Office, 2005b: 15). Published only a month prior to the attacks of 7/7, the Home Office states 'considerable progress has already been made, in terms of interfaith dialogue, citizenship education in schools and by building partnerships between the police service and community groups to combat the risk of young people being drawn into extremism' (Home Office, 2005b: 18). However, it also agrees with the conclusions drawn by the Home Office Select Committee, affirming that the government sees community cohesion as integral to a counter-terrorism strategy, and stating that ministers 'will be taking forward a programme of engagement with Muslim communities in the coming months' (Home Office, 2005b: 18). This heralds a post-7/7 response to the problem of British Muslims becoming terrorists that would situate engaging with the Muslim community as central. By working with, and through, Muslim communities, the approach was one that sought to build cohesion and a sense of belonging, that through doing so, would challenge extremism.

Nevertheless, that Prevent would be implemented through a community-led model was not pre-ordained. Approaches to counter-radicalisation were being developed in these early years that emphasised a partnership model, based upon close working relationships between security agents and members of the Muslim community. This approach is exemplified in the development of the Muslim Contact Unit (MCU), a specialised police unit headed by Robert Lambert, and active between 2002 and 2007. It included a large percentage of Muslim officers and developed close relationships with members and leaders of the Muslim community. Its intent was to provide a space for communication, such that individuals of concern could be discussed. This required the building of trust, leading to relationships that were mutually enabling. These community contacts could provide insight and the police could sometimes provide them with assistance. This might involve enabling peaceful protest or sometimes providing space for critical voices to work to counter dangerous elements in the community (interview with Robert Lambert). This latter aspect was not without controversy. In doing so, the MCU was willing to work with groups who would now be labelled non-violent extremists: those who may disagree with mainstream British society on substantive issues, but who nevertheless reject violence and were seen to be credible voices in the community in moving others away from violence. Perhaps the most notable of these groups was the STREET project, an organisation of Salafi Muslims set-up to counter the narratives of Abu Hamza (a prominent advocate of violence in the name of Islam) and pre-dating Prevent work (Githens-Mazer and Lambert, 2010: 897).

The work of the MCU prefigures a crucial element of Prevent: that it would be possible to identify, and engage with, individuals who were vulnerable to radicalisation. While this period of the policy does not accomplish this goal, it is nevertheless important to establish that the identification of such individuals was always perceived to be a component of the Prevent strategy. Those working on the policy saw important contributions that could be made by emulating the work that the New Labour government had been undertaking in regards to youth criminality and gang-related violence (interview with Senior Civil Servant). In this policy area, the focus had shifted to early intervention, with Youth Justice Boards established that sought to direct 'at risk' youths away from engagement in crime. It was thought the institutions that had developed in this space could be translated, to be used with individuals at risk of radicalisation. Albeit that Prevent self-consciously sought to 'push the boundary a little' of this sort of work, wherein the numbers involved are relatively low, yet the potential risk if these individuals are not spotted is significant (interview with John Wright). In this period, though, such plans had not yet come to fruition. It would not be until 2007 that this approach would start to be implemented.

It was thought that the partnership approach of the MCU could be rolled out nationally as a model for Muslim community engagement work, and there had been discussion with the Association of Chief Police Officers (ACPO; since renamed the National Police Chiefs' Council (NPCC)) and the Home Office in this regard (interview with Robert Lambert). However, these conversations were overtaken by events. The *Terrorism and Community Relations* report, followed shortly by the tragic events of 7/7, entailed that the immediate priority for the Home Office was an approach that sought to enact counter-radicalisation through a community engagement approach with British Muslims, under the banner of Prevent. The political realisation that young men, born and raised in Britain, were willing to enact this violence, led to real questions being asked of the ideas and values of Muslim communities in the UK. A security-focused approach that positions Prevent as a means of identifying and intervening into those vulnerable to radicalisation will emerge. The questions that take on an urgency in this period though are broader, focusing on the identities and values of British Muslim communities, and how government might be able to help these communities tackle violent extremism.

While CONTEST was first outlined to Cabinet in 2003, the analysis contained in the 2006, publicly released, iteration demonstrates the centrality of these broad concerns around community cohesion and mobilising counter-radicalisation through a community relations policy. Stating that the government has a role to play within Prevent, it is nevertheless affirmed that 'this is a battle of ideas in which success will depend upon all parts of the community challenging the ideological motivations used to justify the use of violence' (Home Office, 2006: 3). The policy states: 'Muslims themselves are aware of the risk of radicalisation within certain offshoots of their communities and we must work in partnership with communities to identify and respond to the risks that extremism poses' (Home Office, 2006: 6). Committed to working with local communities, the Home Office states that it has 'supported Muslim and other faith communities and encouraged their contribution to social cohesion and interfaith activities' (Home Office, 2006: 14). At this time, Prevent is focused on three broad areas of activity: first, contesting the battle of ideas through challenging extremist narratives that justify violence; second, tackling economic disadvantage and supporting the Muslim community through encouraging cohesion, integration, community leadership and capacity building; and third, deterring those who facilitate terrorism (Home Office, 2006). The security-focused, targeted approach of the MCU is not mentioned. Instead, the policy provides a broad community-focused response to the problem of radicalisation.

This analysis can be seen in the practices of Prevent that emerge in the aftermath of 7/7. There is a clear recognition that while a police focus on individuals at risk was of value, there needed to be long-term community building work that showed young Muslims could have a decent future in the UK and be part of civic life (interview with Hazel Blears). Government ministers were sent out across the country to build relationships with the Muslim community, to reassure the community that the government did not think that all Muslims were terrorists, and to listen to their grievances (interview with Hazel Blears). Home Office ministers visited nine 'towns and cities with large Muslim populations to consult them about how government could work with communities to prevent extremism' (Home Office, 2006: 14). These community-based dialogues and workshops developed into the Home Office led 'Preventing Extremism Together' exercise (Home Office, 2005c, 2005d). Out of these dialogues, seven working groups were formed on topics relating to Muslims in the UK, and their discussions led to sixty-four recommendations being put to the government.[4] The Preventing Extremism Together exercises gave rise to further programmes that sought to challenge extremism and build cohesion between Muslim communities and the UK. Prominent examples include the 'Scholars' Roadshow', led by British Muslim organisations and in which Muslim scholars and thinkers travelled round the country talking to young British Muslims, and the 'Muslim Forums against Extremism and Islamophobia', which aimed to provide a space to share views and develop ideas for dealing with extremism (Home Office, 2005c: 5, 10). Another project was the Foreign and Commonwealth Office and DCLG sponsored 'Radical Middle Way' roadshows. These began in the aftermath of the 7/7 attacks and sought to establish dialogues towards the creation of a mainstream and moderate Islam, relevant to young people in the twenty-first century (Home Office, 2009a: 82).

In Prevent's early years the response was therefore one of understanding counter-radicalisation as a community relations strategy. Demonstrative of this emphasis, when the DCLG was established in May 2006, the Department gained ownership of Prevent from the Home Office. These early years represent the beginning of an institutional response to the question of how the government can prevent radicalisation. Drawing links between counter-radicalisation and community cohesion, the concern is one of Muslim communities that are understood as segregated and alienated from the mainstream of 'British' society. The concern is that this segregation is conducive to extremism that might lead to radicalisation. While targeted approaches are tested and are a key ambition of the strategy, the response in this period is broader. These early years focus on the ideas and values present within Muslim communities, and the need to work with the community in order to challenge extremism. In this period, it is therefore questions of Muslim identity that come to the fore within Prevent.

2007–10

'Preventing Violent Extremism' and the reorganisation of Prevent

In the years immediately following the publication of the 2006 iteration, the security-focused capacity to identify individuals at risk was developed, although this was not at the expense of the continued focus on Muslim identity and community relations. While articulated fully within the 2009 iteration of CONTEST, this dual approach was in place by 2007. The reorganisation of Prevent in 2007, entitled Preventing Violent Extremism (PVE), states the Home Office would lead 'on protecting those individuals most at risk from violent extremist influences', while the DCLG would lead on enabling local communities to challenge extremists and promoting shared values (DCLG, 2007: 4). The DCLG's work was to be achieved through 'the building of strong communities, confident in themselves, open to others, and resilient to violent extremism' and is explicitly located within a community cohesion framework (DCLG, 2007: 4). The police and Home Office would take the lead on generating intelligence in order to identify individuals vulnerable to radicalisation, working with community groups and the public sector to do so. The cohesion focus remains, but a Home Office capacity for targeted identification and intervention was constituted that was police-led. There thus developed one set of practices that specifically focused on questions of Muslim identity, and the relation of such identities to 'shared' and 'common' 'British values'. There also developed another set of practices targeting individuals thought to be vulnerable to, and at risk of, radicalisation.

Yet that one would have this community-relations approach, housed within the DCLG, was starting to be contested in the Cabinet. Splits start to emerge concerning to what extent, within a Prevent strategy, the government should intervene into the realm of ideas and identities. While it was broadly agreed within government that the DCLG had a role to play in Prevent delivery, there were debates as to whether it should take the lead on Prevent issues, or whether it should all take place within the overarching counter-terrorism strategy at the Home Office (interview with Jacqui Smith). The ideological question was in terms of 'the extent to which we thought that we needed to tackle the overall space of Islamist extremism or whether or not we wanted to simply focus on when people turned violent or not' (interview with Jacqui Smith). Both Jacqui Smith (Secretary of State at the Home Office between 2007 and 2009) and Hazel Blears (who would take over as Secretary of State at the DCLG in June 2007 and remain in position until 2009) were at the maximum extend of this argument, arguing that if one did not occupy the ideological space, a vacuum was created in which extremism could develop, which could lead to people becoming radicalised towards violence (interview with Jacqui Smith).

As Smith went on to argue:

> some of us felt, more or less strongly, that this did need to be not simply about where somebody crosses over into lawbreaking but it needed to go more widely than that. So it needed to be about a challenge to a particular ideology not simply a challenge to a particular set of behaviours which might at that point be illegal. (Interview with Jacqui Smith)

In the Prime Minister's statement on National Security in November 2007, Tony Blair affirmed the government's commitment to this wider focus:

> To deal with the challenge posed by the terrorist threat we have to do more, working with communities in our country [...] It is a generational challenge that requires sustained work over the long term, through a range of actions in schools, colleges, universities, faith groups and youth clubs, by engaging young people through the media, culture, sports and arts, and by acting against extremist influences operating on the internet and in institutions from prisons and universities to some places of worship. (HC Deb 14 November 2007, cc. 669–670)

Thus, while there were those in Cabinet who thought that Prevent should only focus on those at immediate risk, the scope of Prevent in this period is much broader. Both a security and an identity strand are carried forward, housed in separate government departments, yet with combined oversight through containing them within the Prevent strategy.

The communities strand therefore continues to be developed within the DCLG and retains a clear focus on Muslim identities and extremist ideologies. The PVE strategy asserts that the government recognises that 'while a security response is vital it will not, on its own, be enough. Winning hearts and minds and preventing individuals being attracted to violent extremism in the first place is also crucial' (DCLG, 2007: 4). The intention of the strategy was to 'work with mainstream Muslim organisations to tackle violent extremism'; government will still act when it needs to, but will primarily aim to 'provide sustained support and encouragement to those organisations displaying true leadership' (DCLG, 2007: 12). This was to be achieved through four key strategies: promoting shared values; supporting local solutions; building capacity and leadership; and strengthening the role of faith institutions and leaders (DCLG, 2007). Key projects within the framework sought to promote shared values through ensuring the provision of citizenship education at Islamic supplementary schools and promoting faith understanding in schools more broadly (DCLG, 2007: 5–7). Government sought to help build stronger communities that would be able to challenge extremism, through promoting cohesion (DCLG, 2007: 9–10).

This framework was supported by funding through the PVE Pathfinder Fund. The first round of funding committed £6 million and was dispersed to the seventy local authorities in England that had more than 5 per cent of their population as Muslim. In 2008, this was expanded to a three-year, £45 million fund for all local authorities containing more than 4,000 Muslims (Thomas, 2010: 443–444). While Prevent has always been envisaged as an approach that should tackle all forms of violent extremism, it is clear through these funding mechanisms that the focus here is predominantly aimed at Muslim communities. By the end of 2008, it was estimated by the DCLG that PVE projects were attended by roughly 44,000 individuals, with the majority of the projects focusing on shared values, community leadership or community resilience (DCLG, 2008a: 8–9). The 2008–9 programme alone cost £140 million (Home Office, 2009a: 80). Beyond this, the DCLG commits itself to continuing to fund 'Forums on Extremism and Islamophobia' and expanding its 'Tackling Violent Extremism Roadshows', both run by local communities, and providing a voice for those who are not often heard, such as Muslim women and young people, and also a space in which to discuss sensitive issues (DCLG, 2007: 7–8). What emerges in this period is a broad funding platform. Funding was made available to local groups engaged in a variety of tasks contributing to Prevent, ranging through challenging extremism, building capacity and leadership, and promoting shared values and citizenship.

Alongside this communities approach, the targeted security approach is actively developed within the Home Office. Of importance is the constitution of the Office for Security and Counter-Terrorism (OSCT). Formed in 2007, its purpose was to 'bring more cohesion and greater strategic capability' to the government's fight against international terrorism (Home Office, 2009b). One of its six directorates is the Prevent and Research, Information and Communications Unit, 'responsible for implementing strategies to stop people becoming terrorists or supporting violent extremism [...] and for the strategic communications to support this' (Home Office, 2009b). This focus on processes of radicalisation leads to the formation of Channel. Created as a pilot in 2007, it was 'developed to provide support to people at risk of being drawn into violent extremism' (Home Office, 2010: 3). Channel will come to play a crucial role within Prevent, representing the central mechanism for identifying and working with individuals understood as vulnerable to radicalisation. The Channel project will be explored fully in chapter 6.

The whole CONTEST policy was reviewed in 2009. In this iteration, the clarification of Prevent functions is now formally stated within the strategy. Three components are identified: the PVE programme, 'a community-led approach to tackling violent extremism led by the [DCLG] in partnership with local authorities and a range of statutory and voluntary organisations'; the police Prevent Strategy and Delivery Plan with 300 specialised staff and a national and regional counter-terrorism policing structure; and the Channel programme, an 'initiative which utilises existing partnership working between the police, local authority and the local community to identify those at risk from violent extremism and provide help to them' (Home Office, 2009a: 80). This period of the policy therefore focuses on both the community dynamics that might generate violent extremism and those individuals who are at immediate risk. Yet, increasingly during this period, the housing of the identity-focused strand within the Prevent framework had been the subject of critique. Within the policy community, and within the halls of government, the case was being made that in institutionally bringing questions of cohesion and identity alongside questions of security, the Prevent policy was undermining the work of both.

Key criticisms of Prevent

The first way this critique manifests is in terms of Prevent funding, with questions being asked of exactly who the policy was giving money to.

Whether suitable attention had been paid to who was receiving funding was a question raised in an influential report published by Policy Exchange, entitled *Choosing Our Friends Wisely*. It asked serious questions regarding the suitability of local authorities being put in charge of handing out Prevent funding. Funding for Prevent at this time was handled by local authorities who were held to account under National Indicator 35, a reporting framework through which to assess the success of Prevent interventions, and more pragmatically, ensure that this work was carried out in the ways requested by central government. This left substantive decision-making as to what Prevent was to achieve in the hands of local authority officials who possessed varying degrees of knowledge and commitment to the policy. On one hand, this led to wide variation in Prevent delivery. While some targeted funds, focusing on mosque governance or young people at risk, most engaged in generic cohesion and inter-faith projects (interview with Senior Council Official with responsibility for Prevent delivery). On the other hand, there were concerns these officials lacked the ideological or theological knowledge to properly assess the terrain of Muslim groups and know who is best placed to deliver a counter-radicalising message (Maher and Frampton, 2009: 6).

Ultimately, this mish-mash of funding, it was argued, had led to resources being given to non-violent, yet extremist, groups, who were then charged with supporting young people in the community. This may have been based on ignorance or on the assumption that these non-violent extremists were best placed to counter the message of al-Qaeda. Yet, the report claimed, the perverse effect of these decisions was that:

> PVE – however well intentioned – isn't working. Not only is it failing to achieve its stated objectives, in many places it is actually making the situation worse: a new generation is being radicalised, sometimes with the very funds that are supposed to be countering radicalisation. (Maher and Frampton, 2009: 5)

In effect, the policy had underwritten 'the very Islamist ideology which spawns an illiberal, intolerant and anti-western world view' and the effect had been 'to empower reactionaries within Muslim communities and to marginalise genuine moderates, thus increasing inter-community tensions and envenoming the public space' (Maher and Frampton, 2009: 5). Prevent, in trying to build community capacity and challenge violent narratives had, it was argued, perversely empowered the sorts of extremist ideas it should have been challenging.[5] In giving money to non-violent extremists, the government had promoted ideas and values that undermined the shared values being sought through broader goals of cohesion, and upon which a successful Prevent policy was based.

While this funding regime was under fire for giving money to the wrong people, it was also contested on the basis that it was securitising

Muslim communities. Prevent funding had become the primary source of income for a range of Muslim community organisations, many of which were only tangentially involved in the security-focused objectives of supporting at risk individuals. This led to a large amount of 'security' funding being poured into Muslim communities. On the one hand, this had the effect of framing counter-radicalisation and community cohesion as a 'Muslim' problem, situating Muslim communities as *the* problem spaces of Prevent. On the other, it angered other communities who felt they were missing access to funding, even though many of the projects funded engaged with wider questions of cohesion and community development. The effect was to undermine a broader vision for community cohesion that would focus on the UK as a whole (Communities and Local Government Committee, 2010; Thomas, 2012, 2014).

Further, these groups now receiving Prevent funding were, whether they liked it or not, being brought into a security apparatus. It was increasingly being argued that a community-led Prevent agenda was being mobilised in order to surveil and gather intelligence upon Muslim communities as a whole (Kundnani, 2009; Stevens, 2009; Communities and Local Government Committee, 2010; Thomas, 2010, 2012; Home Affairs Committee, 2012). The security strand of Prevent envisaged it as a police tool to gather intelligence which would then enable intervention into those who were thought to be at risk. Yet this intelligence often came from community members and workers who understood their own Prevent role to be one of engaging in broader cohesion work. In supplying detailed information to the police, the concern of many was that community trust in these broader goals of building capacity and cohesion was undermined.

Lastly, concerns were being raised within government that this dual approach, encompassing both a targeted, security-focused strand and wider questions of community identity and cohesion, was leading to confusion as to what Prevent was supposed to achieve. A report by the House of Commons Communities and Local Governments Committee had argued that a major concern for it was the 'lack of agreement between central government departments charged with the delivery of *Prevent*' (Communities and Local Government Committee, 2010: 44). A submission from the UK Youth Parliament to the committee claimed that, 'rather than working as a strength, it's been our experience that the inter-departmental arrangements are actually a major weakness [...] the muddled way of working between departments is perhaps one of the major barriers to operational success' (Communities and Local Government Committee, 2010: 44). This ambiguity led to concerns that '[l]ocal authorities and their partners appear to lack clarity as to what Prevent aims to achieve', with the DCLG and the Home Office 'not providing consistent advice' (Communities and Local Government

Committee, 2010: 49). While supportive of cohesion work in principle, and recognising its value to countering extremism, the committee concluded that 'work focusing on shared values should be decoupled from the *Prevent* agenda and brought under CLG's broader responsibilities', and that it should make greater efforts to focus on all forms of extremism (Communities and Local Government Committee, 2010: 67).

The political debates at this time therefore coalesce around a critique of Prevent that sees the institutional relationship drawn between Prevent's security and identity strands as *the* problem. The perverse outcome of the PVE agenda was that the strategy was undermining both the security and the cohesion agenda. Money was being given to non-violent extremists which then undermined cohesion. Funds were being made available to the Muslim community, but this damaged a vision of cohesion as a universal good, positioning it as a Muslim problem. This undermined trust in both the cohesion and security agendas, and it was perceived as a means of surveilling and spying on Muslims as a whole. Lastly, as a machinery of government question, delivery of Prevent was muddled and its objectives unclear. During this period of Labour government, the Prevent policy was envisaged as a wide-ranging strategy, both targeting individuals at risk, yet also needing to intervene into broader communal spaces, and the ideas and identities that might give rise to radicalisation. In 2010, with the incoming Conservative and Liberal Democrat government, this position is revisited, with the coalition arguing that UK counter-radicalisation policy was in need of reform, 'with a view to separating it much more clearly than before from general communities policy' (Cabinet Office, 2010: 42).

2011–18

The election of the Conservative and Liberal Democrat coalition on 11 May 2010 provided space to take stock of the workings of the Prevent policy and would lead to its next significant iteration. The incoming government was left with a policy that had been the object of sustained critique. Nevertheless, the policy was widely felt within the civil service to be of use, and upon entering government, both the Conservatives and the Liberal Democrats, given access to full view of the information, were able to see the value of the approach (interview with Charlie Edwards). The response was therefore to initiate a review of the Prevent policy. This began in earnest in November 2010. Lord Carlile, a Liberal Democrat peer and Charlie Edwards, who had been brought into the OSCT by Charles Farr (Director of the OSCT from July 2007 to November 2015), would provide oversight of the review (interview with Charlie Edwards).

The coalition published a new iteration of CONTEST in 2011, and the Prevent review led to a separate and extended document addressing the Prevent strand, published at the same time. This iteration contains an explicit critique of the Prevent strategy under Labour, coherent with the broader critiques discussed in the previous section. Theresa May (Home Secretary from 2010 to 2016), in her foreword to the Prevent strategy, states that the programme the new government inherited was 'flawed'. That it, 'confused the delivery of Government policy to promote integration with Government policy to prevent terrorism', had failed to 'confront the extremist ideology at the heart of the threat we face' and that 'funding sometimes even reached the very extremist organisations that Prevent should have been confronting' (Home Office, 2011a: 1). Seeking to clearly demarcate the work of Prevent from the wider communities strategy, Theresa May stated:

> The new Prevent strategy will follow the principles of our counter-terrorism legislation. It will be proportionate to the specific challenge we face; it will only do what is necessary to achieve its specific aims; and it will be more effective. It will be separate from work to tackle wider forms of extremism and to promote integration, which is being led by the Department for Communities and Local Government. (HC Deb 9 November 2010, c. WS13)

The new strategy would thus *not* include broader communities policy, but would maintain a sole focus on those vulnerable to radicalisation. This vision of Prevent is therefore one in which there is a clear, institutional division between communities policy and counter-radicalisation strategy. Yet, as the analysis of this chapter will start to gesture towards, maintaining this division in both theory and practice has proved problematic.

Removing communities policy from Prevent and reorganising Prevent delivery

This new iteration transforms both the organisation and delivery of Prevent, removing the identity strand, situating it solely in the Home Office, yet also broadening the scope of who is responsible for its delivery. Organisationally, the centre of gravity for Prevent was now within the Home Office, focusing solely on individuals at risk of radicalisation. The Prevent review states that while the strategy 'depends on integration, democratic participation and strong interfaith dialogue' it is nevertheless important 'not to overstate the relationship between radicalisation and community or individual isolation' (Home Office, 2011a: 27). Previously, it is stated, the objectives of building community resilience and cohesion had 'implicitly and sometimes explicitly encouraged the use of Prevent funding and delivery structures for a very wide range of projects, some of them more to do with cohesion than with counter-terrorism' (Home Office, 2011a: 27). This had given the 'impression that the Government was supporting cohesion projects only for security reasons and in effect "securitising integration"' (Home Office, 2011a: 30). It is concluded that:

> Prevent depends on a successful cohesion and integration strategy. But, as a general rule, the two strategies and programmes *must not be merged together*. Combining the strategies risks using counter-terrorism funds and delivery structures for activities which have a much wider purpose and whose success will be jeopardised by being given a security label. Moreover, channelling Prevent funding into cohesion projects has the further effect of making it less likely that Prevent will meet its own objectives. (Home Office, 2011a: 30, emphasis added)

As Charlie Edwards relayed, 'Prevent focuses on the tip of the [...] spear, rather than the shaft' (interview with Charlie Edwards). The shaft is the responsibility of the rest of government, local authorities and communities and refers to the dynamics, values and beliefs of the population and the broader challenges of social integration. The tip is the most difficult, where you see individuals 'moving from non-violent to violent extremism' (interview with Charlie Edwards). The sole concern of Prevent is now the head of the spear, with the Home Secretary taking the lead role on the strategy (Home Office, 2011a: 9). This would be a targeted, security-centred approach. Moreover, it would explicitly seek to do more to engage with other forms of violent extremism. While affirming the primary threat is still from Islamism, Northern Ireland related and right-wing extremism are highlighted as areas of Prevent work (Home Office, 2011a: 14–15).

Yet, while Prevent is being centralised in the Home Office, its implementation is shifted from a police-led model to one that would be led by a range of societal and professional groups. If, previously, the lead agency on Prevent work had almost always been the police, the vision for the new Prevent was that the police should *not* play a lead role (interview with Lord Carlile of Berriew). Thus, within this new Prevent, the identity strand is excluded from Prevent work and the security strand is remodelled. Previously, following the MCU partnership model, the police took the lead and would engage community contacts in order to identify individuals and spaces that were deemed to be at risk. The new strategy locates this targeted Prevent work away from the police and into local authorities. The local authority, it is deemed, will be able to mobilise the broader community towards this role of targeted identification, working alongside community and mosque groups. Prevent is now envisioned as working 'where the emphasis is on the community and where most of the work is actually done within the community. You can't impose Prevent. It requires community acceptance wherever possible' (interview with Lord

Carlile of Berriew). Ironically, this vision of Prevent sees a much more community-focused solution to counter-terrorism than the DCLG-led Prevent prior to it (interview with Senior Council Official with responsibility for Prevent delivery). Where pre-2011 Prevent sought to tackle radicalisation and extremism through transforming community relations, encouraging shared values, cohesion and leadership, the post-2011 Prevent sees communities as a vital resource for identifying individuals who are vulnerable to radicalisation.

Further, again shifting the focus away from the police, the 'mainstreaming' of Prevent gathers momentum in this period. This mainstreaming entails that a range of professionals will possess responsibilities for the identification of signs of vulnerability to radicalisation. Sectors with responsibility specifically include education, the internet, faith institutions and organisations, health, the criminal justice system and charities (Home Office, 2011a). This is not a new development, but it is within this iteration that this vision of counter-radicalisation finds its surest footing. From the very beginning of CONTEST it was envisaged that this was to be a whole-government policy. Thus, from its earliest meetings, there were representatives from many different departments around the table, and this entailed the strategy already had buy-in from these groups. However, and reflecting the Youth Justice Board model that Prevent looked towards, when it came to identifying individuals at risk of engaging in criminality, the police had taken the lead as they were the most accustomed to this work (interview with John Wright).

It is clear that in the 2007–9 period there were attempts to ask these sectors to play a part in counter-radicalisation. As Jacqui Smith related, within this period there was 'always a strategic objective that you had to intervene wherever you felt there was a potential for radicalisation and extremism', whether this was the public sector, the third sector, religious groups or internationally (interview with Jacqui Smith). Yet this had been a difficult process. For instance, it took time to convince the education sector that it had a valuable role to play within this. In effect, there were experts from the OSCT working with people from across government who, in some cases, were sceptical about the proposed objectives, and in others, saw this as a very minor part of what they were doing (interview with Jacqui Smith). While one had 'buy in' from across government, this only meant that the initial conversations were easy to start, there was still a long and difficult process to translate these into the daily workings of these institutions (interview with John Wright). The 2011 iteration takes this mainstreaming as a key focus. This would reach its culmination in the Counter-Terrorism and Security Act that was approved in February 2015, making Prevent a statutory duty for a range of public sector bodies, including local authorities, the education sector, healthcare and the probation service.

Following from these shifts, the funding of Prevent changes significantly in this iteration. Whereas previously, local authorities had commissioned local groups to organise Prevent activities, now, central government would manage the Prevent budget, with local authorities being directed to undertake specific Prevent work. This is a response to the concerns discussed previously that money had made its way to extremist groups, with the Home Office seen as best placed to have the expertise to make reliable funding decisions. Prevent funding is also significantly decreased. No longer is it funding large, community projects, and further, the mainstreaming of Prevent is leading to savings. In incorporating this into the daily work of many professionals, this work is now being done at no extra cost, without need for specific funding (Home Office, 2011a: 101).

Organisationally, there is therefore a fundamental shift in the delivery of Prevent. First, the DCLG is no longer involved. It still has a role to play in terms of cohesion and extremism, but these are institutionally distinct from Prevent work. Instead, Prevent will be the sole preserve of the Home Office and will focus only on those seen to be moving towards radicalisation. Further, the implementation of this security strand is remodelled. While the police have a role to play (and are, for instance, heavily engaged within the Channel process), the lead is to be taken by local authorities working through local community organisations. On the one hand, this involves a clearer role for community organisations in identifying vulnerable individuals, and on the other, it reflects the mainstreaming of Prevent work, to be delivered throughout society by a range of professionals.

From 'violent' to 'non-violent' extremism

Nevertheless, while this change in the machinery of government and implementation of Prevent distances it from a focus on identities and values, alongside this move is a clear discursive shift that troubles this distinction. The second important change in this iteration is that of moving away from a language of violent extremism to one of merely 'extremism' or 'non-violent' extremism. The argument is that extremist groups, even those committed to non-violence, provide a theoretical and theological legitimation for certain ideas, which may then be used as justifications for violent actions (Home Office, 2011a: 5). This formulation is made with clarity in the 2012 annual report, which states that, '[w]e have taken a much stronger position on extremism which not only undermines integration and is inconsistent with our British values, but can draw people into terrorist activity' (Home Office, 2013: 10). This focus on non-violent extremism is not new, but the emphasis is. This is therefore a restating and entrenching of previous approaches. Yet this explicit framing also brings with it new measures to tackle extremism, as will be demonstrated through an analysis of the Extremism Task Force and the Counter-Extremism strategy later in the chapter.

The centrality of extremism and its relation to questions of radicalisation takes centre-stage in David Cameron's Munich speech. He states that:

> Islamist extremism is a political ideology supported by a minority. At the furthest end are those who back terrorism to promote their ultimate goal: an entire Islamist realm, governed by an interpretation of Sharia. Move along the spectrum, and you find people who may reject violence, but who accept various parts of the extremist worldview, including real hostility towards Western democracy and liberal values. (Cameron, 2011)

The irony of this mobilisation of extremism is that it further discursively relates questions of radicalisation and violence to questions of identity. Cameron goes on to state that Islamist extremism represents a distinct political ideology, and that an important reason that young Muslims were drawn to it, beyond questions of global politics and inequalities, was a 'question of identity' (Cameron, 2011). That,

> under the doctrine of state multiculturalism, we have encouraged different cultures to live separate lives, apart from each other and apart from the mainstream. We've failed to provide a vision of society to which they feel they want to belong. We've even tolerated these segregated communities behaving in ways that run completely counter to our values. (Cameron, 2011)

This analysis clearly echoes the Cantle Report of 2001. Despite the focus on cohesion since then, Cameron lays the blame for this segregation at the feet of the previous government, arguing that a failure to challenge extremists and a 'hands-off tolerance' has led to the feeling that 'not enough is shared' (Cameron, 2011). This has resulted in a fragmented, fractured society with little communality. The analysis follows that young Muslims, feeling attached to neither their ancestral roots nor their lived society, find in the ideology of Islamist extremism a community to be a part of. The necessary response is thus one of confronting this ideology, and *actively* promoting a shared national identity open to everyone. What Cameron termed 'muscular liberalism' (Cameron, 2011). Thus, while it is envisaged that generic work around cohesion, integration and extremism is solely the preserve of the DCLG (2012), the core analysis retains the problem of extremism as one that is of concern for those working at the tip of the spear, intervening into processes of radicalisation.[6]

In summary, the 2011 iteration significantly narrows the focus of Prevent, concentrating on targeted interventions into those vulnerable to radicalisation and enacting an institutional separation from the DCLG's work regarding cohesion and extremism. Delivery would now be provided by public sector professionals and through local authorities working in partnership with local communities and community groups. Yet, it is also clear that questions of identity and security remain interlinked. While the 'solution' to the critiques levelled at Prevent in the 2007–10 period was to institutionally separate cohesion from counter-radicalisation work, an analysis of radicalisation and extremism that ties these areas of government together remains. In the years following the release of the 2011 iteration, two murders would complicate this relationship further.

The Extremism Task Force

On 22 May 2013, Lee Rigby, a soldier in the Royal Regiment of Fusiliers, was murdered in broad daylight by Michael Adebolajo and Michael Adebowale. They told onlookers that the attack was in response to the deaths of Muslims overseas at the hands of British Armed Forces. The murder of Mohammed Saleem in Birmingham, by Ukranian student Pavlo Lapshyn on 29 April of that year, had gone much unremarked beyond the Muslim press. It was thought that the stabbing could be a revenge attack by the English Defence League for the recent convictions of six Muslims who had planned to bomb one of their rallies. Lapshyn, acting independently of such motivations but nevertheless pursuing a racist and white supremacist agenda, then went on to detonate bombs outside mosques in Walsall, Wolverhampton and Tipton, fortuitously causing no injuries. These attacks, and the different extremisms they represent, led to the establishment of the Extremism Task Force.

The Extremism Task Force was a Cabinet-level group bringing different government departments, the police and intelligence services together to think practically around how the government could do more to tackle extremism. The concept of 'extremism' has been mobilised often in order to ascribe a term to those theological and political identities that may engage in, condone or provide legitimation for violent action. While in common usage since the beginning of the strategy, it is only formally defined in the 2011 iteration of CONTEST. Here it is given as:

> the vocal or active opposition to fundamental British values, including democracy, the rule of law, individual liberty and mutual respect and tolerance of different faiths and beliefs. We also include in our definition of extremism calls for the death of members of our armed forces, whether in this country or overseas. (Home Office, 2011b: 62)

While the 2011 iteration of Prevent sought to separate questions of extremism and identity into the DCLG, the conclusions of the Extremism

Task Force can be read as a recognition that the move had failed. At one level, this is a question of capability, and represents a view that the DCLG had been ineffective when it came to working on questions of extremism (interview with Baroness Pauline Neville-Jones).

Yet at a more fundamental level, it speaks to the debates that have pervaded the policy since its inception concerning to what extent it is necessary to intervene into the realm of ideas and identity within the Prevent policy. If the Prevent review of 2011 had sought to focus the strategy away from broad questions of identity and values, focusing only on individuals vulnerable to radicalisation, the Extremism Task Force reignites the debate of what a counter-radicalisation strategy should do. The report that came out of the Taskforce – *Tackling Extremism* – stated that while efforts to tackle extremism had been ongoing, there was a need to do more:

> This response is broader than dealing only with those who espouse violence – we must confront the poisonous extremist ideology that can lead people to violence; which divides communities and which extremists use to recruit individuals to their cause; which runs counter to fundamental British values. (Cabinet Office, 2013: 1)

The report identifies five areas for further action, arguing the government needs to: disrupt extremists; counter extremist narratives; make delivery of Prevent and Channel legal requirements; promote integration, through supporting communities and promoting projects that bring communities together; and enable institutions to confront extremism (Cabinet Office, 2013). This vision troubles a clear distinction between security and communities policy, bringing questions of values and cohesion squarely alongside questions of radicalisation – both conceptually and institutionally – through the lens of countering extremism.

The other crucial development to arise from the Extremism Task Force is the promise to enact Prevent and Channel as statutory duties, which, as noted earlier, was achieved through the Counter-Terrorism and Security Act on 12 February 2015. If throughout the history of Prevent one of the key struggles has been to make the strategy a priority for a range of sectors and institutions, this represents the culmination of that process. Whereas previously the government had used reporting mechanisms to ensure compliance, it was now felt that a more permanent and decisive mechanism was required. The Act specified a range of authorities who would now be compelled to undertake certain duties within the Prevent framework. This will have crucial implications for who it is that delivers Prevent work, shifting the burden onto specified authorities, especially regarding the need to make referrals to Channel where appropriate, and will be discussed further in chapter 6.

The Counter-Extremism strategy and CONTEST 4

Policy developments since 2015 have only served to further muddy the institutional relationship between questions of radicalisation, terrorism, extremism and values. With the election of the Conservative Party in 2015 and 2017, the focus on extremism is both continued and formalised. On 30 September 2014, the then Home Secretary, Theresa May, used her speech at the Conservative Party conference to outline a vision for a counter-extremism strategy beyond Prevent. She stated:

> I want to see new banning orders for extremist groups that fall short of the existing laws relating to terrorism. I want to see new civil powers to target extremists who stay just within the law but still spread poisonous hatred. (May, 2014)

Pushing beyond a purely Prevent framework, although clearly mobilising the language and analysis of 'extremism' developed through Prevent, she went on to argue:

> yes, not all extremism leads to violence. And not all extremists are violent. But the damage extremists cause to our society is reason enough to act. And there is, undoubtedly, a thread that binds the kind of extremism that promotes intolerance, hatred and a sense of superiority over others to the actions of those who want to impose their values on us through violence. (May, 2014)

Showing an impressive disregard for the history of the strategy and the critiques she had levelled at previous iterations, she stated that 'Prevent has only ever been focused on the hard end of the extremism spectrum' (May, 2014). May stated that the new strategy will go 'beyond terrorism', will be the 'responsibility of the whole of government, the rest of the public sector, and wider civil society' and will 'aim to undermine and eliminate extremism in all its forms' (May, 2014). The intent is to develop 'new civil powers to target extremists who stay just within the law but still spread poisonous hatred' (May, 2014).

Speaking in 2015, Theresa May makes a clear statement that Prevent again needed to engage on this broader terrain of identities and values. In a formulation that does much to reiterate the community cohesion agenda, and the vision of Prevent enacted by previous Labour governments, she stated:

> It also means that the response isn't just about delivering a 'counter-narrative'. It's about promoting a whole set of positive values that define who we are and what we stand for. In promoting the values we believe in, we can set the boundaries and limits of the extremist arguments – on our terms, not theirs. (May, 2015)

If a shift to focus on non-violent extremism discursively troubled an institutional separation between Prevent's security and identity strands, this renewed focus on extremism and promoting those values that define 'who we are' again puts into question these institutional divisions. Countering extremism, developing community capabilities and promoting cohesion again sit alongside this security focus.

The Counter-Extremism strategy was published in October 2015 (Home Office, 2015a), and, while it seeks to address the question of extremism beyond a purely security focus, it is clearly understood to be a key pillar of a response to the threat of radicalisation and terrorism. The strategy focuses on four key areas: countering extremist ideology; building partnerships with those opposed to extremism; disrupting extremists; and building more cohesive communities (Home Office, 2015a). It is supported institutionally through the development of the Extremism Analysis Unit, located in the Home Office, which works to identify individual and organisations deemed to be extremist, which can then inform government decisions such as who not to engage with, so as not to lend credibility to extremist organisatons. The intent of the government has been to support this strategy with legislation. In 2015, an Extremism Bill was announced in the Queen's Speech which failed to materialise, followed by a Counter-Extremism and Safeguarding Bill in the Queen's Speech of 2016, which again did not make it to parliamentary debate. Such legislation would have included the powers needed to ban and disrupt extremist organisations and to close premises used to support extremism, powers which raised concerns regarding the role of government, and whether it is right for ministers and civil servants to be able to intervene in the expression of ideas and values to this extent. At the time of writing, this legislative route has been abandoned, and instead, the government has developed a Commission for Countering Extremism, based in the Home Office, with its Charter published in March 2018. Its intended aims are to identify and oppose extremism, help government develop new policies in this area, to 'support the public sector, communities and civil society to confront extremism wherever it exists' and, finally, to 'promote a positive vision of our core, shared values' (Home Office, 2018a).

The effect of this approach is thus, once more, to focus on extremism and values, and the values of the communities in which extremism is held to exist, as a constituent part of the problem, moving responsibility for these issues back within the Home Office. While formally separate from the Prevent strategy, the Counter-Extremism strategy can be read as an acceptance of previous analyses that argued for a wider engagement with questions of ideas and identities in the fight against radicalisation, even going so far as to reinvoke the language of cohesion, and the promotion of 'shared' values.

The focus on extremism is continued in the latest iteration of CONTEST, published in June 2018 (Home Office, 2018c). At the time

of writing, it is too early to say whether this iteration will lead to significant alterations to the Prevent strand. On the surface, not much appears
to have changed. The Prevent strand, following the 2011 iteration, still
seeks to respond to the ideological challenge of terrorism, to support and
safeguard individuals at risk, and to work alongside communities, civil
society organisations and specified public sector institutions in order
to do so.

There are two practical developments of note. First, the incorporation
of a new objective: rehabilitating those already engaged in terrorism
(Home Office, 2018c: 40). Targeting those returning from Syria and
Iraq, or being released from prison, this 'Desistance and Disengagement
Programme' blurs the line between Prevent and Pursue. They target
those further along the path than traditionally with Prevent, but are still
not juridical interventions. However, unlike Prevent, participation is
compulsory, and non-compliance could lead to criminal charges or being
recalled to prison. The second is to enable greater information sharing
between the intelligence community and other institutions, such as local
authorities (Home Office 2018c: 27). This need is explicitly framed in
response to the terrorist attacks that shook the UK in 2017, where some
of the individuals involved had been known, or previously had been of
interest, to police or intelligence services, but were not the subject of
active investigations (Home Office 2018c: 26). Keeping track of this wider
pool of risky individuals, it is argued, requires better local knowledge,
which it is claimed will improve the breadth and scale of safeguarding
and disengagement interventions. Yet this raises significant civil liberties
concerns. Who will have access to this list? How will it be used? Can one
be removed? And how might this potentially impact the lives of those on
such a list?

These additions, congruent with the wider 2018 iteration of Prevent,
continue to frame Prevent as a security-focused instrument concerned
with individuals at risk. However, this is complicated by the explicit
statement of 'extremism' as one of three key 'strategic factors' (the others
being 'conflict and instability' and 'developments in technology') in the
wider counter-terrorism space (Home Office 2018c: 23–24). Extremism
is framed as strategically central, yet operationally distinct, from counter-
terrorism more broadly. Trying to make sense of this relationship, it is
stated that:

> The Prevent programme counters terrorist ideologies specifically by
> tackling the causes of radicalisation [...] Counter-radicalisation forms
> one part of a wider effort to counter broader extremist messages and
> behaviours. We have an effective Counter-Extremism Strategy to pro-
> tect our communities from the wider social harms beyond terrorism
> caused by extremism. This includes tackling the promotion of hatred,
> the erosion of women's rights, the spread of intolerance, and the

isolation of communities. We judge that communities which do not or cannot participate in civic society are more likely to be vulnerable to radicalisation. A successful integration strategy is therefore important to counter-terrorism. (Home Office, 2018c: 23)

Ostensibly, Prevent thus focuses on individuals, the Counter-Extremism strategy focuses on wider communal issues, and the communities strategy has an overarching, yet ill-defined, role to play in building an integrated society. These distinctions necessarily break down and the issues they raise overlap. Communities are expected to play a key role within Prevent; extremist messaging tackled by Prevent has wider communal implications; and countering extremism and fostering integrated communities are presented as two sides of the same coin.

CONTEST 4 thus represents the latest effort to articulate a clear institutional relationship between the security and identity strands of Prevent. Since the Extremist Task Force – but rooted in discursive shifts to a need to tackle not just 'violent extremism', but 'extremism' more broadly – the Conservative administration has sought to operationally distinguish work on radicalisation, extremism and integration. CONTEST 4 crystallises a vision of a security-focused strand concerned with individuals, an identity-strand concerned with integration and, intersecting the two, a distinct counter-extremism space, located within the Home Office, not within the Counter-Terrorism strategy, yet a key strategic component of it. It demands the separation of the security and identity strands that were central to the 2011 iteration, yet it nevertheless accepts that tackling radicalisation requires intervention into the broader terrain of ideas and values, locating these inside the Home Office, but keeping them operationally distinct from counter-terrorism. This can thus appear muddled. If the 2011 Prevent review had sought to establish a clear institutional division between the security and identity strands of Prevent work, the policy evolution of the past few years has done much to complicate and deconstruct this position.

Conclusion

This reading of Prevent has told the story that is narrated by those responsible for the policy and the policy itself. The political question at the heart of Prevent, prompting debates within and without government, and leading to its different iterations, is whether the policy should focus solely on those at risk of radicalisation? Or should government occupy a broader space? Thus tackling questions of identity, cohesion and extremism that are seen to contribute to and inform vulnerabilities to radicalisation. Is Prevent about those merely on the verge of terrorism, or is it about the ideas that legitimate such violence? Does one concentrate only on the movement of individuals towards violence, or is it necessary to focus on broader communities that may have a role to play in preventing radicalisation?

In Prevent's early years, and especially following the attacks of 7/7, the priority for government was understanding and supporting Muslim communities, framing counter-radicalisation as a community relations strategy. This led to Prevent being housed in the DCLG and mobilised community cohesion policies as one of the core aspects of Prevent work. The 2007 PVE strategy clarified Prevent's organisation. The cohesion focus remained, but a Home Office capacity for targeted identification and intervention was developed that was police-led. There thus developed one set of practices that specifically focused on questions of Muslim identity, and the relation of such identities to 'shared' and 'common' 'British values'. There also developed another set of practices targeting individuals thought to be vulnerable to radicalisation. The subject of much critique for situating Muslim communities as central to the 'problem' of radicalisation, damaging both the security and identity agendas, the reforms of 2011 stepped back from this approach, locating Prevent wholly within the OSCT and claiming that there was no place for broader community initiatives within the policy. Prevent would be purely focused on those individuals at risk. Yet, in expanding the definition to include non-violent extremism, a whole series of questions are opened up around what exactly is defined as 'extremism', and therefore what utterances and behaviours are objects of concern. The renewed focus on extremism following the Extremism Task Force, the Counter-Extremism strategy and the 2018 iteration of CONTEST, bringing it back within the Home Office, represents a recognition that to separate the perceived causes of violent extremism from interventions into them was problematic. While the government's cohesion and integration strategy remains formally within the DCLG, taking a focus on extremism and core values back into the Home Office muddies these waters. Questions of identity are again squarely within the remit of an explicitly security intervention.

The constant debate within government, and the critique Prevent makes of itself, can thus be read as one of the extent to which a relation between targeted intervention into processes of radicalisation, and the wider question of identity and values, is deemed to be strategically relevant. Does one focus on the former? Or must one also tackle the latter? If both, then how should they be institutionally related? The history of Prevent as told by policymakers and the policy documents is therefore one in which the identity and security elements of Prevent can, and perhaps should be, *separated*. The argument of this book is that this story is inadequate. It reduces the development and institution of the Prevent strategy to merely the question of the relation between a security focus and an identity focus.

Through a discursive analysis of the threat that Prevent seeks to minimise, that of vulnerability to radicalisation, this book will demonstrate that there is another possible reading of Prevent. In locating and bringing to the fore this problematic at the heart of Prevent, the book argues that far from being separable, these questions of identity and security within the policy are intimately related. This problematic of vulnerability to radicalisation, explored in chapters 3 and 4, shows that the political debates related in this chapter fail to recognise that Prevent's security interventions are themselves productive of identity. If this is absent from the narrative thus far described, it is because the story the policy tells fails to conceptually account for the important temporality of Prevent's interventions. Prevent intervenes in the present by producing certain identities as risky for the future. In making this problematic central to the analysis, the book shows there is an intrinsic, intimate conceptual relation between security and identity within Prevent. The claim being made here is not that the policy and those responsible for it are seeking to obscure the ways in which the policy works. Rather it is that the policy is blind to the assumptions it makes, and thus the ways in which identity and security come to be conflated within its operation.

Yet the policy narrative is not alone in failing to adequately conceptualise Prevent. The academic literature that has arisen in response to the policy does much to replicate the analysis of security and identity given in the policy documents. It is a literature that, for the most part, also seeks to reduce the 'problems' of Prevent to the relationship drawn between its security and identity strands. In so doing, and even when critical of the policy, it fails to go beyond the questions that the policy asks of itself, analysing the strategy in terms of whether it has established the 'proper' relation between its security and identity elements. It is thus a literature that has failed to understand the importance of Prevent as a particular mode of power that has produced identities as risky or secure for the future, and then intervened into them in the present on that basis. The second reading of Prevent, given in chapters 3 and 4, focusing on the problematic at its heart, allows the book to bring this mode of power to light. First, though, the book turns to the academic literature on Prevent, demonstrating its inadequacies, yet also outlining two theorisations of Prevent that open up the scope for moving beyond them.

Notes

1 The term 'Islamist' is problematic. As a broad definition, it refers to political movements rooted in an interpretation of the Islamic faith. This therefore goes beyond the application of the term to any specific group, and the often negative associations the term now carries. It is used throughout the text as a discursive reflection of the government texts under analysis, not as an affirmation of the term itself.

2 The term al-Qaeda can be translated from the Arabic into multiple different spellings in the English language. It is consistently spelt 'al-Qaeda' in the text, but where quotations give a different spelling, that spelling is reproduced.

3 The notion of a 'Muslim community' (or 'communities') in the UK is problematic. Representing a plurality of ethnic, cultural and linguistic backgrounds, as well as practising different interpretations of Islam, to signify it as a coherent and bounded entity is a fiction. Indeed, and ironically, it is *through* the application of government policies of cohesion and counter-terrorism that the 'Muslim community' attains a reality and is made governable (Lentin and Titley, 2011; Ali, 2014). The text, however, while acknowledging the politics of its production, uses the term throughout in order to mirror the policy discourse.

4 The exercises were the subject of criticism. It was argued that they were rushed, only engaged with the 'usual suspects' and that the government was reluctant to engage with the grievances of the community, such as concerns around foreign policy (Briggs *et al.*, 2006: 14).

5 Although there were those who made the argument that non-violent extremists were of utility, credibly engaging with those who might be on a path of radicalisation, while still committed to non-violence (Bartlett *et al.*, 2010).

6 Discursively, the Conservative-led coalition, while not significantly shifting practices, tends to favour the term integration over that of cohesion.

2

The 'separatist' literature on Prevent (and the way forward)

This chapter will outline the academic literature that has developed around the Prevent policy. The chapter argues that, for the most part, the literature has, historically, failed to go beyond the political debates and policy narratives articulated in the previous chapter. The first section will demonstrate that the literature has often presented the 'solution' to Prevent to be one of separating its identity and security strands. It is a literature that therefore, like the policy's internal debates, positions the identity and security strands of Prevent as separable. It therefore reifies a perceived tension between the policy's targeted, security interventions into individuals vulnerable to radicalisation and the broader interventions into communities and identities. The second section analyses two approaches to Prevent that provide a means of moving beyond this position. First, an approach that argues Prevent has produced Muslims in the UK as a 'suspect community', and second, an approach that argues Prevent represents a strategy of counter-insurgency. It will be shown in this book that the majority of the literature fails to go beyond the political debates outlined in chapter 1 as it lacks an adequate theorisation of temporality. These literatures rooted in concepts of suspect communities and counter-radicalisation move the book closer to this theorisation, showing, respectively, that Prevent operates through producing, and then transforming, identities.

The Prevent literature and the separation of security and identity

A paper by Thomas (2010; see also Thomas, 2009, 2014, 2017) usefully sums up the literature's analysis of the relation between the targeted security strand of Prevent and its broader community cohesion initiatives; an analysis that materialises following the emergence of the full Prevent agenda in 2007 and continues until the alleged separation of community cohesion and Prevent in 2011. The four key problems of the policy are understood to be its monocultural focus on Muslims, its use as a vehicle for surveillance and intelligence gathering, its damaging impact on community cohesion policies and its creation of tensions between government departments and local and national agencies (Thomas, 2010). An accurate summation of the literature, the critical fault line expounded is the *relationship* between the counter-terrorism and community cohesion strands. The focus is upon the damage done to community cohesion initiatives through their singular, security-guided focus on Muslim communities. The result is that Muslim communities are engaged with through security agents, raising concerns of surveillance, and turning what should be a universal cohesion policy into one with a very specific, Muslim focus. This has 'created envy and suspicion from other communities, while also damaging relations with Muslim communities' (Thomas, 2010: 455). These tensions at community level are exacerbated by 'interdepartmental tensions within national government [...] a political impasse between cohesion-focused engagement and security-focused monitoring and intervention' (Thomas, 2010: 455). Thomas concludes that to move forward, the cohesion agenda must move away from its monocultural focus, instead working with all communities, and thus tackling extremism of all kinds (Thomas, 2010: 456). This therefore positions cohesion as a valuable approach, but one that, if it is to work, should be separated from targeted security interventions within the Prevent framework.

This assumption of *separability* is evident across the literature. Briggs (2010: 981) warns against the danger of 'creeping securitization', arguing that building capacity and resilience, tackling grievances and promoting inclusion, while contributing to counter-radicalisation, should be kept from the security arena. Stevens (2009: 518) approvingly references the Labour government's shift to a community cohesion framework that sought to avoid 'the entrenching of physical and ethnic segregation', but, he argues, is now under threat: that 'PVE clearly – and worryingly – reverses this trend'. Prevent, Awan (2012: 1169–1170) argues, 'creates problems where the government shoehorns certain counterterrorism projects into a community based approach' and that this 'risks blurring the boundaries between counterterrorism and community cohesion'. The Runnymede Trust, a prominent anti-racism organisation, has argued that 'the ease with which the notion of community cohesion has become intertwined with the wider Government priority of combatting violent extremism' entailed a danger of 'community cohesion being seen as something that only specific ethnic or faith groups would be required to do' (Runnymede Trust, cited in Richards, 2011: 147–148). Their concern is that under the PVE framework, community relations towards the development of cohesion are expected to take place within an engagement with local police forces. They argue broader cohesion strategies must be separated from developing good police relations in terms of Prevent's counter-terrorism mandate, stating that they 'would recommend dissociation between the concepts of cohesion and prevention of terrorism if positive intercultural and interfaith work is to practically occur' (Runnymede Trust, cited in Richards, 2011: 147–148). Kundnani (2009: 6) praises the 'many progressive elements within the earlier community cohesion agenda' yet bemoans the singular focus of Prevent on Muslims which have undermined them, and the increased security presence within, and surveillance of, Muslim communities.

It is the proximity and associated stigmatisation of the security agenda that is understood as tarnishing the otherwise good, or at least uncritically accepted, work of the communities agenda. In and of themselves, these critiques are valid. It would seem clear that the conflation of the two strands has damaged certain community cohesion initiatives through undermining and alienating Muslim community activists and creating departmental and institutional conflicts over territory. However, the claim the book is making in this section is that such critiques merely insist that if the policy can but separate these spaces of intervention, then the 'problems' of the Prevent policy would be resolved.

The 'problem' of Prevent being who enacts Prevent

One manifestation of this approach is that the implicit solution outlined is that there would be no issue if only the *right* agency, department or institution were in command. This is a common theme throughout the literature. Pantucci (2010: 257), who is a supportive voice for the Prevent policy, claims that '"Spooks" and social workers are an awkward mix'. He goes on to question whether such an example of 'coordinated' government cannot go on to produce 'deleterious side-effects', recounting how local government agents were reaching out to youth workers to ascertain levels of radicalisation and clan structures in their borough. While well intentioned, he argues that 'the impact was to turn longstanding community workers into analytical outposts for security services' (Pantucci, 2010: 257). He assumes that a neat separation between the two can be drawn. He therefore reproduces government concerns that the community elements of Prevent are being unhelpfully brought within a security framing, identifying the problem as the 'securitization of elements of government work that do not benefit from such a process of securitization' (Pantucci, 2010: 257). His concern is not with the practices themselves, but that through labelling certain practices and staff as serving counter-terrorism functions, there may be detrimental consequences.

Likewise, Spalek and Lambert (2008: 258) recognise that Muslims 'are encouraged to work with state agencies in order to help combat extremism' and argue that there has been little in the way of academic reflection on this point. They recognise that this engagement with Muslim communities for the purposes of counter-radicalisation is highly politicised, and is the context in which 'debates around broader, normative issues in relation to citizenship, multiculturalism, including what sorts of behaviour and attitudes should be encouraged, as well as other values, take place' (Spalek and Lambert, 2008: 261). Their position is that 'questions about community and social cohesion, alongside discussions about Britishness, should not define the terms of engagement with Muslim communities' when it comes to counter-radicalisation (Spalek and Lambert, 2008: 261). Rather, they argue these questions should be left to other areas of policy-making, enacted by different agents of the state. What is not at stake is the legitimacy of the project, but the legitimacy of the agent carrying it out. As long as questions of national identity and cohesion are left to other policy domains and actors, the negative consequences of their institutional proximity would, it is assumed, disappear.

The above analyses see the functioning of Prevent to be congruent with the actors who carry out its work. Thus, through separating those who are responsible for the identity-focused aspects of Prevent work from its targeted security functions, the damaging proximity of the two is overcome. The consistent motif is one of the visibility and perception of counter-radicalisation damaging community cohesion work. It is implicitly assumed that the targets of these interventions will also delineate the two strands and understand the distinctions so long as they are administered by different agents.[1] The roles being played are not considered to be problematic, rather, it is who plays them that is at stake. This is representative of a literature that has viewed the problem as an institutional, not a conceptual, conflation.

The reification of government debates

This failure of the literature to recognise the intimate connection between security and identity in the Prevent policy results in the reification of a government narrative that itself positions the problems of Prevent as the institutional conflation of the two. It thus often fails to go beyond the questions the policy asks of itself; questions that concern the proper relation of its identity and security strands. The argument of this book is that the two strands are intimately connected, wherein Prevent *produces* identity through its demand to secure against vulnerability to radicalisation. Yet the literature, in maintaining the two strands as separable, is unable to recognise this. Below are two examples of this failure, all the more important as, at first glance, they would seem to recognise the important renegotiations of identity and security in the policy.

Birt (2009: 54) entitles one section of his article, 'Securitisation of Integration'. He sees this 'conflation of integration and security' as, at least in part, resulting from 'unclear objectives' and spends time focusing on the concerns and resistances to this framework from local authorities and officials, who fear that 'prioritising counter-terrorism over community cohesion would damage the relationship with local communities' (Birt, 2009: 54). The central issue identified is the 'divisive' single-group funding through the institutions of PVE, and the linking of these revenue streams to performance indicators National Indicator 35 and subsequently public service agreement 26, both of which demand a focus on gathering knowledge of Muslim communities and identifying extremism (Birt, 2009: 54–56). This blurring from within central government, this patchwork approach that links Muslim identity, 'British values', community resilience, information gathering, vulnerability and extremism is thus identified as *the* problem, and is most visibly explicated through a focus on funding mechanisms and financial flows. Ultimately, it is concluded that it,

> needs to be considered whether providing core services on the basis of generic need to all communities from mainstream funding streams, without the additional security rationale, would in fact be more effective and less divisive. Similarly, our narratives of shared values and national belonging and citizenship should be de-linked from counter-terrorism. (Birt, 2009: 57)

Thus, while Birt recognises the central conceit of PVE is its renegotiation of security and identity logics that has resulted in targeting generic funds at Muslim communities, merging security and identity in important and novel ways, without a theoretical analysis that makes sense of their conflation, he is left reliant upon a reading that concludes such an outcome as resulting from 'unclear objectives'.

Similarly, Richards argues that it is the use of the term 'radicalisation' that has facilitated Prevent, an approach that has 'confusingly oscillated between tackling violent extremism in particular and promoting community cohesion and "shared values" more broadly'. He advocates that the 'focus of counterterrorism strategy should be on countering *terrorism* and not on the broader remit implied by wider conceptions of radicalization' (Richards, 2011: 143, emphasis in original). Through focusing on radical ideas and not merely on violent acts, certain Muslim voices have been promoted and funded, while others have been politically and financially marginalised. This, Richards argues, may not prove effective in terms of decreasing violence, where radical, but non-violent voices may be best placed to intervene and persuade (Richards, 2011: 148–149).

This analysis fails to take seriously the merging of security and identity within the policy, wherein certain identities are *produced* as representing potential threats. Thus, to disaggregate the two becomes an impossibility. Richards, in positing the possibility of separating violent acts from Prevent's broader identity politics, fails to take seriously an analysis within Prevent that produces both security and identity at the same time.

While ostensibly both approaches analysed here seek the renegotiation of the core commitments of Prevent – Birt's critique of its Muslim focus; Richard's critique of the obsession with ideas not acts – the effect of these analyses is to continue to see the failings of Prevent as a product of this all-too-close relationship between community cohesion and counter-terrorism. The argument in the literature has consistently been one that sees the *solution* to Prevent as the removal of the cohesion agenda from a security framework. It is therefore a literature that has, historically, failed to go beyond the policy debates detailed in the previous chapter. It reinforces and reifies a narrative, dominant within government and policymakers, that positions the question at the heart of Prevent to be that of the correct relation between its two strands. Thus, even when the literature has been critical of the Prevent policy, it has been unable to go beyond the questions the policy asks of itself. The literature has since developed. There have been attempts to more widely theorise Prevent (which will be analysed both below and in chapter 3), and there has emerged a number of studies of Prevent in relation to the various sectors in which it now operates as a statutory duty. Nevertheless, the failure of the literature to fully grapple with and articulate the relationship between the security and identity strands of Prevent represents a conceptual failure that has occluded a full understanding of the function at the heart of Prevent; a function that, it will be shown, constitutively unites questions of security and identity. What is at stake in the rest of the book is thus a desire to re-engage with the history of the Prevent policy, going beyond the failures of the literature to adequately conceptualise this history, in order to articulate the diagram of power that Prevent has enacted.

Theorising Prevent

There is work that does go beyond the failings of the literature detailed above. Such work seeks to provide a theoretical framework through which Prevent can be understood, and in so doing brings together the security and identity strands of Prevent. These approaches are therefore of value, but, as the next section will show, they still fail to grasp the temporal problematic at the heart of Prevent. Two approaches are evident in the literature, both drawing on wider historical traditions of understanding

counter-terrorism. The first mobilises the concept of 'suspect communities', emphasising the parallels with British policing of Irish communities.
The second situates Prevent within a framework of counter-insurgency.

The suspect communities literature usefully, and importantly, shows
how Muslimness is produced *through* the security interventions of
counter-terrorism. The counter-insurgency approach recognises and
demonstrates how the object of intervention within Prevent work is
Muslim identities themselves, with the counter-terrorism policy seeking
their transformation. Both, however, are blind to the analytical work
being done by the other. In focusing on 'hard' interventions, suspect
communities approaches fail to recognise that Prevent seeks to *transform* these identities to render them less threatening for the future.
Conversely, counter-insurgency approaches fail to adequately account
for the production of this Muslimness, and therefore how it is produced
as threatening for the future *through* the security acts of Prevent. Taken
together, and building on this work, the book outlines an approach that
situates the temporality of Prevent as crucial. This allows for an analysis
of Prevent as a policy that constitutes security by *producing* certain identities as threatening for the future, and then acting to *transform* these
identities in the present.

Prevent as producing suspect communities

Amongst those critical of Prevent's operations, an analysis that has
circulated widely, in both academic critique and grass-roots mobilisations
against the policy, is to utilise the concept of 'suspect communities'. Work
in this tradition has provided an excellent analysis of how, through legislation and policing practice, those considered to be part of Muslim communities in the UK have been rendered suspect and subjected to police
powers such as stop and search. First developed by Hillyard (1993) in
relation to the policing of Irish communities, the term denotes the designation of a community as targeted through counter-terrorism powers,
wherein the members of the group are 'suspect' not due to perceived
illegality, but due to the perception that they belong to the said group.
These powers are enforced through security mechanisms such as pro-
filing, stop and search, surveillance and detention and are often abused
and over-extended by security practitioners.

The work of Pantazis and Pemberton (2009), Awan (2012), Mythen
et al. (2012), Breen-Smyth (2014) and Abbas (2018) shows how these
practices have been used to police contemporary Muslim communities
in the UK. Primarily concerned with the analysis of policing work that
comes under the Pursue heading, one of the strengths of this approach is
that it foreshadows the move away from prosecution as the chief goal of

police interventions. While prosecution is still of course a vital tool, the work of Pantazis and Pemberton (2009) shows how the use of detention and stop and search is instead often focused on information gathering. They also highlight the new powers that have been used to pre-empt terrorism such as control orders, deportation and the freezing of assets. These, as opposed to being based on legal statuses of guilt, work through ascriptions of suspicion (Pantazis and Pemberton, 2009: 654; see also Mythen *et al.*, 2012).

Importantly, this suspicion is shown to be produced by security agents. It is perceived membership with the broader, in this case Muslim, community, that is rendered suspect, providing justification for a range of security practices. Pantazis and Pemberton (2009) demonstrate how Muslim communities in the UK have been produced as suspect through the application of legal and security frameworks. They argue that police powers such as stop and search and arrest without warrant are being broadly applied within the UK on the basis of performances of identity that are seen as suspicious; and that, within the context of the War on Terror, this suspicion disproportionately falls on those who appear to be Muslims (Pantazis and Pemberton, 2009). Negative images of Muslims have led to increased scrutiny in the public sphere, with their actions constantly being observed for signs of danger, leading to increased police action against them (Mythen *et al.*, 2012: 388–389; see also Mythen *et al.*, 2009). This leads to what Mythen *et al.* (2012: 390) have termed 'risk subjectification', wherein respectful and law-abiding people come to be considered as dangerous due to sharing certain traits, such as visible ethnic or religious appearances, that correspond with that of a 'typical' terrorist.

Taking this analysis further, Breen-Smyth (2014) argues that this sus-picion is produced through the discursive othering of the Muslim com-munity. The security practices of the War on Terror, she claims, have served to produce an account of the secure self and that which threatens it. Emphasising the sociological processes through which suspicion is constituted, her work shows that suspect communities do not pre-exist as stable spaces and identities, but are produced by state practices, they are '*constructed in the imagined fears of its non-members*' (Breen-Smyth, 2014: 230, emphasis in original). Abbas' (2018) account serves to decentre the state in understandings of the suspect community and to foreground the role of members of the suspect community in themselves producing suspicion. She demonstrates how, to understand the produc-tion of suspicion, it is crucial to foreground the creation of internal sus-pect bodies, wherein community members internalise the fear of state targeting, precipitating internal disciplinary measures (Abbas, 2018). This draws attention to the complicity of members of the suspect commu-nity in reproducing suspicion. But, in distinction to the highly discursive work of Breen-Smyth, Abbas' (2018) account stresses the embodied nature of suspicion, reproduced through the real and imagined terror of state targeting. In sum, the concept of suspect communities therefore recognises the productive identity politics at stake within counter-terrorism policy. It shows that the 'Muslim community' is not a pre-given entity, but is produced through the application of police and juridical powers, the ascription of suspicion, and the internalisation and internal policing of this suspicion.

Yet this analysis maintains a blind spot as to how this production manifests in a demand to *transform* these identities that are rendered as threatening. The heritage of this approach, rooted in the application (and misapplication) of legal frameworks, entails that it overlooks the pre-criminal interventions that specifically make up Prevent work. It is an approach that sees the production of Muslim identity in terms of the extension of police powers of proscription, detention and stop and search. In so doing, it powerfully critiques the legal framework of the War on Terror. However, by failing to recognise Prevent's temporal demand to intervene *prior to* the criminal act, this approach misses the pernicious power of a counter-radicalisation strategy that seeks to transform these identities on the basis of this suspicion. This blind spot leads to perverse outcomes, wherein those advocating this approach have, like the literatures surveyed in the first section, taken a position where the negative impacts of the creation of suspect communities are seen as detrimental for the broader, positive goals of cohesion (Awan, 2012). Similarly, this approach often situates 'hard' policing methods associated with suspect communities, such as stop and search and detention without charge, as jeopardising positive, 'soft', policing methods, such as community engagement, that make up aspects of Prevent work. As Pantazis and Pemberton (2009: 660) argue, 'it is difficult to see how such skilful, yet ultimately fragile, "soft approaches" can thrive, when the weight of state suspicion and the brutality of "hard" methods have fallen on these communities' (see also Spalek *et al.*, 2008). This therefore misses the power these 'soft' methods themselves mobilise, producing Muslims as suspect, but also trying to transform this Muslimness itself.

Prevent as a counter-insurgency strategy

If the suspect communities approach recognises the productivity of the counter-terrorism strategy, yet overlooks its desire to transform, the next theorisation does the obverse. This approach locates the policy within a history of counter-insurgency practice. One such attempt that is critical of CONTEST is the work of Miller and Sabir (2012). Their analysis also focuses on elements of Pursue as well as those of Prevent. They contend that counter-insurgency consists of four principal elements: the integration of civil and military powers; the key role of intelligence and surveillance; the use of exceptional legislation and pre-emptive controls; and the importance of strategic communication. The claim they make is that there is a deliberate integration of this approach within CONTEST. In doing so, they provide an informative reading of the bureaucratic role of military theorists of counter-insurgency within Prevent, and their contributions to its development. They argue these operations of power target Muslims as a whole, and that this is not a 'by-product of mistakes, ignorance or arrogance' (Miller and Sabir, 2012: 13). They then make the further claim that these laws and programmes 'have been created intentionally and purposefully to coerce and instil fear within the Muslim community and those who stand with it' (Miller and Sabir, 2012: 13). Writing independently, Sabir (2017) further articulates the centrality of surveillance and strategic communication within Prevent, which in his analysis, demonstrate mechanisms of discipline, exclusion and the prevention of Muslim agency and identity, as opposed to the narrative of safeguarding and inclusion put forward by Prevent's proponents. While coercive and exceptional measures such as shoot-to-kill policies and control orders exist, the broad thrust of this approach is that information is gathered, civil bodies are co-opted and civil society groups are set up in order to explicitly tackle the 'problem' of Muslim communities in the UK. Muslims, in this reading, are targeted indiscriminately through programmes of coercion and propaganda as an enemy within, taking action against the community that allegedly 'hosts' the 'insurgents' (Miller and Sabir, 2012: 22). Miller and Sabir (2012: 28) conclude by stating that the policy can thus be understood as 'the conscious planning of a campaign of coercion against dissent in general and Muslims in particular'.

Taking a similar approach, the work of Jackson (2013) argues that Prevent represents a model of pacification, a term often applied to counter-insurgent violence. Jackson (2013: 155) contends that Prevent is 'driven by the desire pacify [sic] any flickers of resistance, no matter how embryonic, and produce the docile citizen-subjects necessary for the maintenance of bourgeois order'. In doing so, Jackson relies upon the work of Neocleous (2011), which explicitly links conceptions of pacification to the promotion of capitalist order, securing particular economic relations and economic subjects. Jackson clearly accepts this premise in stating that 'counter-radicalisation needs to be understood in line with the police dream of pacified workers', explicitly referring back to the work of Neocleous (Jackson, 2013: 156). Yet beyond a broad idea that opposition to Western liberal norms displayed by 'extremists' may well lead to their non-participation within capitalist labour relations, there is no discursive support within the Prevent documents, and indeed, the counter-terrorism strategy and practices of the UK more broadly, to support such a claim. Put another way, while preventing radicalisation may well produce subjects who are willing to engage in capitalist labour relations, this disregards the discourses mobilised within the policies and the diagram of power they enact.

In framing Prevent as a counter-insurgency operation, the above work does recognise the important intent of the Prevent policy to secure Muslim identities in the UK. In framing Muslims as a problem, what is required is their transformation, and in the above readings, this is found in ensuring that Muslim communities are quiescent and docile. However, this is problematically achieved through designating Muslim communities as an internal enemy, coercively targeted by the British state. This book reads these interventions into Muslim communities differently. It does so through the work of John Mackinlay. Also mobilising a counter-insurgency framing, Mackinlay's (2009) reading of the policy demonstrates how the intent of Prevent is not to coerce docility, policing an internal enemy, but is rather to transform societal conditions, producing them as environments out of which enemies will not emerge.

Utilising a counter-insurgency framing, albeit in support of the Prevent (and broader CONTEST) strategy, Mackinlay argues that, despite its limitations, the CONTEST strategy as a whole 'is – in evolutionary terms – hugely significant and may turn out to be a prototype for the next generation of counter-insurgency operations' (Mackinlay, 2009: 7). He claims there exists a 'post-Maoist' campaign of Islamist violence that has an internationalised 'frontline', able to tap into the alienation and dislocation of Muslims worldwide. This represents a diffuse, networked archipelago that does not necessarily have concrete territorial goals or even an end-game; it consists of multiple overlapping populations, and it is a struggle that has no clear centre of gravity (Mackinlay, 2009).

What his analysis illuminates is that, in responding to networks of potential terrorists, the British state has had to adapt. Security interventions have had to go beyond merely identifying actual plots, but involve engaging with processes of radicalisation, and the threat of individuals becoming terrorists. He claims that one of the failures of the early War on Terror was in treating it as a counter-terrorism intervention, targeting what it saw to be socially disembedded actors organised within hierarchical lines. He argues that the expeditions of the War on Terror 'had addressed the mosquitoes but not the swamp' (Mackinlay, 2009: 190).[2] Speaking positively about the transformations enacted through Prevent, Mackinlay draws attention to the networked and localised responses that allowed threats to be identified and intervened into *before* they emerge. In the concluding pages, Mackinlay (2009: 229) praises the 'chaotic swarm' of local Muslim organisations which had been effective at diverting young, disaffected Muslims from engaging in violence.[3] While only taking full effect after the publication of this text, the same approach is at work in the utilisation of professionals such as teachers and social workers to identify and act on signs of radicalisation.

Mackinlay asserts – and clearly supports – an idea that Prevent must take as its object *all* Muslims, ranging through 'uncommitted', passively and actively 'disaffected' to those being 'groomed and mentored' (Mackinlay, 2009: 216). This allows him to make a key claim that, '[i]n the British experience the key to shutting off the flow of attackers lay in altering the situation earlier when the insurgent was still in a formative state' (Mackinlay, 2009: 209). This approach problematically locates all Muslims – by virtue of their Muslimness – as outside of 'domestic' Western populations. This in turn positions all representations of Muslim politicality within a narrative of domestic insurgency, a claim he notably makes in regards to the so-called 'race riots' of 2001 (Mackinlay, 2009: 202). Nevertheless, it importantly recognises the temporal innovations of Prevent. The policy does not target Muslims as an explicit, internal enemy, but it seeks to understand and act on Muslim identities in order to ensure that they are unthreatening.

In contrast to the suspect communities approach, this counter-insurgency framing positions the importance of Prevent in its ambition to transform Muslim identities on account of the potential threat these identities are seen to hold. Yet, contrastingly, it does not account for the production of this Muslim identity as threatening. In contrast to Mackinlay, the post-structuralist approach of the book enables a critical reading of Prevent's desire to transform the environments in which insurgency emerges. As opposed to essentialising the potentialised threat incumbent within all Muslims as Mackinlay does, this book will demonstrate that the security practices of Prevent themselves act to establish certain identities as risky, and certain identities as secure. In essentialising Muslims as always potentially risky, Mackinlay thus denies the politics that, as the suspect communities literature shows, is involved in the identification and the production of certain identities as risky.

In so doing, this book follows in the footsteps of the work of Heath-Kelly (2012, 2013) and de Goede and Simon (2013), both of whom situate the key innovation of Prevent to be its ambition to intervene *prior* to individuals becoming terrorists. Working within a Foucauldian framework, they both analyse counter-radicalisation practices as a means of governing, producing knowledge concerning the future potentials of individuals to radicalisation in order to make such individuals governable in the present. Within this reading, the concept of radicalisation attains a centrality. It is through the constitution of expert knowledge of radicalisation that potential to terrorism can be governed, ascribing categories of risk to behaviours, such that those deemed risky can be intervened into (Heath-Kelly, 2013: 396). Concerned with what Anderson has termed 'anticipatory epistemic objects' (Anderson, 2007, cited in de Goede and

Simon, 2013: 321), this approach locates Prevent in general, and the concept of radicalisation in particular, within a growing literature on preclusive governance (a literature that will be analysed in the next chapter). This literature argues that what is important within modern security practices is the way in which risk is mobilised and produced in order to render the uncertainty of threats contained in the future as governable. As such, when analysing radicalisation, this approach is not concerned with testing the validity of the concept, but is instead interested in what the concept of radicalisation produces; it 'makes it possible for British counter-terrorism to act upon futurity' (Heath-Kelly, 2013: 398).

The analysis given in this book seeks to deepen these interventions. Building on this approach, it too seeks to demonstrate that radicalisation functions to produce terrorism as governable. Yet the book seeks to extend this insight, detailing the specific identity politics at stake within counter-radicalisation policy. It does so through textually analysing the problematic of Prevent and then showing how this has resulted in the concrete practices of Prevent's assemblage. In so doing, the book hopes to show that the concept of radicalisation at the heart of Prevent has established a coherent diagram of power, encompassing both Prevent's targeted security interventions and its broader interventions into communal identities. Combining the insights of the counter-insurgency and suspect communities approaches, this framing of Prevent goes beyond the analysis of the literature given in the first half of this chapter. It demonstrates the importance of the policy is to be found in the way it establishes a relation between the concepts of temporality, identity and security.

Conclusion

In opening up this question of temporality, the book is able to articulate the implicit problematisation of threat that underwrites the Prevent policy. While authors in this field do highlight the ways in which security and identity frameworks have become increasingly intertwined within the policy, without an analysis that sees Prevent as an assemblage of coherent interventions that produce and then act upon identity, such analyses maintain the illusory position that it is possible to separate these two strands. In doing so, the literature merely reifies and reinforces government interpretations of the key problems that inform Prevent work, limiting it to asking questions only of the *relationship* between the community cohesion and counter-radicalisation strands. In opposition to the debates that have framed both the political and academic discourse on Prevent, this approach illuminates a key coherency within Prevent. It locates as crucial within Prevent the problematic of stopping people from becoming radicalised. In so doing, a temporality is invoked that demands intervention in the present in order to mitigate the risks of the future. The relation within Prevent of identity and security is therefore not merely a question of institutional design, but is one of centrality to the theorisation of threat within Prevent. As the next two chapters will show, this problematisation of threat that informs Prevent is one that produces *both* its security and identity strands. The centrality of identity is the subject of chapter 4. First, though, the book needs to situate the problematic of Prevent within an account of temporality, to outline Prevent's radical temporal ambition.

Notes

1 On this point, it is therefore interesting that, while government in the 2011 Prevent review proclaims this need for separation, many functions, although programmatically distinct, are still carried out by the same individuals. It is stated there is a need to separate individuals who carry out security roles from those involved in cohesion, yet it is then stated that: 'we also accept that many staff working on Prevent, notably in policing and local authorities, will continue to have cohesion-related functions, something that is more rather than less likely as local authorities look for opportunities to make efficiency savings' (Home Office, 2011a: 30; see also Thomas, 2014 for an excellent discussion of the practical tensions and overlaps in the delivery of cohesion and Prevent work).
2 This resonates with statements by David Cameron in his time as prime minister. The need to 'drain the swamp' was a phrase he used in a statement to the House of Commons in the aftermath of the murder of Lee Rigby (Wintour, 2013).
3 Albeit he agrees that there were good critiques to be made (such as that quoted in chapter 1 by Maher and Frampton (2009)) about the use of funds and the ideals of some of these groups (Mackinlay, 2009: 228–230).

3

The temporal ambition of Prevent: stopping people becoming terrorists

In this chapter and the next, the book intends to present a very different, second reading of the Prevent policy, a reading that brings to the surface the *problematisation of threat* at the heart of Prevent. The previous reading emphasised the political debates concerning Prevent and how these have informed the institutional development and implementation of the policy. They demonstrated that the political debates concerning the policy, which have all too often been replicated in the literature, are of the extent to which the security and identity strands of Prevent can, and perhaps should, be separated. On the one hand, there are targeted, security interventions into those at risk. On the other, there are broader questions of identity, belonging and values. These questions of identity might have a role to play in ensuring security, but, nevertheless, the policy questions posed are whether they should be part of the same strategy, or whether they should be demarcated as separate areas of government. The driving assumption is, therefore, that it is possible, and perhaps desirable, to separate Prevent's security and identity interventions. A methodology rooted in a Foucauldian understanding of problematisation allows this book to tell a different story. This analysis focuses on the problematised site of Prevent: *vulnerability to radicalisation*. Instead of taking vulnerability to radicalisation to be self-evident, it is a methodological approach that instead asks how the subject of vulnerability to radicalisation is produced: how is Prevent's object of threat problematised as a site of knowledge and intervention?

A close, textual analysis of this object of threat that Prevent seeks to manage allows the book to make the claim that to separate Prevent's identity and security focus is an impossibility, as they are already conceptually conflated. This second reading shows Prevent to be productive of *both* these security and identity strands, in that they both result from the *same* problematisation of the threat of *vulnerability to radicalisation* that sits at the heart of Prevent. That this is occluded within the analyses of the policy given in the previous two chapters is because the political debates and much of the literature fails to recognise the conceptual significance of the *temporality* at the heart of this problematic. Prevent deliberately and self-consciously seeks to intervene *prior to* an individual becoming a terrorist. It thus seeks to act on the *potential* for an individual to become violent. In so doing, it must produce an account of that which is risky and threatening, that which, if left alone, may lead to terrorism. The next chapter will argue that this is achieved through an understanding of vulnerability to radicalisation that interprets certain identities as risky, due to being seen as alienated from, and outside of, a conception of 'Britishness' and 'British values'.

First though, and the subject of this chapter, it is necessary to outline a general theorisation regarding how the concept of radicalisation makes this early intervention possible. The first section locates Prevent as a demand for early intervention. The threat posed by Islamist terrorism is represented as novel, requiring a new strategic response. It is, as will be shown, therefore a *problematisation* that produces the threat of Islamist terrorism as requiring early intervention. In contrast to previous counter-terrorism strategies, Prevent represents a novel temporal ambition that one can, and should, intervene into the process of someone *becoming* a terrorist. The policy, therefore, explicitly seeks to act within conditions of uncertainty, arguing that it is necessary to act on the potentials identified in individuals lest such individuals become violent. In so doing, this ambition ties into a range of contemporary security issues, which are seen to increasingly demand action within uncertainty. The second section of this chapter links Prevent to these wider developments, arguing that this literature provides a framework for analysing security practices that seek to act within conditions of uncertainty. Yet this literature has a tendency to ontologise these recent developments, which has the effect of neutralising and effacing the politics of these securing acts. Rather, the argument made here is that, through a focus on problematisation, what comes to the fore are the ways in which security actors produce future threats *as* knowable and actionable. The third section then shows that, in regards to Prevent, the threat of people becoming terrorists is made knowable and actionable through the concept of radicalisation. Radicalisation envisages all life as in the process of becoming, and that, through understanding this process, the individuals who might become terrorists, and the environments that might allow such becoming, can be identified and then acted upon.

A new form of terrorism

The attacks of 9/11 were not the first acts of violence carried out by al-Qaeda, yet they changed the perceptions of the threat to the UK substantially. Followed by 7/7, they resulted in a new problematisation of the threat posed by this particular form of terrorism. Speaking later to the Chilcott enquiry, Tony Blair stated: 'my view after September 11th was that our whole analysis of the terrorist threat and the extremism had to change [...] the calculus of risk had to change and change fundamentally' (The Iraq Enquiry, 2011: 4–5). As the first iteration of the CONTEST strategy articulates, between its adoption by Cabinet and its official publication, 'the threat has grown and it has changed in character' (Home Office, 2006: 3). The purpose of the strategy is to identify the 'range of issues which need to be addressed in implementing an effective counterterrorism policy against the type of threat we *now* face' (Home Office, 2006: 3, emphasis added). In response to the attacks of 7/7, and the full realisation that British citizens were willing to enact terrorist violence on home soil, Tony Blair stated 'the rules of the game are changing' (*BBC News*, 2005).

While the CONTEST strategy notes that the UK had faced terrorism before, notably as a result of the Troubles in Northern Ireland, it nevertheless affirms 'the threat that we currently face does have certain distinctive characteristics' (Home Office, 2006: 6). Differentiating this threat, four factors are identified. First is that the threat is 'genuinely international', attacking a wide range of targets across many countries (Home Office, 2006: 7). Second, the threat comes from a 'variety of groups, networks and individuals' who may work together but may also pursue separate goals (Home Office, 2006: 7). Third, 'these terrorists intend mass casualties', are 'indiscriminate' and are willing to attack civilians on a scale not seen before (Home Office, 2006: 7). Finally, they are driven by a 'particular and distorted form of Islam', which terrorists argue legitimates this violence (Home Office, 2006: 7).

This analysis draws on a body of literature within Terrorism Studies that identified a so-called 'New Terrorism'. Theorists arguing for the application of this term (see, for key examples, Laqueur, 1999 or Benjamin and Simon, 2002) stress that recent terrorist groups could be characterised by their religious basis. As a result, rooted in a religious belief in salvation, they possessed a willingness to engage in mass casualty and indiscriminate attacks, including the use of self-sacrificial violence. These claims inform the analysis of the threat given in CONTEST documents, with the 2009 iteration stating that a 'new form of terrorism emerged overseas in the late seventies and early eighties [...] These militant groups had an explicitly religious agenda and justified terrorism on religious grounds' leading to the creation of al-Qaeda in the 1980s (Home Office,

2009b: 20). In reproducing this account of 'new' terrorism, what emerges in this period is an analysis of the threat that differentiates it from previous threats posed to the UK, an analysis that informs and demands new thinking.

The assessment of the threat posed by this new form of terrorism differs from previous British experiences with terrorism in at least three substantive ways. First, there is a clear organisational difference, resulting in problems of identification. Unlike the threat posed to the UK by Irish Republican terrorism, Islamist threats often are not from organised and hierarchical groups who would give warnings, but individuals acting in loosely connected networks who are prepared to commit self-sacrificial attacks with no notice (interview with Lord Carlile of Berriew). These groups and networks may be 'motivated by the Al Qa'ida ideology, but have no connection to the Al Qa'ida organisation' and might be small enough that a single police operation could arrest the key members (Home Office, 2009a: 32). This networked and cellular organisational structure poses difficulties for police and intelligence work, as individuals involved may know little when it comes to the activities of others, making detection much harder. This is further compounded by the problem of 'lone-wolves' or 'self-starting' terrorists (Home Office, 2009a: 30; interview with Jacqui Smith), a problem that has only increased (Home Office, 2011a: 14). In these cases, individuals 'who have little or no direct contact with any existing terrorist groups' may emerge and yet be capable of causing immense harm (Home Office, 2009a: 32). These individuals may have radicalised themselves, often through accessing online material. Or they may appear as self-radicalised, yet have been radicalised through online contact and are thus less visible to police and security agents. Organisationally, this threat therefore generates problems of identification, where there may not be traditional police or intelligence mechanisms for picking out such individuals.

This question of identification gains a further urgency in that it is understood this becoming violent can occur very quickly. Specifically, in the wake of 7/7, the Inquiry into the attacks concluded that:

> extremists could be created at any time through a very quick process [and therefore] the window of opportunity for identifying and disrupting potential threats could be very small [...] greater efforts are being made to identify individuals being groomed for terrorism (and those doing the grooming) at an early stage, in the knowledge that progression to attack planning may occur very rapidly, and with a view to *intervening before terrorism has a chance to develop*. (Intelligence and Security Committee, 2006: 29, emphasis added)

The hope, in the immediate aftermath to 9/11, was that threats could be profiled, that there would be some discerning feature amongst those engaged in violence that would allow for early identification. Yet this was not the case. The attacks of 7/7 forced a recognition that radicalisation could occur in people of all ethnicities, and that there was 'no clear profile of a British Islamist terrorist' (Intelligence and Security Committee, 2006: 29). It also became apparent that becoming violent was not always a process that went through a series of neat, identifiable stages that took time to complete. Incidents such as Operation Crevice demonstrated that if something went wrong and the plan needed another person, the group was able to find them quickly and persuade them to join up (interview with Tony McNulty). It showed that there was a wider environment of extremists who could be persuaded to engage in violence. The decision to engage in terrorism need not be a process that takes years to come to fruition (interview with Tony McNulty). These organisational differences of 'New Terrorism', and the speed with which individuals might become involved, therefore posed new problems for identifying threats.

Second, the form of attacks being undertaken differs from previous threats. While engaging in bombing and assassination campaigns both in Northern Ireland and on the British mainland, Northern Irish terrorism infrequently targeted civilians, and often provided warnings if doing so. By contrast, this 'new' terrorism aimed for mass casualty attacks. Al-Qaeda is judged to have 'popularised and given spurious legitimacy to suicide bombing and aspires to use chemical, biological, radiological and nuclear weapons' (Home Office, 2009a: 35). Further, its exponents were willing to sacrifice themselves in doing so, with their religious motivation providing the succour of belief in a plentiful afterlife. As a result, argues Omand (2010: 90), 'society cannot rely only on effective detention and prosecution after the event' nor on the deterrence of long prison sentences; '[p]re-emption is needed' (see also Pantucci, 2010: 256). As opposed to deterring terrorists, and, if necessary, prosecuting after the event, the problematic here is that one must intervene prior to the bomb going off.

Third, Islamist extremism is understood as an entity that cannot be brought to the negotiating table. In a speech by Jacqui Smith at the launch of the 2009 iteration, she stated that for al-Qaeda, 'there can be no meeting of minds between the Islamic and non-Islamic worlds – or even between Muslims and non-Muslims in Britain'; its goal is for a 'state of relentless hostility and confrontation between us' (Smith, 2009). Conversely, the threat in Northern Ireland was territorial and had clear political objectives. While the UK government did not negotiate openly with terrorists, it was a conflict that was amenable to political solution, as history has shown.

These three differences combine to paint a very different picture of the threat to which the UK had to respond. The threats now faced could emerge with little to no warning, unmonitored by the police and intelligence services. They aimed for mass destruction with no regard to their own survival, and there was no reasoning to be had with them. On the basis of this analysis, the CONTEST strategy consistently articulates the Islamist threat as unlike that Britain has faced previously, stating that: 'their *modus operandi* has not been directly comparable to that of Irish-related terrorists or to international organisations which have threatened this country before' (Home Office, 2009a: 36). The problematic produced by Prevent identifies the threat of contemporary terrorism as containing a series of drivers that provide a strong rationale for early intervention. Thus, while only a small number of individuals might ever go on to commit acts of terrorism, the consequences of not catching those who did were unthinkable. Much better, it was thought, to ensure that individuals did not become terrorists in the first place. To intervene early into the processes that might lead an individual down that path. This framing thus impels Prevent's temporal ambition, which is to act before an individual has made a decision to engage in violence. Drawing on approaches to youth criminality and gang violence, as noted in chapter 1, Prevent represents an ambition to manage the threat of someone becoming violent, prior to, or in the early stages of, the process of becoming violent.

The innovation of this temporal demand to intervene early can be drawn out through comparison to previous British approaches to threats of terrorism and subversion. This ambition of Prevent goes beyond previous British state responses to terrorist violence, most notably in regards to the conflict in Northern Ireland. As has been alluded to in previous sections, the British state response to Irish terrorism consisted of internment, arrest, deterrence, propaganda and, ultimately, a political settlement. Propaganda was mobilised to generate support for the UK and seek to dissuade people from joining the armed conflict against the British state. Yet, at no point was there an ambition by the British state to proactively intervene into the processes by which people became terrorists. That state agents, utilising community contacts, would seek to identify individuals vulnerable to becoming violent and then intervene in order to manage the threat of such violence, is not a part of the security response. One former security minister went as far as to say, 'the IRA [Irish Republican Army] experience says nothing about [Prevent] at all' (interview with Tony McNulty).

A second comparison of note is with the threat seen to be posed to the UK by communism during the Cold War. Similarly envisaged as a battle of ideas, Prevent draws on a lineage of counter-subversion established in the UK in the early Cold War as a response to the threat of communism. The British response at that time consisted primarily of disseminating anti-communist propaganda, often through influential and seemingly 'neutral' channels, in order to avoid the appearance of official propaganda (Maguire, 2015: 643–644). The intent was one of immunising workers against communism by providing counter-arguments against Soviet propaganda (Maguire, 2015: 658–659). Other measures taken included the disruption of foreign communist leaders, such as making it difficult for them to acquire visas, and investigating and purging communists from the civil service (Maguire, 2015: 655, 645). Further, other organisations, notably the BBC, worked with the Security Service in order to vet potential or actual employees, and affiliation with subversive organisations might be a bar to appointment or promotion (Hastings, 2006). The contestation of ideas is at the forefront of the response to the communist threat, and the need to contest the narratives that justify violence is evident in Prevent. Yet these anti-communist initiatives had no ambition to intervene *prior* to any individual becoming a communist. For those who became communists, there might be repercussions, such as making it difficult to work in various institutions. However, that one could identify individuals as potentially vulnerable to *becoming* communists, and then manage that potential, is not discussed. While early intervention as a concept is clearly not novel, in applying this to the processes by which someone may become a terrorist, the Prevent policy broke new ground.

It is this threat of individuals becoming violent that is the chief and innovative concern of the Prevent policy. In taking these processes of becoming violent as an object of intervention, this approach will generate new knowledges, expertises and means of intervention. In identifying the threat of becoming violent as central to the policy, Prevent explicitly and self-consciously attempts to intervene within conditions of uncertainty. That is, it seeks to act on the potential of an individual to becoming violent. There is a categorical uncertainty as to whether that potential might ever be fulfilled. Yet, on the basis of the harm that would occur if the intervention did not occur, this early intervention is impelled.

The relation between temporality and security

In seeking to explicitly act within conditions of uncertainty, the Prevent policy is representative of a shift in contemporary security practices. Recent years have seen the development of a wide range of scholarship arguing that there has been a transformation of the means through which security is produced. Notably emerging in the disciplines of critical security studies (Massumi, 2007; Amoore and de Goede, 2008a) and criminology (Zedner, 2007; McCulloch and Pickering, 2009), it is a literature that argues there has been a contemporary shift towards preclusive security. Preclusive security is used here as a term that encompasses a wide range of security practices seeking to intervene prior to the manifestation of that which it intends to secure. A distinction drawn by Massumi (2013) between dangers and threats is of pertinence here. Dangers, in this reading, represent an immediacy and localisability of harm. The harm exists in the future, but there is a linear line between the present and the future harm. It is a harm that is, therefore, clear and present. Threat, on the other hand, exists in a future space that cannot be related to the present along linear pathways. Thus, a threat retains a categorical uncertainty; it exists only in its potential. Within British counter-terrorism, the danger of the terrorist attack is the ultimate object to be secured. Pursue targets this danger explicitly, utilising a criminal justice framework to apprehend those actively engaged in terrorism. Prevent operates at the level of threat. The objects of Prevent's preclusive interventions cannot be said to represent a definitive harm. They exist in the future as potentials. But due to the possibility they might become a danger – and the harm that would entail – they require some form of action in the present.

This framing is common across a number of different contemporary security arenas. The problem is one of identifying the emergence of an extremely low number of actual dangers – in this case terrorists – where the damage of non-identification is potentially devastating. Alongside terrorism, the risks of pandemics and climate change are also seen to represent problems that, while very difficult to predict or pinpoint in their emergence, contain a grave threat to human life. In response, state actors have increasingly had to find new approaches to securing these threats, explicitly acting within conditions of uncertainty as opposed to a past in which things were presumed to be much simpler.

The literature on preclusive security has emerged in response to these transformations, seeking to explicate and analyse the novel state security practices that have developed in response to these threats. This literature is of utility to an understanding of Prevent, in that it foregrounds the problems of epistemology when trying to secure the uncertain, and provides an analytical framework for critically analysing these practices. Yet, within this framing, the literature has often claimed the nature of contemporary threats has qualitatively shifted, demanding new security practices. These claims of novelty are ill-judged and problematic, framing changing government security practices as responding to an ontological shift as opposed to being based in the shifting problematisations of security actors. Before showing how the literature provides a framework for understanding the concept of radicalisation and the role it plays within the Prevent policy, it is first necessary to engage with and tackle this limitation.

Accounts of a new security paradigm

Two broad approaches that underpin much of the current literature can be identified. The first approach is that made by Ulrich Beck. Beck (2002, 2003) has argued that the contemporary 'world risk society' has entered an era within which dangers are unpredictable and uncontrollable. While 'risk' as a concept demands the calculation of the incalculable, and for Beck, represents a master narrative of first modernity, there is now an era of uncontrollable risk, a knowing contradiction in terms that for Beck describes the multiplicity of human-made, manufactured uncertainties within which life now exists (Beck, 2002: 41). Beck's work is important in that it traces the novel geographies and temporalities of 'risk'. Contemporary risks faced, such as the ecological, the financial and the terrorist, are understood to be different from those that went before. The contemporary world is defined by its hyper-complexity and interconnectedness, and these cannot be conceptualised in any meaningful way. These risks share a framing that goes 'beyond rational calculation into the realm of unpredictable turbulence' and is irreducibly global (Beck, 2002: 43). The threat is so infrequent or singular that it cannot be reliably foretold, and in its global, albeit uneven effect, it demands a global response: a global risk community. The point, within this framework, is that threat is no longer insurable: it is explicitly non-quantifiable, and moreover, the damage it might inflict is devastating beyond calculability. As such, the central, yet hidden, issue in contemporary world politics is '*how to feign control over the uncontrollable*' (Beck, 2002: 41, emphasis in original). While previous risks existed, the nature of these risks was such that they could, with a relative degree of certainty, be calculated and thus managed. Contemporary risks, it is argued, surpass this manageability.

The second approach, most evident in the work of Massumi (2007), is that, with the end of the Cold War, approaches to security have qualitatively changed, and that these shifts have generated new pre-emptive logics that signal a transformation in how societies are now governed. Massumi argues that in the post-Cold War world, understandings of threat shift from an idea of calculability to one of radical unknowability. Thus, in the calculation of nuclear grand strategy, for state actors to make sense of the threat posed by the enemy (and thus their optimal response), all that was needed was more knowledge; one might not have all the information, but it did exist. Unknowns were the product of a failure of intelligence, not of the radical unknowability of the world (Massumi, 2007). While the interrelation of cause and effect combine to result in enormous complexity, it was nevertheless a vision of the future that could be ever more accurately known if one had access to the right data and statistical methods. There is thus an epistemology of retrievable and disclosable knowledge that would allow these made-knowable and predictable threats to be managed (Massumi, 2013: 25).

With the end of the Cold War, this epistemology breaks down. The future comes to be conceptualised as exceeding calculation, entering into an epistemology of radical uncertainty. Massumi distinguishes between a pre-Cold War ontology of security in which threat is knowable (although may be unknown) and a post-Cold War ontology of pre-emption which explicitly acts upon that which is unknowable. The driving imaginary of the Cold War was one in which, however problematic it might have been, knowledge that would make judgement and calculation possible existed. For Massumi (2013) this emergence of unknowability as *the* central problem within contemporary security thinking triggers a shift into a logic of pre-emption. In seeking to act on these unknowable threats, the processes and methods of security change. The example Massumi (2013) gives is that security shifts from tackling the present danger to explicitly acting to produce the threat that is presumed to exist. This is best expressed through the doctrine of pre-emption underpinning the invasion of Iraq. The invasion was not a response to a danger, but a pre-emptive flushing out of the threat Iraq was held to contain. For Massumi (2013), the logic was one in which, through acting, one would force the threat to emerge, thus allowing it to be targeted.

Thus, Beck establishes a vision of a simple world now overrun with complex interconnections which render social problems, such as terrorism, unmanageable. Massumi treads a similar path but, instead, emphasises a past security landscape of knowability and cumulative knowledge, compared with a modern world in which threats are rendered unknowable. Both works are of value, demonstrating that how security is understood by state actors has changed. Yet both problematically posit some form of break between a past that was manageable and a present that is not. Beck roots this transition in one of ever-increasing complexity. This complexity is important, informing how problems of terrorism are understood and governed. Yet, contrary to Beck's warning of unmanageability, there are a whole range of technologies that seek to make knowable these incalculable and indeterminate risks in order to make them actionable. As Aradau and van Munster (2007) argue, Beck's commitment to an historicisation, which locates the advent of 'risk society' within a process of reflexive modernisation following from 'industrial society', fails to grasp the manifold ways across time and space through which risks come to be understood and made governable.

Massumi recognises that this uncertainty can be managed, highlighting the mechanisms that allow contemporary threats to be governed, and action to be taken within conditions of uncertainty. Yet he is mistaken in his sharp ontological division established between Cold War technologies of knowable calculability and post-Cold War technologies of unknowable incalculabilities. Even within the Cold War, there are many examples of 'unknowable' threats which security actors negotiated within conditions of uncertainty. Collier and Lakoff (2009), for instance, locate the development of what they term 'vital systems security' as a means of generating knowledge regarding the vulnerability of US infrastructure to enemy attack. Such knowledge was produced not through statistical analysis but through enacted knowledge. Security agents enacted potential futures through imaginative practices of scenario planning and modelling concerning, in Massumi's language, 'unknowable' future events (Collier and Lakoff, 2009: 11). Indeed, the study of security practices and their epistemological relation to the future is now being extended back, to rethink how security knowledges were generated in, for instance, the Cold War (Collier and Lakoff, 2008, 2009; van Munster and Sylvest, 2014). Moreover, even the classical conception of the 'security dilemma' takes as its starting assumption the unknowability of the intentions of other states, and thus the question of whether armaments are intended defensively or aggressively.[1]

As opposed to an ontological account that sees a shift in the nature of modern threats, instead, these practices should be read within an ontological reading of threat. Threats, following Massumi, presuppose acting within conditions of uncertainty. It is here the book introduces the term 'preclusive'. While, as the next section will clarify, there are numerous ways through which the future can be made knowable, the intent of using the term 'preclusive' is to provide a general term which accounts for the specific relation of security-temporality outlined in this section. The term 'preclusive security' thus clarifies an ontological position, drawing on the above literature, which makes clear that *all* attempts to act upon a threat must necessarily produce a means of making this threat knowable. Preclusive security thus provides an ontological account of the relationship between security and temporality, allowing the question of security epistemologies to come to the fore as the object of analytical importance. This approach to security epistemologies thus meshes with a methodological approach of problematisation, shifting the analytical gaze to security actors and policymakers, and their discursive production of threat. In summary, there has not been a shift from a controllable, pre-reflexive society into a reflexive modernity that eludes management. Rather, governing through risk can be seen as a socially embedded set of practices and knowledges that change over time and *bring into contestation the subjects and objects of risk*. Risk can thus be viewed as a means of ordering our world through articulating and managing social problems (Aradau and van Munster, 2007: 97).

Crossing the 'temporal gap'

When securing within conditions of uncertainty, what therefore comes to the fore is the need to produce the future as knowable such that action in the present becomes possible. There exists a 'temporal gap', defined in this book as the temporal space that exists between the present and the envisaged future harm. To secure threat then requires crossing or traversing this space (Anderson, 2010b; Massumi, 2013). This analysis thus demands that threats cannot be read as epistemologically given phenomena. Threat, in its unresolvable uncertainty, therefore exists primarily as an affect; it is, for Massumi (2013), something that is felt and intuited. It is the feeling itself that becomes the truth content of the possible harm, and thus, within preclusive security, becomes the key driver of interventions. Processes of securing threats thus generate a dangerous or promissory supplement to the present (Anderson, 2010b). The question of securing threat always generates an excess, an indeterminacy, a gap into which the security intervention is deployed and must seek to find legitimacy.

To secure therefore requires the traversal of this gap. That is, to disclose the future-object of security will always require work, some form of discursive, material or practical means of making-knowable. Intimately related to this legitimacy thus comes the possibility of making a truth-claim, not in a positivistic sense of objective truths, but in the sense of how particular statements of knowledge – of epistemology – come to contain actionable truths. In these processes of making knowable, while threat formally retains its irresolvable uncertainty, different mechanisms are employed that rationalise and attach thresholds of epistemologisation that govern what is understood to be legitimate knowledge of the threat in question. While at one level the affect of threat informs the production of these mechanisms of making knowable, at the level of their utilisation, this affect is effaced and neutralised through a variety of rational, technical and bureaucratic methods of making threats known.

There are two ramifications of such an analysis for how security can be understood and analysed. The first is methodological, the second is political. Methodologically, this literature brings to the fore the importance of questions of epistemology within an analysis of securing threats. Following Anderson (2010a), two stages of analytical inquiry can be identified within the context of intervention into uncertain threats. First, there is the constitution of a temporal relation, a relation to the future that provides the context within which claims to knowledge can be made. Second, there is the production of a knowledge that can then be deployed in order to traverse the temporal gap, such that claims as to the reality of the threat can be made. Anderson (2010a) labels these 'practices', and includes the examples of calculation, imagination and performance. These practices govern how knowledge of the future can be produced and attain a truth-content, rendering them knowable in the present. Folding back on the methodology followed in this book, this coheres with the act of problematisation, constituting a problematised object of threat.

Within the context of this book, this temporal relation is established through the concept of radicalisation, enacting an account of individuals as on a trajectory through time, towards or away from violence. The book then utilises two of the concepts developed by Anderson (2010a) to analyse the relation radicalisation draws within uncertain future threats. First, is that in relation to environments that may produce vulnerability to radicalisation, a pre-emptive logic is invoked. Second, in relation to individuals who may be vulnerable to radicalisation, a precautionary logic is invoked. These concepts will be mobilised and further defined in chapters 5 and 6, respectively. A range of knowledge practices are then used to understand radicalisation, the environments that may enable them and the signs that might provide evidence of the movement of individuals. The temporal relation of radicalisation will be analysed shortly. The knowledge that has then been produced to make knowable such threats is the subject of the next chapter, and reveals how Prevent is productive of an identity politics.

The second ramification is political. While the futures with which security actors might be concerned are limitless, the production of the future will necessarily be partial – conceptualising and visualising only a portion of actual potential futures that will be culturally and epistemically limited (de Goede, 2008). Emphasising the space of uncertainty at the heart of securing threats thus opens up the possibility of a political analysis that puts the *constitution* of those objects at its heart. Through analysing the means through which the temporal gap is traversed, analysis can ask questions of how particular futures become rendered as threatening, and how their mediation becomes possible. If Beck and Massumi thus problematically ontologise the changing nature of threat across time and space, the intention here is to provide an ontological account of threat that enables a political reading of the epistemological relations that are constituted in regards to threat. Put differently, it is to bring to the fore the role that security practitioners have in representing threats, and constituting them as objects of both knowledge and action. Thus, in constituting and traversing the temporal gap, security actors *structure the promise of future threats.* Every act of securing threat is thus a performative traversal that constitutes its own political terrain. It is within this traversal that the politics and the operations of power within security acts and processes can be identified. The political ramifications of Prevent's traversal of the temporal gap is the subject of chapter 7.

*The contemporary centrality of security within conditions
of uncertainty*

Before analysing the temporal relation enacted by radicalisation, it is first
necessary to outline the literature's identification of a shift in security
practices within which Prevent can be located. Within this context, and
despite the limitations outlined, the literature has identified contemporary problematisations of threat that seek to go beyond previous state
security practices. While all acts of securing threat require the production and traversal of a temporal gap, in response to threats such as contemporary terrorism, climate change and epidemics, security policies
have explicitly and self-consciously sought to deploy security practices
within conditions of categorical uncertainty, preclusive to the threat they
seek to manage. This ambition has, in turn, led to a shift in contemporary
security practices.

Central to the literature is a perception that approaches to security
have, in recent years, gone beyond previous statistically driven and calculative technologies. In its place, the role of imaginative and specula-
tive practices are foregrounded. Aradau and van Munster (2008) term
contemporary approaches to security as existing within a '*dispositif* of
risk', emphasising the centrality that risk management techniques from
commercial and environmental practices have attained within the War
on Terror.[2] For Grusin (2004), this contemporary relationship to threat is
one of 'premediation'. The concept entails that the contemporary world
is, in part, governed by a plurality of public, media-driven futures. That,
through the imagining of a plurality of possible futures one can act upon
them in the present in order to deny the future's surprise. It insists that,
'the future itself is already mediated, and that with the right technologies
[...] the future can be remediated before it happens' (Grusin, 2004: 19).
Building upon this formulation, Anderson (2010a) argues that previous
ways of envisioning the relationship between liberal rule and the uncertainty of the future had revolved around either the logic of foresight or
probability – either good judgement or mathematical induction from past
events. Yet the threats that are envisaged in modern society cannot be so
easily discerned. Instead, they demand governance of highly improbable
and indeterminate events that contain the potential for massive damage
to life and the conditions of life on this planet. In relation to this type of
threat, no longer can one manage the present based on only likely, plaus-
ible events (within the paradigm of foresight) – one must now expect the
implausible. Nor can one apply probabilistic calculation – these 'low-n'
events escape calculation (Anderson, 2010a).

This relation of premediation therefore demands new modes of
knowing the future such that action can be taken in the present. In its
self-conscious arrangement of a radical plurality of imaginations, it

'simultaneously *deploys and exceeds* the language of risk' (de Goede, 2008: 156, emphasis in original). While both seek to commodify and harness an uncertain future, premediative logics are not about getting the future right (de Goede, 2008). While risk logics aim for calculative predictions, premediation seeks to create as multiplicitous a number of futures as possible, in order to most effectively minimise and mediate the surprise of the future. The book borrows from Grusin this language of *mediation*, using it as a term that denotes security action in the present, in order to effect a future that is produced as threatening. Emphasising the centrality of these premediative logics within contemporary security practices, there is an emerging range of scholarship outlining the numerous mechanisms through which the future can be made knowable and actionable through these non-calculative methodologies. Recent work has, for instance, focused on the centrality of imagination (van Munster and Sylvest, 2014), conjecture (Aradau and van Munster, 2011), scenario planning (Collier and Lakoff, 2008) and emergency response preparation (Anderson and Adey, 2012).

For Grusin, this is primarily a media-driven process. However, what is apparent within the study of Prevent, and in the development of the broader literature, are the ways through which questioning how future uncertainty might be acted upon has attained a central policy and bureaucratic concern, informing the problematisations of threat by security actors. Famously, the report into the attacks of 9/11 argued that there had been a 'failure of imagination' and that the United States needed to find ways to bureaucratise imagination within its security practices (National Commission on Terrorist Attacks Upon the United States, 2004: 344–346). Similarly, in the UK, the National Security Strategy states that while the Cold War was 'largely predictable', the country 'no longer face[s] such predictable threats' (Cabinet Office, 2010: 18). Rather, the UK must 'scan the horizon, identify possible future developments and prepare for them. We must be prepared for alternative futures based on key trends, building in the adaptability to respond to different possibilities' (Cabinet Office, 2010: 15). Summing up this contemporary framing, Sir David Omand, writing on the nature of modern intelligence, states, 'there will be less inductive reasoning, and rather more hypothesis formulation and testing, for example in relation to the *possible intentions of groups that may not yet themselves know their potential capabilities*' (Omand, 2009: 13, emphasis added). In this self-conscious engagement with an uncertain future, this has led security actors to privilege non-calculable approaches to making the future knowable.

The importance of these transformations is evidenced by the wider strategic shift that these preclusive security ambitions have foregrounded. De Goede *et al.* identify an 'ideal of emergent security', wherein that which is privileged is the ability for security actors and processes to emerge with, and respond to, the emergence of the threat itself (de Goede *et al.*, 2014: 415). This emphasis on emergence signals a change in the problematisation of threat away from linear and knowable concerns, towards a fixation on the chaotic, complex and non-linear. It is a security framing that moves from long-term strategic planning, and instead emphasises the ability to identify and respond to threats at the moment they manifest. As the discussion of the problems posed by contemporary terrorism earlier demonstrates, it is the need to spot the emerging terrorist that comes to the fore. Radicalisation can occur rapidly and without prior warning, and the results, if left unmediated, could be devastating. Emergent security thus emphasises flexibility, adaptability and the need to join up disparate data points that might point to the emergence of threat, stressing interoperability and data sharing across public and private partners (de Goede *et al.*, 2014). In seeking to act prior to illegality, the responsibility to secure goes beyond security agents such as the police and intelligence services, extending to a range of non-traditional security agents (Zedner, 2007). In order to act on uncertainty, it is a security framework that seeks to embed itself into the environment, an ambition that is clearly visible in the Prevent strategy, and the need to locate expertise regarding radicalisation wherever such radicalisation may occur. The intent is to fabricate within the structure of social relations and institutions the means and mechanisms of response, such that response can co-emerge with the threat (Anderson and Adey, 2012: 30).

The key contribution of the literature should thus be understood as foregrounding the question of security epistemologies. What emerges as crucial is that acts of security are acts of intervention into uncertain futures, and that, as such, they require the generation of knowledge in the present as to the shape that such futures take. The literature, therefore, enables and demands analyses of (preclusive) security that privilege how uncertain futures are produced as knowable and actionable in the present. This focus on the production of knowledge that renders the future as governable, and the strategies through which uncertainty can be made knowable, thus has broader ramifications for how security can be understood and analysed, informing how this book frames the question of epistemology at the heart of Prevent. The question it enables is: how does the Prevent policy produce as knowable the potential future terrorist, such that mediative action in the present is possible? Or, in other words: how does Prevent cross this 'temporal gap' that sits at the heart of securing uncertainty? The answer is to be found within the concept of radicalisation.

Radicalisation: constituting the temporal relation

Prevent structures its relation with an uncertain future through understanding processes of radicalisation. Here, the book outlines how this concept structures the temporal relation of Prevent, before the next chapter will detail how the subject who is vulnerable to radicalisation is made knowable. From its inception, this question of understanding and preventing radicalisation has been the modus operandi of Prevent. The policy documents state that the Prevent strand is concerned with 'tackling the radicalisation of individuals, both in the UK and elsewhere' (Home Office, 2006: 9) and that it sought to understand '[t]he processes whereby certain experiences and events in a person's life cause them to become radicalised, to the extent of turning to violence to resolve perceived grievances' (Home Office, 2006: 9). By 2011, it is possible to simply state that the purpose of Prevent is to 'stop people becoming terrorists or supporting terrorism' (Home Office, 2011a: 10). The promise held by the concept of radicalisation is that it becomes possible to conceptualise movement towards violence. In opening up this space of movement, it becomes possible to identify why and how such movement occurs.

The academic literature on radicalisation contains two broad interpretations of why an individual might become violent,[3] both of which have informed the Prevent policy documents.[4] First, there is a sociological approach that privileges questions of globalisation, community and identity within a decision to enact violence (see, for example, the work of Roy (2004) and Kepel (2004, 2008)). Roy (2004), for instance, argues that second- and third-generation immigrant Muslims in the 'West' occupy a particular space within a globalised world and are in the continual process of redefining and balancing a plurality of identities. Lacking a traditional, spiritual community, religion is reshaped in order to make sense of its application to a new culture and choices must be made as to the primary identity through which one sees oneself. Centrality is thus attached to the idea of the 'ummah' within Islam, which ascribes a communal identity on account of inclusion within the Muslim faith. Questions of politics and economic marginalisation recede. The factors that are understood to influence radicalisation are a lack of social inclusion, alienation, and the need for a sense of belonging to a community, which, it is held, participation in violence can bring. Moreover, one might act not necessarily due to one's own position within society, but out of solidarity and vicarious care for one's co-religionists, seen to be suffering throughout the world.

Second, there are a number of approaches that stress the importance of social movements and networks. Both Wiktorowicz (2005) and Sageman (2004) use empirical data to argue that what is of chief importance are individual ties and small group dynamics, wherein peer pressure and bonding shape collective identities and generate momentum towards engaging in violence. Individuals may join such groups due to political concerns, experiences of discrimination or some form of personal crisis, but it is within the dynamics of the group that a movement to violence is achieved. Such groups are likely, at least in Sageman's work, to be peer groups within a shared locale. It is also possible though that these interactions could take place online.

Both these approaches are represented in Prevent. The 2011 iteration refers to radicalisation as follows:

> So far as Al Qa'ida-related terrorism is concerned, this review has found that our earlier analysis of the key drivers of radicalisation remains largely valid. So we believe that radicalisation – in this country – is being driven by: an ideology that sets Muslim against non-Muslim, highlights the alleged oppression of the global Muslim community and which both obliges and legitimises violence in its defence; a network of influential propagandists for terrorism, in this country and elsewhere, making extensive use of the internet in particular; and by specific personal vulnerabilities and local factors which make the ideology seem both attractive and compelling. (Home Office, 2011a: 18)[5]

There is thus a narrative of global oppression that justifies violence. This is mobilised by social networks and driven by psychosocial vulnerabilities that derive from a sociological focus on identity and belonging. Indeed, the two broad theories articulated here work best when combined. Vulnerabilities explain why an individual may become engaged in a network, and social networks explain how vulnerabilities may become mobilised towards violence.

There have, increasingly, been contrary voices within the literature. However, the terrain of such interventions is mostly limited to the applicability of the methodology, and thus the empirical basis of such claims. One argument put forward is that of over-complexity: that such a plethora of pathways towards violence exist that to search for any 'cause' becomes futile. Githens-Mazer (2010), utilising first-hand data from interviews with former recruiters and participants, argues that there are multiple, complex variables involved in the process of radicalisation, such that they only attain meaning within specific cases, and to search for any generalisable principle is a folly (see also Githens-Mazer and Lambert, 2010; Pisoiu, 2013; Schmid, 2013). Another is that the term lacks analytical precision. Sedgwick (2010) demonstrates this, locating three contexts in which 'radicalisation' is differentially used (see also Richards, 2011). Similarly, Silva (2018: 40) argues that the literature is subject to confirmation bias, wherein the majority of studies begin with a predefined data set of Islamist terrorists and extend their 'findings' to the broader question of radicalisation in general. Kundnani (2012, 2014) goes further, arguing that, as a discourse, the key theoretical claim of radicalisation studies does not hold up. Regardless of the specific mechanism identified by the academic study, such as the identification of a particular cultural or psychological variable, what radicalisation studies fail to achieve is to demonstrate any causal relation. There are many who may display particular indicators, but only a tiny number of this much larger population may engage with violence. The literature cannot pick out this minority and the theorisations invoked thus lack any explanatory power.

What is lost in this debate, however, are the important ways in which such knowledges, and the practices they inform, are themselves productive and generative. Rather, and following Heath-Kelly (2012, 2013) and de Goede and Simon (2013), radicalisation knowledges function as anticipatory objects that make Prevent interventions possible and necessary. As de Goede and Simon (2013: 321) put it, the 'political rationality of radicalisation as a security problem rests upon the belief that there is a process of becoming radical and that it is possible to intervene upon it'. These analyses demonstrate that what the concept of radicalisation produces, and is shared across both sociological and social movement approaches, is an understanding of violence as a movement in time: a *becoming* violent. The concept invokes a temporal movement from a present space of normalcy to a future one in which violence is justified.

The radicalisation literature posits there are stages through which an individual will move on the way to engaging in violence. In a review essay by King and Taylor (2011), they identify five models of radicalisation, of which four are marked by a linear pathway towards violence. For instance, they cite the work of Wiktorowicz (2005), who understands radicalisation as consisting of four linear stages based upon a case study of Al-Muhajiroun in the UK. First, there is a cognitive opening, often a crisis of some form, and then, second, a 'religious seeking' which provides some form of answer. Third, there is a 'frame alignment' wherein the religious worldview is brought into line with that of the terrorist, and finally, socialisation, where the individual joins the group. Similarly, Moghaddam (2005, cited in King and Taylor, 2011: 606), sees radicalisation as a 'staircase' of six steps, starting with a feeling of deprivation on the ground floor and moving through other steps such as blaming others and establishing 'us and them' thinking, before the final step of being willing to commit violence. At all steps, an individual may, or may not, stop. Lastly, by way of contrast, King and Taylor identify the work of Sageman (2008) as the only case in which factors that may contribute to radicalisation are not linear. Instead, Sageman posits four prongs: moral outrage; an aligned interpretation of the world with the terrorist group; resonance with personal experience; and a network of like-minded individuals. While non-linear, it is expected that a terrorist will have collected all four prongs on their journey to violence. As Sageman (2004, cited in de Goede and Simon, 2013: 320) states in his earlier work, '[t]here's really no profile, just similar *trajectories* to joining the jihad.'

What this approach to modelling radicalisation allows, in a practical sense, is for the identification of where individuals exist on this progression, which direction they are travelling in, and what particular traits or characteristics are common, or even necessary, within these stages of advancement. This has led to an academic literature, which, rooted in positivistic ontology, has focused on testing the validity of isolated variables in terms of the potential of individuals to be 'radicalised' (Horgan, 2008; King and Taylor, 2011). This understanding of radicalisation is most notable in the metaphor of the 'conveyor belt' that is often put forward. Radicalisation thus envisages life to be in a process of becoming, and that with the right understanding, the trajectories of life that may become threatening can be identified. Radicalisation as a concept can thus be read as a family of knowledges that enacts a particular temporal relation. Processes of becoming violent can be generalised, such that the steps towards violence can be recognised. What is therefore produced through radicalisation knowledge is a temporal relation that connects the display of signs or factors in the present with the potential movement on a path towards violence. The uncertainty of the future terrorist is disciplined through a conceptualisation of movement that allows one to see, imagine and map future trajectories. While the future retains a formal uncertainty, this disciplining allows for particular truth-claims to be made. The crucial question, and that of the next chapter, is therefore: how is vulnerability to radicalisation in the present articulated and made knowable? The answer, as this book will show, is through rendering identities and performances that are seen to be outside of 'Britishness' or 'British values' as risky.

Conclusion

The argument of this chapter has been that all acts of securing threat necessarily exist in relation to an uncertain future; a future space which is *produced* through the act of security. The term 'preclusive security' has been introduced to highlight this ontological position, arguing that *all* attempts to act upon a threat necessarily have to produce a means of making the threat knowable. Locating this analysis within the contemporary critical security literature on security-temporality, it was argued that the literature draws important attention to contemporary framings of security practices that privilege novel approaches which self-consciously seek to act within conditions of uncertainty. Yet, it was demonstrated that this should not be ontologised as a juncture, but rather requires an analysis that privileges how security actors constitute threat. Of analytical importance is thus the particular mode of relation to the future that the security acts in question presuppose. The object of analysis must be the discursive and practical means through which the uncertainty of a particular threat is disciplined and made knowable in the present. Methodologically, this entails that, first, it is necessary to articulate the relation to the future that is established within a particular security framing. Second, it is then possible to analyse the knowledge that is produced which makes the objects of threat intelligible in the present.

Within the context of counter-radicalisation policy, the temporal ambition of Prevent, it has been shown, is to intervene early, preclusive to an individual becoming a terrorist. This ambition goes beyond previous state approaches to tackling political violence, actively seeking to intervene into these *processes of becoming violent.* This has required that it be possible to identify such processes. It is the concept of radicalisation that has enabled this and structures the relation with a categorically uncertain future. The concept of radicalisation thus informs a problematic that sees life processes within a state of becoming, and the possibility of an analysis that might identify becoming which is considered risky. In the next chapter, the book will demonstrate how the Prevent policy orders such processes of becoming into those that are secure and those that carry a threat which requires mediation.

Notes

1 Thanks to Shane Brighton for raising this point.
2 Aradau and van Munster (2008: 24, 25) define *dispositif* as 'a heterogeneous assemblage of discursive and material elements for governing social problems' which here relates to the creation of 'a specific relation to the future, which requires the monitoring of the future, the attempt to calculate what the future can offer and the necessity to control and minimize its potentially harmful effects'.
3 This follows the analysis of Dalgaard-Nielsen (2010), although she includes a third category of case-study driven analyses that, to this reading, are of far less academic and policy consequence.
4 Not least as many of the texts that will be cited in the following section are also cited in key Prevent policy documents. The 2009 iteration (Home Office, 2009a), for instance, cites Wiktorowicz (2005), Hoffman (2006), Sageman (2004, 2008) and Kepel (2008). The selected bibliography contained in the 2011 iteration of Prevent (Home Office, 2011a) has an even wider representation of the literature, although, as Silva (2018) shows, this engagement is only with elements of the academic literature, and not that within a critical terrorism studies framework.
5 A similar account is given in the 2009 iteration (Home Office, 2009a: 41–43).

4

Crossing the temporal gap: vulnerability, extremism and the ordering of identities

The previous chapter demonstrated that the key innovation of Prevent is in its temporal ambition to intervene into processes of becoming, and that it therefore seeks to make knowable and actionable the movement of an individual towards violence. Radicalisation establishes a temporal framework that allows for an understanding of the processes an individual might go through on the path towards violence. Yet, a mere outline of this temporal framework does not itself identify who is a threat and who is not. Central to the problematic of Prevent is, therefore, the following question: how can potential to radicalisation be identified in the present, such that the threat held for the future can be mediated? If radicalisation is envisaged as a process, there remains a question as to why certain individuals engage with this process and others do not. This chapter makes the argument that Prevent traverses the temporal gap by discursively situating the subject of vulnerability to radicalisation and extremism as outside of, or alienated from, 'Britishness' and 'British values'. The next two chapters, in articulating the assemblage of counter-radicalisation that implements Prevent, will show how this takes concrete effect, targeting specific behaviours, identities and communities.

Here, though, the intention is to show the problematic of vulnerability to radicalisation renders an uncertain future as knowable. Vulnerability, it will be shown, is positioned within the policy, as those subjects and spaces that are deemed disassociated from 'Britishness' and 'British values'. Then, in analysing the mobilisation of the term 'extremism', it can be made clear that 'Britishness' is rendered securing of vulnerabilities, whereas extremism, defined in explicit opposition to 'British values', furthers this potential to radicalisation. Thus, in traversing the temporal gap, the Prevent policy produces an account of identity in which identities that cohere with 'Britishness' and 'British values' are deemed secure, whereas those which are understood to disassociate from this 'Britishness' are read as potentially threatening and thus requiring some form of mediation. Therefore, in taking seriously the temporality of Prevent, and its ambition to intervene early, this book shows that the security and identity strands of Prevent cannot be separated in the ways envisaged by the political debates that narrate the policy or the academic literature, as discussed in chapters 1 and 2.

The first section of this chapter provides a discursive reading of the ascriptions of 'vulnerability' and 'extremism' within the policy. It demonstrates a problematisation wherein vulnerability and extremism are positioned as outside of 'Britishness' and 'British values' and therefore as threatening. The second section then argues that in approaching these discursive ascriptions through a post-structuralist framework, Prevent can be understood as a set of productive practices, producing, through the security act, an account of 'Britishness' and that which lies outside. 'Britishness' is thus produced as secure and securing – it is normalised – while that which is produced as external is rendered threatening and in need of mediation. Once produced, once this boundary is established, vulnerable or extreme identities are positioned as in need of trans-formation on account of the threat they pose. Through bringing them into coherence with this 'normalised Britishness', their 'secure-ness' is established.

Ordering identities as secure and risky

In contrast to the reading of Prevent's institutional history given earlier that showed evolution, adaptation and transformation, this section provides a discursive reading of the Prevent policy that brings to the fore a key continuity which has existed since it began. It analyses that which is designated as threatening within Prevent, the individuals and spaces that represent a potential towards radicalisation. Radicalisation, and the future potential terrorist, are made knowable through the ascription of the terms 'vulnerability' and 'extremism', and their discursive relation to 'Britishness'. This problematised threat, which has run throughout the Prevent policy, is one that situates that which is threatening as that which is located outside of 'Britishness' or 'British values'. This section, in con-trast to a literature that sees Prevent as consisting of disjuncture and different iterations, seeks to bring out a key coherency that runs through the history of the policy.

Articulations of vulnerability

In the first iteration of CONTEST, the knowledge production that would go on to inform the policy is still very much in development. It provides broad, generalised statements and the focus is very much on the big picture. Radicalisation, it is explained, cannot be reduced to a single explanatory radicalising factor (Home Office, 2006: 10). Three broad factors are presented and discussed. First is the 'development of a sense of grievance and injustice' arising from a 'negative and partial' interpretation of history, and the relationship between the West and Islam, and 'often a simplistic, but virulent anti-Westernism' (Home Office, 2006: 10). This could derive from the misperception of Western intentions and actions, the presence of Western actors and forces in Muslim countries, a perceived inconsistency in Western foreign policy, or even an isolated incident that may 'be used to convince susceptible individuals that the West is antipathetic to Islam' (Home Office, 2006: 10). The second factor identified is a 'sense of personal alienation or community disadvantage', a sentiment of socioeconomic deprivation that may be felt vicariously, nationally and internationally (Home Office, 2006: 10). The third factor identified is an exposure to radical ideas, which may come through reading radical literature in a physical format, or through the internet, but is more likely to be through a local contact, a 'forceful and inspiring figure, already committed to extremism' (Home Office, 2006: 10). Accepting that these factors are not conclusive, and that the generation of radicalisation knowledge is still in its infancy, the policy argues that they should be viewed as 'considerations which may affect radicalisation' (Home Office, 2006: 10). Outlined in this way, the themes that will characterise the discursive construction of the radicalised subject already begin to appear, though they are yet to attain coherence. There is a clear statement that there is a narrative to such violence, a broad idea of alienation and a conception that this usually involves some form of network.

The focus here remains at a communal, rather than individual, level. Nevertheless, the articulation of the 'radicalised' individual already starts to point towards questions of identity and belonging. The policy states that, '[a]n alienated individual who has become highly radicalised is not necessarily a terrorist' (Home Office, 2006: 10), pre-supposing that radicalisation entails a prior alienation from society. As Hazel Blears (who would take control of Prevent shortly after this document was published) stated, what was happening at this time was the beginning of an understanding as to how the narrative of al-Qaeda played out in British communities. So, for instance, she argued that while there was anger around foreign policy, it was far more complex and concerned people's identity, their role in Britain, economic issues and their place within their own community. These issues were then mobilised by a small group of radical preachers running very sophisticated operations (interview with Hazel Blears). Overall, this conception of the problem thus positioned communal disadvantage and alienation from 'British society' and values as central to radicalisation. In response, it is integration into, and equality within, 'British society' that is required; 'the drive for equality, social inclusion, community cohesion and active citizenship in Britain strengthens society and its resistance to terrorism here in the UK' (Home Office, 2006: 9).

In the 2007 reiteration of the Prevent policy, the critical discursive shift is the introduction of a language of 'vulnerability'. It emerges in 2007, becoming commonplace in the 2009 strategy, and is ubiquitous in the 2011 and 2018 iterations. The subject of radicalisation becomes the individual who is 'vulnerable to violent extremist messages' (DCLG, 2007: 10), 'vulnerable to radicalisation' (Home Office, 2009a: 12) and 'vulnerable to recruitment' (Home Office, 2009a: 80). Such properties are located as inherent to the individual, such that 'radicalisers' are said to target 'specific personal vulnerabilities' (Home Office, 2011a: 18). In the 2011 iteration, the second objective of Prevent is even titled 'Protecting Vulnerable People' (Home Office, 2011a: 55). The 2018 iteration states Prevent is designed to 'safeguard and support those vulnerable to radicalisation, to stop them from becoming terrorists or supporting terrorism' (Home Office, 2018c: 10).

It is a language of vulnerability that enables government policy and intervention to more explicitly focus on the individual, beyond – although still including – the broader focus on communities found in earlier documents. It is no surprise that this language of vulnerability emerges in 2007, at the same time as the development of capacities to target individuals. Central here is the establishment of the specialist Channel agency in 2007, tasked with identifying such subjects (Home Office, 2009a: 90) and analysed in chapter 6. Thus, trained specialists, such as the police, are now understood to be able to 'identify places where radicalisers may operate and where vulnerable individuals may be located and provide assistance to them' (Home Office, 2009a: 85). This specialist knowledge is understood as trainable and transferable, and it is expected that members of other professional bodies, such as teachers (DCSF, 2008a, 2008b; ACPO, 2009; DfE, 2015), local government officials (Local Government Association, 2008), healthcare professionals (Department of Health, 2011; NHS England, 2017) and those providing further and higher education (ACPO, 2012a, 2012b; Home Office, 2015b, 2015c) be educated in, and maintain vigilance towards, potential threats.

Most importantly though, this discourse represents a move towards the psychological, and shifts the emphasis away from external factors (see also Jackson, 2013 on this point). Where earlier, misperceptions of foreign policy or communal disadvantage were emphasised, the focus is now upon the individual's mental wellbeing. Vulnerability is defined as:

> not simply a result of actual or perceived grievances. It may be the result of family or peer pressure, the absence of positive mentors and role models, a crisis of identity, links to criminality including other

forms of violence, exposure to traumatic events (here or overseas), or changing circumstances (eg a new environment following migration and asylum). (Home Office, 2009a: 89)

And it is stated that:

> In many countries, including the UK, people are not only vulnerable to radicalisation because of political and economic grievances. A range of social and psychological factors are also important. Radicalisation seems to be related *directly* to a *crisis in identity* and, *specifically*, to a feeling of *not being accepted or belonging*. (Home Office, 2009a: 44, emphases added)

Further, it is stated that intervention providers must be 'able to reach and relate to people who will very often be alienated and separated from mainstream society and Government' (Home Office, 2011a: 61).

Within this discourse, questions of identity and belonging attain a clear centrality to Prevent. In its understanding of radicalisation, the Prevent policy traverses the temporal gap through conceptualising the subject who is 'vulnerable' as outside of, or alienated from, 'British society', and therefore risky. What the discourse of vulnerability therefore envisages is that identities in the UK can be ordered as secure and as risky. Those that are deemed to not belong are framed as vulnerable through this alienation. Thus positioned, it becomes those who (are seen to) exist outside of a framework of 'British' belonging, and the norms and behaviours associated with this, who threaten the British state.

Britishness as securing; extremism as risky

Thus far, this section has shown that vulnerabilities come to be articulated in a psychosocial framing that stresses an alienation from 'Britishness'. The centrality of identity and values can be further shown through an analysis of the concept of 'extremism'. This analysis shows that 'Britishness' is rendered capable of securing vulnerable identities, and conversely, distance from this 'Britishness' is rendered risky. To make this argument, it is necessary to make sense of the ways in which Prevent understands and constructs the question of ideology and ideas. In doing so, the book can show how 'British values' are able to secure those who are vulnerable.

The language of vulnerability implies certain ascriptions of agency and responsibility within the Prevent policy. This is most apparent in the dichotic line drawn between the 'radicalised' and the 'radicalisers'. From its first enunciation in 2006, a distinction has been explicitly made in terms of their ability to think and act meaningfully and purposively and their subsequent power relations. If the 'radicalised' are vulnerable, it is those 'radicalising' who exploit their vulnerabilities. This differentiation is most explicitly spelled out in 2009, stating that, '[w]ithin terrorist networks the motivation as well as the background of those in leadership positions differs from those who are not' (Home Office, 2009a: 43). Thus, the 'radicalising' subject is described as 'a forceful and inspiring figure, already committed to extremism' (Home Office, 2006: 10). Such figures are understood to play the part of a 'a charismatic role model and ideologue' and are able to 'exploit and create grievances' (Home Office, 2009a: 44, 91). This is played against the language of the vulnerable subject, when it is claimed that these individuals need support from 'being groomed to terrorism by those who claim religious expertise and use what appear to be religious arguments' (Home Office, 2011a: 80). These radicalisers, and the groups they represent, seek to 'manipulate, mislead and take advantage of young people' (Home Office, 2011a: 83).

Importantly, this analysis situates 'British values' as able to defend against the pernicious impact of radicalisers and their extremist ideology. It constitutes certain spaces as potentially threatening on account of the ideas and identities they are seen to contain, and it positions 'Britishness' as key in mediating such problematic potential. This construction can be explicitly seen in the attention paid to particular problem spaces within the context of vulnerability to radicalisation. In the first iteration of Prevent, one of the central concerns was to deter 'those who facilitate terrorism [...] changing the environment in which the extremists and those radicalising others can operate' (Home Office, 2006: 2). In the 2009 iteration it is contended that '[r]adicalisers exploit open spaces in communities and institutions' (Home Office, 2009a: 88). The point being made here is that the ideology of radicalisation requires 'open' spaces in which the extremist ideology is unopposed and uncontested. This is stated most explicitly in the 2011 iteration, which claims that, 'radicalisation tends to occur in places where terrorist ideologies, and those that promote them, go uncontested and are not exposed to free, open and balanced debate and challenge' (Home Office, 2011a: 63). Thus, there 'should be no "ungoverned spaces" in which extremism is allowed to flourish without firm challenge and, where appropriate, by legal intervention' (Home Office, 2011a: 9). The presumption is that, when confronted with such debates and challenged by differing arguments, the 'radicalising' ideology will likely fail. Such ideology is vapid, appealing to the vulnerable, but yet unsustainable against reasoned objections. Hence the response must be to generate this debate, to expose the radicalising ideology to challenge. A central task of Prevent is to therefore 'ensure that [radicalisers'] views are subject to civic challenge and debate' (Home Office, 2011a: 83).

This analysis demonstrates a central tenet of Prevent, visible in the earlier discussion of radicalisation, which holds that certain environments are more threatening than others. Certain environments come to be positioned as more vulnerable, in that they are seen to be disassociated from, to be outside of and lacking, 'British' identities and values. As was shown in chapter 1, the language of extremism has assumed a central space in the 2011 and 2018 iterations. Yet this concern around particular, extreme ideologies has been a long-standing factor within the Prevent policy, with the first iteration stating that '[s]ince early 2003, the United Kingdom has been implementing a long-term strategy for countering international terrorism and the extremism that lies behind it' (Home Office, 2006: 9). The concept of extremism clearly carries an explicit identity politics, being formally defined in 2011 as:

> vocal or active opposition to fundamental British values, including democracy, the rule of law, individual liberty and mutual respect and tolerance of different faiths and beliefs. We also include in our defin-ition of extremism calls for the death of members of our armed forces, whether in this country or overseas. (Home Office, 2011a: 107)

What is at stake is that environments that are removed from normalised British identities and values, those which are deemed to be closed and extremist, are considered more vulnerable to the possible emergence of individuals committed to political violence. Within an ascription of extremism is therefore a mutual exclusivity with a 'British' identity or holding of 'British values'. In regards to Islamist extremism, Prevent understands it to represent that:

> the West is perpetually at war with Islam; there can be no legitimate interaction between Muslims and non-Muslims in this country or else-where; and that Muslims living here cannot legitimately and or effect-ively participate in our democratic society. (Home Office, 2011a: 20)

The Muslim extremist is thus set apart from the normalcy of 'Britishness' in terms of the identities to which they will not subscribe, and is intrin-sically linked to the problem of potential terrorist violence through this devoid identity.

Discursively, the implication of a language of 'vulnerability' not only demands rehabilitation, as Richards (2011) highlights, it also implicitly positions 'British values' as an antidote or preventative measure. As Stevens (2009: 518) articulates, for Prevent to make sense, it must assume that the decision to join a violently radical group (or, it might be added, to undertake violent action alone), is due to a 'lack of exposure to viable alternatives or the capacity to reason appropriately'. This framework can also clearly be seen in one of the central metaphors invoked to represent the threat of radicalisation, that of the virus. Tony Blair, in a speech to the US Congress in 2003, framed the threat to the West as resulting from poverty and a lack of freedom elsewhere: 'in the combination of these afflictions a new and deadly virus has emerged. The virus is terrorism whose intent to inflict destruction is unconstrained by human feeling and whose capacity to inflict it is enlarged by technology' (Blair, 2003).

Relating this directly to radicalisation, Norman Bettison, the former Prevent lead for ACPO, has argued that al-Qaeda represents

> a virus that has carriers and that can infect some who come into contact with the source. The 'virus' metaphor is particularly useful in thinking about strategies to target the most susceptible and vulnerable in our communities. We also need to learn more about the way the virus spreads and mutates. This sort of endeavour will help to provide barriers to infection and to identify the symptoms better than we do at present. (Bettison, 2009: 130–131)

This representation of Prevent works to establish the ideology as one that flows across societal networks: a disease that infects those who are vulnerable to its message, yet one that can be immunised and defended against.

Thus, since its inception, Prevent has maintained a spatial analysis that sees, within the flow of particular ideas, the possibility of establishing threatening spaces. That is, spaces in which such ideas are not challenged and opened up to contestation are rendered as problematic. It can be stated that:

> We judge that communities who do not (or, alternatively, cannot) participate in all civic society are more likely to be vulnerable to radicalisation by all kinds of terrorist groups [...] A stronger sense of 'belonging' and citizenship makes communities more resilient to terrorist ideology and propagandists. (Home Office, 2011a: 27)

This is also extended to particular institutions that can also be designated as 'vulnerable' (Home Office, 2011a: 29). Schools that have been promoting conservative Islamic theology, as seen in the Trojan Horse affair, reflect what this means in practice. These extremist spaces are problematic as they foster extremist ideas – isolated from 'British' identities – which render individuals within them more vulnerable to radicalisation due to this alienation. Spaces in which extremism has taken hold are thus established as a dissociative milieu, giving meaning and potential recruits to the terrorist cause: an *en masse* not-belonging that represents a potential threat in and of itself.

The problematic of counter-radicalisation thus establishes, through the ascription of vulnerability and extremism, the possibility of traversing the temporal gap, identifying both problematic environments and individual characteristics in the present which indicate potentials towards becoming violent. This will result in two broad approaches within the assemblage of counter-radicalisation. The first, analysed in the following chapter, addresses the environments that are generative of radicalisation. The second, analysed in chapter 6, will identify individuals vulnerable to radicalisation. This reading of Prevent's problematisation of threat shows that it is through identifying identities in the present that threats in the future are made knowable. Vulnerability is associated, both individually and spatially, as being outside of 'Britishness'. 'Britishness' becomes both indicative of secure identities and, in relation to identities that have strayed from 'Britishness', it becomes deployed as a way of securing such identities. To disassociate, to be alienated from the mainstream of 'British society', comes to represent a security concern due to the potential for radicalisation it creates.

Identity and (preclusive) security

It must, of course, be recognised, that to posit an intrinsic relation between security and identity is not new. Such an analysis has been a mainstay of post-structuralist scholarship in International Relations, which has, since its emergence in the late 1980s and early 1990s, drawn attention to the means through which practices of security have been productive of state identities (see, for example, Ashley, 1988; Connolly, 1991; Walker, 1993; Campbell, 1998a). The starting point here is that, through designating that which is outside, states are, in fact, performing particular identities, that carry with them exclusions and boundary-drawing processes. Ontologically, there can be no pre-figurative 'I' that acts out a response to an objective and external other. Rather, it is in the process of articulating and performing threats, that the 'I' and its outside are produced. As Campbell demonstrates, this demands that the practices of International Relations are not those of pre-existing, ahistorical entities that interact across, and with reference to, pre-given boundaries. Rather, analytical concern must be towards the processes and practices that establish boundaries between the internal state and external international (Campbell, 1998a: 61). Therefore, to understand the identity of the 'British' state, the processes through which it produces, performs and secures itself against its outside must be examined. Such boundary-producing practices are often the product of ascriptions of danger or threat to that which is considered other, establishing the internal community as normalised, safe and coherent, in opposition to the dangerous outside.

Within this context, the term 'preclusive identity politics' serves to bring together literatures on security-temporality and security-identity, signifying that Prevent produces an account of identity in the present that makes intelligible future threats to security. Prevent, to this reading, can be situated as productive of the boundary between that which is designated as 'British', and therefore secure, and that which is designated as outside. Prevent should thus be read not as the securing of an extant, and pre-existing 'British' identity, but rather, it is through Prevent that this 'Britishness', and that which is alienated from and outside it, is produced. Through Prevent, certain identities are produced as risky on account of the potential they are deemed to contain for the future. At an abstract level, Prevent is a process where certain identities are ordered as risky, and this riskiness is understood to be constituted by an alienation from 'Britishness' and 'British values'. Prevent thus orders identities in the present. Certain identities are produced as external to a 'Britishness' and thus risky, others are normalised as 'British' and secure. In this abstracted understanding of Prevent, the content of what may or may not be 'British' recedes in importance. The point is that Prevent produces, through its security acts and ascriptions, certain identities as alienated from 'Britishness', and thus risky and in need of securing. It is, therefore, *through* the security act of Prevent that identities not considered as containable within 'Britishness' or 'British values' are produced and ascribed. These 'acts' can be understood both in terms of the narration and representation of that which is deemed risky in the policy and Prevent guidance, and also in the concrete interventions of Prevent by security actors.

This reading of Prevent therefore sees 'Britishness' and 'British values' as relatively empty signifiers in terms of their content, demarcating that which requires no intervention. They are relatively empty in that attempts at definition are given, defining 'British values', in opposition to extremism, as promoting human rights, democracy, tolerance and freedom. The key point though is that they are defined and situated through their productive ascription. It is through the security act, in its targeting of those groups and individuals who are constituted as alienated and vulnerable, that the constitutive outside of these terms is produced. Yet, in mobilising ascriptions of 'Britishness' and alienation, it is a discourse and series of operations that nevertheless retains a power in ascribing that which belongs within the British state, and that which does not belong, and, therefore, *requires some form of transformation in order to belong*.

One of the concerns raised in response to Prevent has been the ambiguity that the language of extremism and 'British values' contains. Yet, viewed through the lens of security-identity, this problem can be reformulated. Rather than being ambiguous signifiers, it is rather through the operation of Prevent that their content *is* inscribed. It is thus through analysis of Prevent, as a series of security interventions into the 'vulnerable' and 'extreme', that the outside can be read. In mapping the assemblage of Prevent, the knowledges it constitutes and the practices it instantiates, the book is able to locate the concrete forms that are ascribed to these identity practices within Prevent. In charting the interventions of Prevent, both in terms of how they are envisaged in the documents and how they are actualised, it becomes possible to specify those identities which are deemed to fall outside of a normalised Britishness, and thus demand some form of mediation. In so doing, it is possible to map the boundaries of a normalised Britishness, charting where the line of inside and outside is drawn. Concretely, the subjects of Prevent have, significantly, been Muslim communities in the UK. As will be demonstrated in the next two chapters, the security interventions of Prevent order Muslimness, and Muslim political and religious expression, to be indicative of alienation from 'Britishness', and thus in need of securing. In being produced as outside of a normalised Britishness, it is these concrete identities that then require being brought within this 'Britishness' in order to secure them.

Through intervening to secure that which is produced as at risk of radicalisation, British identity and its outside are constituted. If 'Britishness' and 'British values' signify a secure identity, then that which Prevent narrates as risky and intervenes into is, in the moment of that intervention, *produced as* alienated, outside of 'Britishness' and thus a risk. It is in the utterances, behaviours and identities that Prevent ascribes as risky, that this outside is narrated. It is through the active interventions into vulnerable individuals, communities and institutions, that the outside of 'Britishness' is actively produced and then acted upon. Conversely, Prevent produces that which is secure and 'British' by virtue of its silence, thus signifying a lack of threat. For those produced as threatening *due to* being outside of this 'Britishness', these identities are then acted upon through Prevent, in order to bring them more in line with a secure, 'British' identity. Identity is produced in the present as a threat, and then it is the identity that is the subject of mediation in the present on this basis. It is this framing of identity that the book understands in terms of the production of a 'normalised Britishness'. 'Britishness' becomes produced as that which is both secure and securing. The identities that are produced as outside and alienated from this 'British' identity are rendered threatening, to be secured through their greater coherence with 'British' identity and values. This is the preclusive identity politics of Prevent, a politics which orders identities as risky or threatening in the present, on account of the potential they are seen to contain for the future, and which seeks their transformation on that basis.

Prevent, therefore, operates as a function that produces its own boundary; a boundary that is established between the secure, 'British' interior, and that which is placed outside of this interior. This is a boundary that is not coterminous with territory, seeking as it does to identify British citizens who, nevertheless, in the alienation they are seen to contain, are held to pose a threat. Nor does it cohere with the law, seeking, as the last chapter demonstrated, to intervene prior to any illegality, or even the thought of illegality. Rather, it produces a boundary between those whose coherence renders them secure, and those who, in their perceived disassociation, are produced as outside of 'Britishness', requiring mediation. This boundary is of significant political consequence, serving to

deny political expression and participation on account of these productive identity practices. These political consequences are the subject
of chapter 7.

Read against the existing post-structuralist literature on security
and identity, this analysis of Prevent radicalises the questions posed
by a scholarship that understands security practices as productive of
the self and other. This reading of preclusive identity politics, building
upon the analysis of chapter 3, recognises that all acts of securing necessarily intervene within conditions of uncertainty, producing an account
of that which is being secured through the security act itself. Through
this reading of Prevent, it is therefore possible to open up a conceptual
space between the self and the other. There is still the production of the
core, 'British' self, and there is still clearly the outside of the terrorist, the
radicaliser. Yet, and of crucial importance when contemporary security
practices seek to intervene into life as a continual process of becoming,
not only is there a spatiality of the inside and outside but there exists a
temporality of the life that may become outside, and the life that will
likely not. In emphasising the temporal ambitions of Prevent, this book
therefore troubles an analysis that serves to merely demarcate the self
and its alterity. Prevent provides a vision of life that is always in the process of becoming, wherein it becomes possible to make claims as to the
trajectories that such processes of becoming are following. On the one
hand, this analysis therefore pushes scholarship to consider the ways in
which threats are produced as knowable and actionable in the present.
In regard to identity, this entails that it is not merely the other who must
be mediated, but those who are seen to exhibit potentials for becoming
other, and the environments seen to be conducive to such movement.
On the other hand, this analysis therefore has implications for the production of contemporary 'Britishness'. In taking potential as its object of
intervention, Prevent extends the relation of identity and security into all
those spaces in which identity is both produced and potentially, therefore,
mediated. As such, all life must now be watched on account of the potential signs of radicalisation that could, at any moment, be displayed. In
order to effectively maintain vigilance of all life as becoming, the security
imperative of Prevent is installed throughout society. Going beyond traditional security institutions, the need to monitor and understand this
potential becoming violent has become embedded across society, such
that the intervention can emerge alongside any potential threat.

Conclusion

Through making explicit the temporal ambition of Prevent, the book has
shown the intimate and co-constitutive role that identity and security

have played in forming Prevent's object of threat. The demand to intervene into processes of becoming has produced an understanding of a movement towards violence that makes possible the generation of particular truth-claims. Prevent, therefore, constitutes the vulnerability of individuals, and their movement in time through a process of radicalisation, as an object of thought. This account of vulnerability, as this chapter has shown, is then produced as a disassociation from a space of 'Britishness'; a 'Britishness' that is defined in opposition to extremism.

Prevent's problematisation of threat thus mobilises identity as the key mechanism through which to make articulable and visible its object of security concern. In making this claim, the book goes beyond the policy's internal self-critique and the literature on Prevent. These both narrate Prevent as a question of the relation between its identity and security strands. Rather, in bringing to light this problematisation at the heart of Prevent, the book demonstrates that the two are co-constitutive. The problematic of Prevent is constitutive of both the security and identity policies identified in chapter 1, with both policies producing an account of threat through ordering identity in the present. 'British' identities are deemed secure and securing, while those produced as outside of this normalised Britishness are rendered threatening. Individuals deemed vulnerable to radicalisation, and environments that generate vulnerability, are understood on account of their extremism, their alienation, and their disassociation from a normalised Britishness.

The problematic of vulnerability to radicalisation thus enables future threats to be made knowable and actionable through ordering identities in the present. Yet, so far, this threat has only been articulated in general terms. The intent of the next two chapters is to demonstrate the specific identities, that, through the implementation of Prevent, are produced as outside of a normalised Britishness, and thus rendered in need of securing. They therefore outline the *assemblage* of Prevent, and the specific knowledges and practices through which this problematisation of threat has been mediated in the present. They identify how vulnerability to radicalisation is produced as intelligible, allowing Prevent to be implemented as a concrete assemblage. In doing so, the next two chapters articulate the function of power that Prevent mobilises. They outline the practices that identify individuals and spaces in need of mediation, and the steps that are taken to effect this. The next two chapters thus demonstrate how the locations and subjects of vulnerability and extremism are inscribed upon the world, and how and where the boundaries of the contemporary British internal are constituted.

5

Governing threatening environments: community cohesion and problem institutions

In response to this problematic, an assemblage of counter-radicalisation has been developed. Representing practices, knowledges and institutions, it is an assemblage that aims to identify those identities and performances that are considered to be alienated and risky, in order to enable their transformation. Within this assemblage, two approaches can be identified. The next chapter will outline how 'at risk' individuals are identified and secured. This chapter details how this problematisation informs an understanding of problem environments, which are then acted upon by the Prevent assemblage. In doing so, the chapter details how British communities policy and the Prevent agenda come to be intimately bound together.

The problematic identified in the past two chapters renders environments within which becoming takes place as a central concern. In this chapter, the book analyses these environments, exploring how certain communities and institutional spaces come to be seen as problematic, conducive to radicalisation. In analysing the government response to these spaces, a pre-emptive governmental power can be identified, seeking to manage the identities in these spaces, in order to make radicalisation less likely. This chapter starts with an overview of the history and discourse of community cohesion, going on to demonstrate how the problematic of Prevent, and its understanding of vulnerability to be a disassociation from a normalised Britishness, integrates community cohesion into its analysis. While, as will be demonstrated, cohesion always imposed an implicit limit on who can legitimately participate in constituting that which is shared, within Prevent and the problematic of vulnerability and extremism, it attains an explicit directionality towards the generation of secure, 'British' identities. In so doing, it can also be seen to alter the governmental power being mobilised, embracing this directionality. This analysis of problem spaces, it will be argued, can also be seen in Prevent's approach to institutions considered to be risky. This aspect of

Prevent has been in place since it began, but comes to the fore in the 2011 iteration. Environments such as prisons, schools and universities are seen to be at risk, potentially containing, in part or in whole, closed spaces, in which secure, 'British' identities are unable to circulate. Efforts have, therefore, been made to open up these spaces, and ensure that secure identities are being circulated and promoted. The analysis put forward in this chapter demonstrates that, far from being a separate and separable area of government policy, the UK's approach to problem spaces, specifically through communities policy such as community cohesion, is an integral part of the counter-radicalisation assemblage, responding to the problematic outlined in the previous two chapters.

Community cohesion, the 'death' of multiculturalism and the 'race riots' of 2001

The summer of 2001 saw disturbances across towns and cities in England, encompassing people of different cultural backgrounds, mobilised primarily along racial lines between white and British-Asian youths (Home Office, 2001a). The violence prompted internal reflection on the ethnic make-up of British cities, and notably, the position of Muslim communities in the UK. Disorder was most widespread in Oldham, Burnley and Bradford, but there were lesser disturbances across a number of other towns, mostly in the north of England. The Ministerial Group on Public Order and Community Cohesion reported that there were 395 arrests in connection with the disorders in Bradford, Burnley and Oldham; hundreds of police were injured, and the cost of the damage was over £10 million (Home Office, 2001b: 7). After the dust had settled, the question of why the disturbances had occurred came to the fore. Independent reports were published detailing the cases of Oldham (Oldham Independent Review Panel, 2001), Burnley (Burnley Task Force, 2001) and Bradford (The Bradford District Race Review Panel, 2001). Ted Cantle led a team to produce an overview of the causes of the violence and make a series of policy recommendations, and the Rt. Hon. Jon Denham led the inter-departmental Ministerial Group on Public Order and Community Cohesion to provide recommendations at the level of central government (Home Office, 2001a, 2001b). These responses to the disturbances set in place a new agenda for communities policy that lasts to this day. Subsequently followed by the attacks of 9/11, this is a moment that represents a transition in how questions of identity, difference, belonging and security are understood within the British state, and how the boundaries of this Britishness are constituted.

The key theme that emerges upon investigation into the riots is a concern regarding segregation. It is the distance and differences between ethnic communities in the UK that are understood to have become entrenched, at the expense of that which is held in common. It is identified that, in many areas affected by the 'disorder or community tensions, there is little interchange between members of different racial, cultural and religious communities' (Home Office, 2001b: 3). As the Cantle Report famously stated, they were struck by the 'depth of polarisation of our towns and cities' (Home Office, 2001a: 9). This segregation is understood to be the result of state multicultural policies that had emphasised the positive aspects of ethnic, cultural and religious difference. Yet, and problematically, this emphasis on difference had led to physical segregation between these groups. Different communities were housed in different parts of towns or cities, and were found to be living 'parallel lives' (Home Office, 2001a: 9). Not only were they living in separate housing estates, but these differences were compounded by separate 'educational arrangements, community and voluntary bodies, employment, places of worship, language, social and cultural networks' (Home Office, 2001a: 9).

These separate habitations were originally with the best of intentions. Communities, particularly those coming into the UK, wished to live together. It was also the result of anti-racism policies by local government, seeking to minimise the potential for violent encounters between, at times, hostile white communities towards newer, racialised minority communities (interview with Professor Ted Cantle). However, the disturbances catalysed an understanding that this excess of separation was itself the problem; multiculturalism had, for laudable reasons, 'sowed the seeds of its own destruction' (interview with Professor Ted Cantle). As Trevor Phillips, then Chair of the Committee for Racial Equality, would later state, Britain was 'sleepwalking' into segregation (Casciani, 2005).

The problem identified is that this segregation was the cause of tensions, distrust and clashes between communities. The lesson taken from the violence that erupted in 2001 is that segregation is a 'growing problem' and is understood to have been a 'significant contributory factor to the disturbances' (Home Office, 2001b: 3). Emphasising that, within these towns, citizens of white and South Asian origin might never meet in their day-to-day lives, the Cantle Report states there is 'little wonder that the ignorance about each others' communities can easily grow into fear, especially where this is exploited by extremist groups determined to undermine community harmony and foster division' (Home Office, 2001a: 9). A lack of contact between different groups is thus read as producing the conditions out of which the violence emerged.

The framing of the 'riots' thus emphasised cultural, ethnic and religious difference, with the question being whether these differences had become too entrenched. Without a common and inclusive national identity that provided a vision of what it meant to live in a modern, multi-racial Britain, communities instead looked inwards. Some white communities looked back to the 'supposedly halcyon days of a mono-cultural society', and émigré communities alternatively looked to their country of origin for their identity (Home Office, 2001a: 9). This inward focus is then seen to lead to a lack of understanding of different groups, resulting in misunderstandings and tensions. These tensions can then generate, and be exploited by, extremists. Within this context, what comes to the fore is a focus on increasingly vocal Muslim youth coming into conflict with 'indigenous' white youths. While British Muslims represent many different ethnicities and faith practices, there had been, since the late 1980s, a perception that they also constituted a community of faith that was becoming increasingly politicised. This was notably mobilised in opposition to Salman Rushdie's book, *The Satanic Verses*, published in 1988 and considered blasphemous to the Muslim faith by many (Hewitt, 2008; Bleich, 2009, 2010).

This problematisation of the disturbances marks a watershed in terms of UK communities policy, signalling a shift from an approach of multi-culturalism to one of community cohesion. Prior to 2001, questions of societal division were largely articulated within a multicultural paradigm. Within this context, it was understood to be of importance that minority ethnic, cultural and religious groups were able to make claims on the state, both in terms of the collective identity of the nation, and materially, in the form of access to resources (for classic statements of this position, see Taylor (1994) and Kymlicka (1995)). While a coherent multicultural project in the UK has never existed in policy terms, the response to the disturbances marks a crucial move away from this approach (Lentin and Titley, 2011). While there are no easy answers, the broad solution to addressing the 'deep fracturing' of communities is to remould them into 'cohesive ones, uniting people around a common sense of belonging regardless of race, culture or faith' (Home Office, 2001b: 3).

Community cohesion is defined as a 'common vision and sense of belonging for all communities', where people from diverse backgrounds are all valued positively, have similar life opportunities and are able to develop strong relationships with others (Local Government Association, 2002). Rooted in the work of Putnam (1995), it is argued that the focus must move away from 'bonding' capital towards 'bridging' capital: from developing strong intra-group identities to strong bridges across groups. As David Blunkett, the then Home Secretary, stated, the societal problem to be faced was the existence of towns and cities which lacked 'any sense of civic identity or shared values'; the solution was to be a renewed citizenship, allowing 'a common place for diverse cultures and beliefs, consistent with the core values we uphold' (*Guardian*, 2001). In the Cantle Report, community cohesion is advocated on the basis that it is 'based upon a greater knowledge of, contact between, and respect for, the various cultures' of the UK, coupled with 'a greater sense of citizenship based on (a few) common principles which are shared' (Home Office, 2001a: 10).

The violence arguably had deeper roots, located in the economic decline of northern mill towns (Kundnani, 2001; Amin, 2002). Yet this complexity is reduced to an analysis that places the ultimate focus on ethnic and cultural difference (McGhee, 2003, 2008: 54; Werbner, 2005: 748; Kundnani, 2007). The effect of this response was to reframe identity politics in the UK into one within which cultural diversity comes to be seen as threatening (Kassimeris and Jackson, 2012). Community cohesion envisages that, through providing positive encounters and contact across spaces of difference, these segregations and distances between communities can be lessened, and thus too the violence such distance is seen to potentially contain. This understanding of the problem is clearly summarised in the Denham Report, where it is stated:

> A positive approach to celebrating diversity has undoubtedly been a key factor in enabling some communities to deal with the *inevitable tensions between different groups* more effectively than others, as the Cantle Team found in Birmingham, Leicester and Southall. The most successful have been those which have, in addition to this, *succeeded in uniting diverse groups through a shared sense of belonging to, and pride in, a common civic identity.* (Home Office, 2001b: 11, emphases added)

Differences between communities are ascribed an inherent potential towards tensions and possible violence, and are established as a site of problems if they are not adequately managed. Diversity is understood as 'a source of rich cultural interactions', yet 'in other areas segregation has led to fear and conflict, which has been exacerbated by political extremists who capitalise on insecurities to promote their own narrow objectives' (Home Office, 2004: 5, emphasis added). Cultural difference becomes problematised as a potential condition for emergent disorder. Cohesion thus posits a particular relation to an uncertain future, in that, through managing the flows of identities and their differences, it is possible to generate more secure future environments. The uncertainty of the future is mediated through a theorisation of cultural segregation that holds that too much distance between ethnic, cultural or faith groups can lead to future outbreaks of disorder and violence. A shared vision and a common, core identity is held to mitigate such threats.

Community cohesion and the limitations on mixing

The development of cohesive communities is not, at least in these formative years, dependent upon integration into an overarching 'British' identity. Nevertheless, community cohesion, at least within official policy documents, does seek to go beyond merely fostering interaction, seeking the creation of something 'shared' or 'common', often explicitly at the civic level. However, this does not mean that this dialogue is open to everyone. Constituting that which is shared, and who can mix, is already always limited. It is stated that:

> Respecting and valuing diversity is an essential part of building a successful, integrated society. But *respect for diversity must take place within a framework of rights and responsibilities* that are recognised by and apply to all – *to abide by the law, to reject extremism and intolerance and make a positive contribution to UK society.* Different ways of living our lives, different cultures or beliefs all coexist within this shared framework of rights and responsibilities. (Home Office, 2004: 7, emphasis added)

And moreover that:

> Recognising that integration can mean changes for established communities does not mean abandoning the values that we share as citizens: respect for the law and democratic structures, fairness, tolerance and respect for difference. (Home Office, 2004: 8)

Even in the formative stages of community cohesion, there are clear limits placed on the ideas and identities that are allowed to engage in dialogue and mixing. Already, those designated as 'extreme' are placed outside of this framework, denied the possibility of constituting that which is shared. It is thus crucial to recognise that the positive mixing of cohesion is circumscribed. The flows of identification and values that are desired are not open-ended, and have always been implicated within restraints that have sought to promote certain types of mixing, and isolate those identifications, ideas and values that are thought problematic. What is at stake within the project of cohesion is thus a conception of the limit, of those identities that cannot be contained within the UK, and which must therefore be mediated, lest they pose a future threat.

There is therefore a tension between those who promote an approach that focuses purely upon the opening of flows (see, for example, Cantle, 2005; Thomas, 2012) and a political implementation that asks questions of the direction these flows of ideas, values and identifications *should* take. While mixing in itself is represented by the discourse as a good (McGhee, 2008; Fortier, 2010), what is also apparent is that distinctions are being drawn between what is sharable, and that which is considered the basis upon which dialogue can exist. Within community cohesion's vision of mixing is thus a statement of the limits of the public sphere. Certain ideals and values come to be seen as the precondition of dialogue. There are thus implicit constrictions and exclusions at work within a narrative of dialogue and mixing.

Governmentality and the pre-emptive generation of security

In the following section, the book makes the claim that the form of power that is mobilised in this vision of cohesion has important genealogical connections to Foucault's articulation of governmentality. Cohesion, it will be shown, can be understood as a means of acting upon social relations through identifying and managing flows and circulations of bodies and identities, in order to generate positive mixing which produces cohesive, shared identities. It is a vision of power that seeks to direct and regulate flows of the population towards a normalised space of 'core' and 'shared' values. The utility of invoking Foucault at this point is that it allows the book to make visible operations of power that may otherwise be obscured, but that are constitutive of how cohesion is conceptualised, and will come to play a key role in Prevent.

Rather than the act and law of the sovereign, or the regulation of discipline (although not replacing these mechanisms), governmentality is, for Foucault, a technique of power that seeks to manage populations. Predicated on the freedom of subjects, it aims to guide, acting indirectly, through the incentive (Foucault, 2007: 353). In short, it can be defined as the 'conduct of conduct', the desire to, in Dean's (2010: 22) words, 'structure the field of possible action, to act on our own or others' capacities for action'. Writing with regard to the development of this modality in the eighteenth century, this new expression of power would require that the ruler take on the role of the 'regulator of a milieu' (Foucault, 2007: 29), representing both that in which circulation is carried out – the natural (such as rivers and hills) and the artificial (such as agglomerations of people and houses) – and the affects that bear on those who live in such spaces. It is in acting upon this space of circulation that governmentality finds its expression, and it is within this terrain of intervention that the 'population' comes to exist (Foucault, 2007: 21).

Confronted with such complexity, the governance of the population becomes the management of an indefinite number of open series, circulations and events. This planning for the indefinite required a new relation to the future, a new way of thinking, and was concerned historically with the town. It 'involved responding to what is, paradoxically, a fairly new and fundamental question of how to integrate *possible future* developments within a present plan' (Foucault, 2007: 18, emphasis added). It would thus require actively working on the future: 'the town will not be conceived or planned according to a static perception that would ensure the perfection of the function there and then, but will open onto a future that is not exactly controllable, not precisely measured or measurable' (Foucault, 2007: 20). Governmentality, from this reading, thus acts upon the milieu of the population – the complex circulations of cause and effect – to govern flows. It is through the governance of such flows in the present that uncertain futures can be mediated.

This is clearly evident within cohesion, wherein it deploys an operation of power that does not seek to actively direct outcomes, but rather produces effects through working to influence the natural flows and rhythms of social life. Rather than attempting to prevent certain events or flows in advance, governmentality seeks to install an apparatus that works within the reality of any fluctuations, operating through the free choices of individuals (Foucault, 2007: 37). It is a form of power that intervenes not directly, but at right-angles; it 'lets things happen' (Foucault, 2007: 45). The individual as a natural phenomenon can be seen as possessing certain desires that, once aggregated, form the desires of the population. What therefore appears as a series of variables can be naturalised as a constant, allowing for an understanding of causation within the circulations of the milieu (Foucault, 2007: 72–74). It is such analyses that then allow the identification of the aberration, the crisis or the epidemic, the occurrence that does not fit within the normally recognised pattern (Foucault, 2007: 61). Through the identification of such divergences, those things that are 'unnatural' to the population can be identified and acted upon. It is this process that Foucault calls 'normalisation', and is defined as consisting of 'establishing an interplay between these different distributions of normality and acting to bring the most unfavourable in line with the more favourable' (Foucault, 2007: 63). Folding back on the analysis in chapter 3 that demonstrated that 'Britishness' is assumed to successfully challenge and disrupt extremism, such a 'Britishness' can be conceptualised as a normalised constant, and the natural outcome of open flows of ideas and identities.

Within cohesion, through managing the circulations and flows of bodies, ideas and identities, it is presumed that 'Britishness' can be generated, minimising the potential for future disturbances and disorder. Within this context, and utilising the typology of relations to the future offered by Anderson (2010a), of utility here is the concept of pre-emption. Within pre-emption, the future and the threats it contains are established as unknowable and indeterminate. One knows that threats can emerge, yet the location of such emergence cannot be known in advance. These are the 'known unknowns' of a Rumsfeldian epistemology. To this extent, the impulse of action in the present is directed towards 'the conditions of emergence of a threat, ideally occurring before a threat has actually emerged' (Anderson, 2010a: 790). The threat is itself only a possibility due to the specific conditions of the present that allow a series of potential futures to unravel. The present then becomes that which must undergo transformation, such that the emergence of the future can be better regulated, and its dangers diminished. Thus, crucially, pre-emptive logics are *generative* of the present, demanding the (re)creation of life in order to mitigate the threat of the future (Anderson, 2010a). The governmentality of cohesion thus seeks to act upon circulations of bodies, ideas and identities in order to produce less threatening environments. The future threat contained within these environments is produced as knowable through an understanding of the community relations in the present. Through constituting as intelligible the existence of tensions, and whether certain environments are contained within an understanding of 'core' and 'shared' values, the possibilities of future violence can be read.

Directionality: generating Britishness

In making sense of community cohesion as enacting a particular modality of power, what comes to the fore is that through the problematic of Prevent post-9/11, cohesion does not entail a neutral ideal of mixing and bridging, but a directional demand to demonstrate one's inclusion within a normalised British identity. Or, within the post-structuralist reading given in this book, it is through the security acts and ascriptions of Prevent that certain communal identities are produced as threatening and thus require being brought into coherence with that which is also produced as a normalised Britishness. As demonstrated in chapters 3 and 4, at the heart of the problematic of Prevent is a reading of radicalisation, in which it is an alienation from a normalised Britishness that is indicative of vulnerability to extremist messages and radicalisation. While the discursive language used within the early years of cohesion is careful not to position cohesion as a move towards assimilation or integration, within its merging into the Prevent agenda, it becomes increasingly clear that the limits to cohesion, identified previously in the chapter, transform into a demand for those who do not cohere to move towards a normalised Britishness. It is a discourse that attains a directionality. The mobilising ideal of 'British values' becomes increasingly important, not just as the prior assumption within which positive mixing may take place, but also as a set of immunatory affiliations that can contain and reverse processes of becoming violent. 'Britishness' and 'British values' are both normalised and normalising.

Discursively, it is with the 2007 reworking of Prevent that the merging of cohesion and Prevent work, and the centrality of 'British values' within this, is first explicitly stated. The PVE strategy, outlined by the DCLG in 2007, starts by affirming that this is not a clash of civilisations, but is instead a question of standing up to a small fringe of terrorists and their extremist supporters, and that the government is committed to working with 'the vast majority of Muslims who reject violence and who *share core British values* in doing this' (DCLG, 2007: 4, emphasis added). It is stated that:

> As a society we must defend and *promote* our shared and *non-negotiable values*: respect for the rule of law, freedom of speech, equality of opportunity, respect for others and responsibility towards others [...] Government needs to support individuals and organisations who uphold those values and to respond robustly when those values are transgressed. (DCLG, 2007: 5, emphasis added)

What is clearly at stake in this narrative is, thus, not a question of finding those values that British citizens hold in common, apparent in the immediate responses to the 'riots' of 2001. Rather, there is a de facto understanding of that which is already held to be shared, which must now be promoted, and which is the basis upon which further interrelation is possible.

Interwoven in the text, extremists and terrorists stand to one side, and those Muslims who share core 'British values' stand to the other. In advice given to local Prevent partners, it is stated that:

> The Government is committed to promoting cohesion and our shared values more clearly and strongly across society. The Government regards the promotion of shared values – including fairness, respect and tolerance, democracy and the rule of law – as a key element of building strong, empowered and resilient communities; tackling all forms of hate crime; and promoting equal opportunities. (Home Office, 2009c: 21)

While the history and academic understanding of Prevent, as shown in chapters 1 and 2, has often attempted to demarcate communities and security policy, this movement in the text shows how the problematic of Prevent is mobilised *through* communities policy, governing interventions into communal identities produced as outside of a normalised Britishness, and therefore as threatening. Thus, it can be stated in the 2011 iteration of Prevent, that:

> There is evidence to indicate that support for terrorism is associated with rejection of a cohesive, integrated, multi-faith society and of parliamentary democracy. Work to deal with radicalisation will depend on developing a sense of belonging to this country and support for our core values. (Home Office, 2011a: 5)

And that a 'stronger sense of "belonging" and citizenship makes communities more resilient to terrorist ideology and propagandists. We believe that *Prevent* depends on integration, democratic participation and a strong interfaith dialogue' (Home Office, 2011a: 27).

This promotion also requires a concomitant challenge towards those views that undermine such a shared vision, jeopardising community cohesion and creating 'a climate in which people may be drawn into vio-lent activity' (Home Office, 2009a: 13). The other side to this emphasis on 'Britishness' and 'British values' is the designation of the risky out-side, and the discursive space occupied by Muslims and 'extremists'. Muslimness, as the literature on suspect communities argued, occu-pies an ambiguous and risky relation in regards to 'Britishness' (Richards, 2011). A key way through which this 'risk' is positioned is by understanding that to be Muslim is conceptualised as on the bor-derline of the British internal. To give but one example: in response to the attacks in France at the beginning of 2015, the Secretary of State for Communities and Local Government sent a letter to Muslim organisations, intended to reassure them in the face of potential hos-tility and ask them to continue to reject extremism in their communi-ties (Pickles and Ahmed, 2015). Yet, as the Muslim Council of Britain (MCB) pointed out (Wintour, 2015), the letter makes certain implicit and problematic assumptions, stating that, '[y]ou, as faith leaders, are in a unique position in our society. You have a precious opportunity, and an important responsibility: in explaining and demonstrating how faith in Islam *can be* part of British identity' (Pickles and Ahmed, 2015, emphasis added). Islam is positioned as continuously needing to establish an inclusion; its coherency within 'British identity' is never quite proven, always requiring work. This framing of Muslims as vul-nerable carries on a legacy of representing Muslimness as in tension with a normalised Britishness (Sobolewska, 2010; Gutkowski, 2011). To be Muslim, and especially to represent Muslims in the UK, requires constant affirmation of one's 'Britishness' and coherence within a normalised account of the British interior.

This demand of directionality transforms the governmental power deployed within cohesion. The question becomes, how does one gen-erate optimal flows of ideas and identities that are able to move prob-lematic environments and spaces towards ideas and identities deemed secure and securing? Prevent's approach to problematic spaces therefore differs from the vision of governmentality articulated by Foucault. While governmentality sees normality as being a natural state to which other flows can be directed, the shared 'British values' that Prevent seeks relies on an analysis that produces certain identities as secure, and others as risky, on account of their potential. 'Britishness' is thus both normalised as that which is the natural state of open flows of ideas and identities, yet also an objective that requires an explicit focus to work towards. To this end, there are practices within Prevent that would fall outside a purely governmental focus on flow, for instance, in active interventions to restrict and promote those identities deemed negative and positive. In this regard, Prevent could be said to adopt a more disciplinary impera-tive. Here, Foucault, retroactively discussing the objective of disciplinary power, uses the term 'normation', wherein the optimum subject is established towards whom all others would be compared, and to which all movements and actions would be expected to conform (Foucault, 2007: 56–57). Whereas a Foucauldian statement of governmentality sees flows as natural and neutral, within Prevent, flows of identity, in themselves, can be deemed of value or of harm. Prevent as cohesion can then be read as the process of governing environments towards the creation of secure identities, and that this includes a language of shared, bridging and mixing that increasingly entails a demand for 'British values' and 'British' self-identifications.

In so doing, it is, at the same time, productive of those identities and performances that are deemed secure and those rendered threatening. Within this framework, this problematisation of threat takes effect at two levels. First, it most clearly takes effect at the level of the population and the Muslim community. Here, the lineage of community cohesion is strongest, wherein obligations are placed upon the Muslim community to tackle extremism and promote secure, 'British' identities through regulating flows of ideas and identities. Second, there is a clear focus on certain problematic spaces and institutions which are seen as liable to extremism. The clearest examples of these are prisons, mosques and education establishments. Within both, the concern is that environments which are alienated from a normalised Britishness are potentially productive of vulnerability to extremism. They are therefore spaces that are more likely to generate radicalisation, and as such, must be mediated. It is in the process of this mediation that British security and communities policy are conflated.

Prevent as the management of flows towards secure identities

Opening flows

Within a framework that sees normalised Britishness as both secure and, crucially, securing, the opening of flows is itself framed as a good. As demonstrated in chapter 4, 'British values' and identities are seen to win out when confronting extremist values and identities. Opening up closed spaces – those in which extremist ideas have taken hold, or could take hold – to circulation is therefore understood to be mediative, providing the opportunity for 'British' ideas and values to challenge extremist ones. There is the contention, as discussed in chapter 4, that radicalisation occurs in places where extremist ideologies are uncontested, and 'not exposed to free, open and balanced debate and challenge' (Home Office, 2011b: 63). Environments exist which, due to being closed to the flow of differing identities, are generative of the conditions of radicalisation.

These closed environments, in which radicalisers and extremists operate, must therefore be opened up (Home Office, 2006: 2).

It is in this space that a series of community cohesion projects have been developed that seek to generate this openness, focusing on establishing dialogues within and across communities. While, in principle, this places responsibilities on all communities within the UK in its integration within the Prevent framework, the effect has been to place greater obligations on Muslim communities. At the level of the community, the overall aim is to create 'strong, prosperous and empowered communities: positive environments of which we can be proud' (DCLG, 2008c: 12). These must enable 'positive relationships between people of different backgrounds' and create a 'sense of belonging and a shared vision for the future' (DCLG, 2008c: 12). This is most clearly demonstrated in a series of cohesion projects that produce and situate the question of Muslim belonging alongside, and in tension with, a broad idea of shared, core and 'British values'. The PVE Pathfinder Fund was the primary mechanism for distributing Prevent funds to local authorities and was launched in 2006. The fund was distributed to local authorities who were responsible for further allocating funding and planning projects. The three strategic objectives were to develop a community in which Muslims: identified themselves as part of a wider British society and were accepted by the wider community as such; rejected violent extremism and worked with the police; and were able to develop their own capacity to deal with problems and support those at risk (DCLG, 2008a: 13). Funding, as detailed earlier, was allocated on the basis of the size of the Muslim population in local authorities. This was first based on authorities with over 5 per cent of the population identifying as Muslim, and subsequently, was allocated to any authority containing more than 4,000 Muslims (see Thomas, 2010: 443–444).

This funding was used for important cohesion projects that were, especially in the period between 2001 and 2006, focused primarily at Muslim communities within the UK. High-profile examples include the Preventing Extremism Together exercises and the subsequent Radical Middle Way roadshows. These sought to create space for dialogue in order to engender a mainstream and moderate British identity (Home Office, 2009a: 82). Another is the 'Muslim Forums against Extremism and Islamophobia', which sought to provide a space to discuss how to combat extremism in the Muslim community (Home Office, 2005c: 5, 10). In 2008, the DCLG mapped the work being undertaken under the PVE agenda, stating that 44,000 individuals had attended PVE projects. Of these, 61 per cent of projects had a direct focus on Muslim communities, with 64 per cent of the projects funded focused on developing shared values and 61 per cent engaged in supporting and nurturing civic and theological leadership (DCLG, 2008a: 6–8). What is clear from these numbers is that the project of cohesion has always maintained an uneven distribution of responsibility to cohere. The burden has fallen on Muslim communities to demonstrate leadership and resilience, and their coherence within an idea of 'shared', 'core' or 'British' values.

Alongside this focus on communities and Muslim leadership, the focus on opening up circulations is clear in terms of concerns and policies regarding particular institutions. One early example in this regard is the space of the prison. As early as the 2006 iteration, prisons were highlighted as particularly worrying environments, with evidence that radicalisation was occurring in these spaces. There is a clear concern that, within the prison walls, there are a large number of individuals searching for meaning, and that such people may be susceptible to those already travelling down a violent extremist path. While prisons are highly regulated environments, there are nevertheless worries that such stagnation of flow might result in radicalisation, and, thus, there is a need to make these flows intelligible and open to monitoring. This can be seen in the following statement in the Home Affairs Committee report on radicalisation. Regarding prisons, it states:

> The current thinking in the prison service was that dispersal of terrorist prisoners around the estate was the best method for containing the spread of terrorist views but some argued that concentration would be more effective. (Home Affairs Committee, 2012: 40)

The closure, both physical and conceptual, and the assumption of vulnerability, combine to create the prison not as the illuminated panopticon, but rather as a series of closed spaces that must be thought through in terms of the potential flows of ideas within them. Does one aim to quarantine negative identities or open them up to the potentially pacifying flows of differing identities? The prison becomes a space within which ideas and identities circulate, and these circulations must therefore be managed.

Further, such an analysis explains the focus on universities and, particularly, Islamic societies. The Home Affairs Committee reported that, in as far as there was a problem, 'it was in London and linked to the fact that universities provided "free space" whose use was difficult to regulate' (Home Affairs Committee, 2012: 41).[1] There has been a consistent desire to thus open up these spaces to the free-flow of ideas. This is reflected in the discussions that have taken place around external speakers at universities, and the need for university administrations to monitor who is speaking on campus (now a part of the statutory duty of universities under the Counter-Terrorism and Security Act 2015). Moreover, there is a clear idea that potentially extremist speakers should not speak unopposed. In ensuring that speakers are challenged in debate, one is not constituting closed spaces, but is rather allowing for the flow of ideas, and, as argued earlier, the assumption is that extremist arguments will wither under such contestation. Speaking to the Home Affairs Select Committee, Charles Farr stated:

> It is about ensuring a broad spectrum of speakers rather than a consistent series of speakers representing one particular point of view. It is about ensuring that it is open to everyone and it is not, in effect, a closed meeting, which is what many of them are. It is about, in some cases, ensuring that there is more than one speaker speaking, so that people hear a varied and broad range of views rather than simply one. (Home Affairs Committee, 2012: Ev. 63)

Through unblocking the circulation of ideas, these closed spaces, where extremism has taken hold, can be opened to the flows of ideas. In so doing, extremism is opened up to challenge, and secure 'British' ideas and identities will win out.

Further, this prism allows for a clear interpretation of the threat seen in the Trojan Horse scandal with which this book started. As quoted in the introduction, the 'problem' identified in the official report was that, 'instead of enjoying a broadening and enriching experience in school, [young people] are having their horizons narrowed', and there is evidence they 'are being encouraged to accept unquestioningly a particular hardline strand of Sunni Islam [which] raises concerns about their vulnerability to radicalisation in the future' (Clarke, 2014: 13). The object of concern is not the active radicalisation of the children involved, nor even the explicit promotion of an ideology that would be termed violent or extremist. Rather, it is the promotion of an Islamic ethos and a lack of promotion of 'British values' and ideals. It is a distance from a normalised Britishness that renders these children as vulnerable, and thus seen to be less able to resist radicalisation in the future. Through opening up the school to the flows and circulation of 'British' identities, these risks can be managed.

Promoting 'British values'; negating extremism

In addition to merely opening up flows of ideas and identity, Prevent seeks to manage problematic spaces through the promotion of secure 'British' identities and the negation of those deemed extremist. This has often been located under the heading of promoting 'British values', but there are a number of ways this has been achieved. From the launch of PVE within the DCLG in 2007, one of the core planks of official Prevent work has been to promote positive identities and values, envisaging the strategy as 'winning hearts and minds' (DCLG, 2007). One clear demonstration of this is the focus on Islamic supplementary schools. The

DCLG and DfE developed lesson materials for an Islam and Citizenship Education programme, designed to be used in these spaces. These materials sought to 'provide teachers with the tools to demonstrate to young Muslims that their faith is compatible with wider shared values and that being a Muslim is also compatible with being a good citizen' (Home Office, 2011a: 81). This is also encompassed within a wider focus on education that seeks to deepen understandings of faith and Islam in Britain across the sector (DCLG, 2007: 5–6).

Up until the 2009 iteration of CONTEST, this is talked about in a language of 'shared values'. Under the Conservative-led government from 2010, the policy is much more comfortable talking in a language of 'British values', as is most notably attested to in David Cameron's Munich speech, where he stated that:

> Frankly, we need a lot less of the passive tolerance of recent years and a much more active, muscular liberalism. A passively tolerant society says to its citizens, as long as you obey the law we will just leave you alone. It stands neutral between different values. But I believe a genuinely liberal country does much more; it believes in certain values and actively promotes them. (Cameron, 2011)

This is reflected in new duties placed upon educative establishments to promote 'British values', as a part of their citizenship education, in response to the concerns raised by the Trojan Horse scandal. In guidance issued in November 2014, it states it expects schools to promote the 'fundamental British values of democracy, the rule of law, individual liberty, and mutual respect and tolerance of those with different faiths and beliefs' (DfE, 2014: 5), with the definition of 'British values' explicitly referencing the 2011 iteration of the Prevent policy. This is to be achieved through actively challenging opinions or behaviours contrary to the above values. While this guidance is non-statutory, it is nevertheless the case that schools will be assessed on this metric by Ofsted, who are specifically tasked with looking at:

> how well the school prepares pupils positively for life in modern Britain and promotes the fundamental British values of democracy, the rule of law, individual liberty and mutual respect for and tolerance of those with different faiths and beliefs and for those without faith. (Ofsted, 2015: 38)

The education sector thus carries a key responsibility for promoting the values that it is envisaged will lead to the secure identities of the next generation.

Another manifestation of this approach to identity is in the emphasis placed on promoting those voices deemed to be beneficial, and monitoring those where it is thought that problems could arise. It is within this framework that the focus on support for Muslim women and young people comes to be important (DCLG, 2007: 9–10, 2008b: 38–50; Home Office, 2009a: 90–91). The work in regards to women and young people often takes place within a framework of empowering marginalised voices. Managing spatial flows of identity, values and belonging is therefore gendered. From an early stage, promoting female Muslim voices was a key part of community cohesion and Prevent work. Hazel Blears, while at the DCLG, set up a Muslim Women's Advisory Group who met with her every four to six weeks to keep her up to date on community issues, and it also acted as a space to train these women on how to speak to the media (interview with Hazel Blears). It is stated in the policy that, '[w]omen can play a vital role in building strong communities and tackling violent extremism. It is important to enable their voices to be heard and empower them to engage with disillusioned youths' (DCLG, 2007: 9). Muslim women are understood to 'possess a largely untapped potential to challenge the attitudes that can foster violent extremist ideas' (DCLG, 2008c: 30).

What is at stake is the moderating influence that Muslim women are seen to be able to exert over traditional and patriarchal flows of identification and values within Muslim communities. Resting upon tropes and assumptions regarding Muslim women as under-represented in public life, necessarily pacifistic and lacking in confidence (to be remedied with 'leadership training'), it is a narrative that seeks to open up the flows of identity to those less (potentially) dangerous. This is not to denigrate the position of Muslim women, both within Muslim communities and within British society more broadly, nor is it to oppose attempts to encourage their involvement in public life. But it is to position this within a narrative that sees their promotion as generative of less-threatening identities, and thus serves to essentialise the roles that women are seen to play within Muslim communities. Similarly, young people are framed as best able to speak out against violent extremism, but that they need to be equipped with the tools to challenge the prejudices and preconceptions that can otherwise be exploited by extremists (DCLG, 2008c: 33).

Another example of the promotion of secure identities is evident in Labour attempts to promote versions of Islam that were deemed more acceptable to the government. A key example is the setting up of the Sufi Muslim Council in July 2006. It explicitly sought to mobilise an apolitical Islam, as opposed to the work of the MCB, and was launched with the active support of politicians from across the political spectrum, including strong endorsement from Ruth Kelly, then Secretary of State at the DCLG (see Casciani, 2006). The links between Kelly and the Council are uncertain, but it is clear that it was formed prior to amassing any form of grass-roots mobilisation, something that it was unable achieve before closing in 2010. Its formation was primarily a political move, being launched in parliament and set up as an alternative voice in opposition to the established MCB. It was the subject of much criticism, in that it was seen as an attempt to engineer a passive, depoliticised British Islam (see, for example, Ghannoushi, 2008).

More broadly, the management of identities is evident in the focus on mosques and their governance and leadership. In regards to faith leaders, there are clear concerns expressed about the quality of faith guidance. While it is accepted that the overwhelming majority of Muslim faith leaders condemn terrorism, concerns have been raised that they are not always able to convey this message. It is stated that many imams 'still come from overseas; we have introduced new immigration rules for all Ministers of Religion to ensure that those seeking to enter the country meet certain requirements such as basic English skills' (DCLG, 2007: 10). There has also been much work over the course of Prevent to ensure there are clear standards for imams and other faith leaders who are engaged by the state. Within these initiatives, there was a clear focus on challenging the al-Qaeda ideology, and ensuring that the Islam being preached in the UK was not supportive of extremism. This was reflected in concerns around whether imams spoke English or not, and led to a focus on mosque management and the place of origin of imams working in the UK (interview with Senior Civil Servant). What is at stake within this is thus a desire to ensure that negative messages, while not illegal, are minimised. Imams who are deemed problematic might therefore not be allowed entry to the country. The focus on language ties into broader questions of cohesion and participation. There is a need to make the teaching and preaching of Islam visible, that by ensuring tutelage is in English, the flows of ideas and identities at play become visible. There is also a clear ambition to promote positive values and identifications through strengthening faith institutions. One of Prevent's core ambitions, from its inception, has been to improve standards of governance in mosques. The independent Mosques and Imams National Advisory Board was established to this end. Its role is to provide guidance and consultation on accreditation of imams, governance of mosques and inter-faith activity (Home Office, 2006: 14, 2009a: 82).

Moreover, this need to promote secure identities, and to marginalise extremist identities, is seen as the responsibility of the Muslim community, and particularly leading Muslim organisations. Despite more recent Conservative claims, the policy has always sought to make access to funding conditional upon a demonstration of commitment to shared 'British values'. Early DCLG work stated that the 'Government will work with the vast majority of British Muslims who reject violence and who share *society's core values*' (DCLG, 2007: 9, emphasis added). The 2011 iteration of Prevent is clearly concerned that the previous Labour government had funded groups who may not support these core 'British values' and seeks to redress this (although it has to admit that no groups were funded that should have been excluded). A key justification put forward by the Conservatives for removing funding from local community groups was that there were concerns regarding 'whether these organisations comprehensively subscribe to what we would consider to be mainstream British values' (Home Office, 2011a: 34). Prevent has therefore always possessed a disciplinary element, making funding and engagement conditional on demonstrating coherence with the mainstream of 'Britishness'.

As well as promoting secure identities, there is a need to restrict flows of ideas, identities and information that are deemed undermining and detrimental. One of the focuses of the Prevent policy, since its inception, has been a concern regarding the internet as a tool of propaganda. This is recognised as early as the 2006 CONTEST strategy as a factor within radicalisation, where its 'ability to connect people, to pass ideas between them, and then pass those ideas on to others has had a significant impact on the accessibility and flow of radical ideas' (Home Office, 2006: 10). At this stage, it is still seen to be of less importance than local, face-to-face networks. While this is still the case, there has been evidence in the intervening years of so-called 'self-radicalisation', where individuals have decided to undertake violent action outside of any local network. The most notable example is that of Roshonara Choudhry, who attempted to murder Labour MP Stephen Timms in his constituency office on 14 May 2010. She claimed that she had been influenced to take action by watching sermons given by Anwar al-Awlaki, a popular al-Qaeda figure who was later killed by the United States in a targeted drone strike. These flows of information therefore continue to be a concern. In early 2010, the police, with the Home Office, launched the Counter Terrorism Internet Referral Unit tasked with assessing and investigating internet-based content. Current policy is to both limit access to content in specific sectors (such as schools through filtering software) and to try to remove unlawful and harmful content from the internet (Home Office, 2011a: 77).

Conclusion

British counter-radicalisation policy has thus constituted a modality of power that seeks to regulate and promote flows of identity, in order to pre-emptively generate secure and securing environments, on account of the threat that disassociations from a normalised Britishness are understood to contain. This chapter has sought to demonstrate that central to Prevent's assemblage is the development of a range of practices that seek to mediate these environments through acting on the identities, values and ideas contained within them. In so doing, a range of approaches have been developed, within a cohesion framework, in order to manage and produce environments in which radicalisation is deemed less likely to occur. Prevent is thus a logic of security, identity and temporality that, in part, functions through environmental effects. Through these processes of securing, it is Muslim identifications and spaces that have been targeted and produced as risky.

This power can be seen in the mobilisation of community cohesion towards the problematic of vulnerability to radicalisation. Counter-radicalisation utilises communities policy towards the generation of communal spaces that oppose and reject extremism, and that promote the circulation of positive, 'British' identifications. While formally separated in 2011, communities policy has still clearly responded to this same problematic. Labelled explicitly as integration, the same themes found within cohesion remain. Integration, it is stated, 'benefits us all' whereas 'extremism and intolerance undermine this as they promote fear and division' (DCLG, 2012: 2). An integrated society, it is claimed, is better able to counter and marginalise extremists, and is thus central to counter-extremism (DCLG, 2012: 2). Integration is consistently framed in the strategy as providing communities with the possibility to come together, engage in dialogue and create solutions. The motifs of cohesion thus run throughout. The key difference, though, is that any semblance of that which is 'shared' as being open to contestation and co-constitution is removed, replaced with a clear statement that the strategy believes 'core values and experiences must be held in common. We should be robustly promoting British values' (DCLG, 2012: 4).

It is an analysis that continues to inform thinking on this issue. On the one hand, it clearly motivates the wider Home Office-led strategy on counter-radicalisation, which explicitly situates community cohesion as a constitutive part of this project, as detailed in chapter 1. On the other, the recent Casey review (Casey, 2016), into opportunity and integration across Britain, on behalf of the DCLG, did much to reproduce the analysis of Cantle and Prevent detailed in this chapter. While the benefits of cohesion and integration are framed in terms of positive impacts concerning social mobility and employment, what is also central is the analysis that, 'where communities live separately, with fewer interactions between people from different backgrounds, mistrust, anxiety and prejudice grow', and that 'integration and shared common values and behaviours [...] are inhibitors of division, hate and extremism' (Casey, 2016: 8). And that, while:

> the argument for a stronger approach to integration is justified on a much wider basis than counter-extremism – with very significant social and economic benefits for the nation – we also believe a more integrated society would reduce hate crime and sectarian violence and improve our resilience in responding to extremism and terrorism. Conversely, the less integrated we are, the more vulnerable

communities and individuals become to the divisive narratives and agendas of extremists and, potentially, the greater the likelihood becomes of hate crime, sectarian violence and terrorist attacks. (Casey, 2016: 145)

Nevertheless, the recently released government Green Paper on *Integrated Communities* (MHCLG, 2018) does start to step back from this analysis as a driving force for communities policy. It still frames segregation of communities as key, wherein opportunities 'to mix and form meaningful relationships with people from different groups are more limited, potentially leading to higher levels of mistrust and anxiety' (MHCLG, 2018: 43) and sees the Commission for Countering Extremism as playing an important role in this area (MHCLG, 2018: 59). Yet, it also brings to the fore a different emphasis, indicative of a potential move away from this analysis. Focusing instead on the barriers faced by newly arrived migrants to the UK, and explicitly stressing that integration cannot be assimilation – while still stressing the concept of 'British values' – it recognises that integration is the active responsibility of both new and settled communities. The extent to which this shift in approach is maintained through the policy process remains, at time of writing, to be seen.

It is, nevertheless, a power and a logic of government that also continues to be central in the approach taken to potentially problematic institutions. The 2011 and 2018 iterations of Prevent, supported by the ongoing mainstreaming process and the enacting of Prevent as a statutory duty in 2015, entails that it is institutional spaces that are an increasing focal point of Prevent work. The problematic at play sees within certain spaces an intensity of circulation of ideas, which thus require monitoring, and perhaps, opening up, lest extremism takes hold within them. This aspect has become more prominent over time, with spaces such as schools (as evidence in the Trojan Horse scandal) and universities under increasing pressure.

It is a power that shares commonalities with, yet goes beyond, an account of governmentality, in that it actively intervenes at times, promoting and restricting flows on account of their secure-ness. Prevent thus represents a crucial site in the conflation of belonging, identifying and securing. What is thus at stake is the process of the constitution of the British inside, and those perceivably threatening subjects who, in being deemed so, require mediation towards the creation of a safe future. In this sense, Prevent is important, in that it functions to set the limit of that which can belong, and establishes a means through which the (re)definition of that which belongs can be iterated. Such a reading goes beyond the literature identified in chapter 2, in that it enables the book to make the argument that cohesion and Prevent are functionally and analytically coherent; therefore, to merely separate them institutionally is redundant, and to separate them conceptually an impossibility.

The threat of the uncertain future, and the potential terrorist contained within it, is managed at the communal and institutional levels through the pre-emptive (re)production of environments that are deemed secure and securing. This analysis therefore demonstrates that to separate cohesion from counter-terrorism is to misread the means and ends of cohesion work. Rather, it allows for a theorisation of both cohesion and counter-radicalisation as a response to a shared problematic. Thus, a key component of the assemblage of Prevent is the mobilisation of a power that seeks to operate through the circulations of ideas and identities within the population, such that it can generate more secure and securing identities. It is a power that acts on environments in order to promote 'British values', negate the voices of extremism and open spaces up to the circulation of identities. Yet, if cohesion is a means of managing problematic spaces through focusing on the flows of ideas and identity in the population, it has not yet been an account of how the individual who is vulnerable to radicalisation is manifested and made actionable within Prevent. This process takes place on a quite different terrain, mobilising its own knowledges and power. It is to this that the book now turns.

Note

1 University Islamic societies are also of interest in that there have been cases where members of such societies went on to commit terrorist acts. For instance, Umar Farouk Abdulmutallab, who tried to detonate plastic explosives hidden in his underwear on 25 December 2009, had been president of the Islamic Society at University College London.

6

The Channel project: identifying individuals who are vulnerable to radicalisation

Responding to Prevent's problematic, the second way through which the assemblage secures the threat of future terrorism is through a focus on the movement of individuals towards violence. Prevent's temporal framing understands radicalisation to be a process. Of central concern is thus the individual who, if not mediated, may one day commit an act of terrorist violence. Here the temporal ambition of Prevent is most explicit, demanding that those who may *potentially* become radicalised – those deemed vulnerable to radicalisation – be identified and made amenable to intervention. It is through the production of this vulnerability that the temporal gap between the present and the uncertain future terrorist will be crossed. The institutional space in which this occurs is the Channel programme. Not referring to any specific institutional body, this defines an approach and framework for managing these interventions. Channel represents perhaps the clearest component of Prevent's assemblage, combining radicalisation knowledge with clear institutional processes, encompassing a range of professionals, in order to govern individuals identified as at risk.

This chapter will start by charting the historical and institutional development of the Channel project. The second section then establishes the key mechanism through which it traverses the temporal gap: the 'vulnerability indicator'. These indicators identify the behaviours and identities that are considered risky, thus requiring attention and perhaps intervention. It is then through a close textual analysis of these vulnerability indicators that the chapter seeks to articulate the power that is produced and mobilised through Channel interventions. First, these interventions are deployed through a power of care; a power that produces the truth of those it looks after. Second, through these indicators, it is possible to locate the concrete instantiations of that which, in its disassociation from a normalised Britishness, is established as threatening. Combined, Channel can be shown to produce an individualised power of care, watching for and mediating those who are seen to have strayed from a normalised British identity.

The Channel process

As shown in chapter 1, one of Prevent's key commitments has been to identify and support vulnerable individuals. Indeed, that the new counter-terrorism strategy would require a means to focus on individuals seen to be at risk of *becoming* terrorists was present even in its formative stages.[1] The recent implementation of New Labour's Youth Justice Boards was seen as a useful model for intervention in order to disrupt engagement in criminality or violence, and their process of multi-agency panels came to play a key role in Channel interventions (interview with Senior Civil Servant). Youth Justice Boards sought to identify young people who were at risk of falling into gangs, and then, through targeted investment in youth services, divert them away from that path. Channel would apply this method to those at risk of radicalisation. In April 2007, Channel was rolled out as a pilot programme, operative in twelve police forces representing localities understood to be at particular risk. It was operative nationally by April 2012 and, through the Counter-Terrorism and Security Act 2015, has now been placed on a statutory footing within a range of listed specified authorities.[2]

The active work carried out by a Channel process consists of three principle tasks: to identify individuals at risk from violent extremism; to assess the nature and extent of the risk; and, if considered suitable for a Channel intervention, to develop the most appropriate support for the individual concerned (Home Office, 2010: 7). Any referral is first screened to ensure that it is not malicious, misinformed or already involves illegality. If considered appropriate, it will then go through a preliminary assessment. At this stage, there will be an assessment of the level of risk, both to the individual and to society. It will also be considered whether the vulnerability identified is to violent extremism, and thus whether Channel is the most appropriate pathway (Home Office, 2010, 2012). If accepted onto the Channel programme, a support package will be tailor-made by a multi-agency panel, depending on the needs of the individual.

In practice, especially in the early days of Channel, the pragmatic use for the process was that it provided a means for the police to deal with individuals on the periphery of violent events, whom they might not have been able to otherwise engage with. For instance, within a national security incident, the investigation may come across a range of people, some highly involved, some only marginally so. With those on the margins, traditionally, there might not be a lot one could do with them. Channel provided a means to come to an understanding of the threat they might pose, intervene with their consent, knowledge and understanding, and hopefully move them away from negative influences that might impact on them (interview with John Wright). On a similar note, where one sees an individual who is involved in violence, such as perhaps travelling abroad, the police experience is that this will impact on friends and family. In these cases, there is clearly no wrongdoing, but there may be individuals who are of concern for the police: 'Channel also enables us to look at that wider contact group and to try and identify people who may be subject to influence and been affected by that, and absolutely to put them through a program that will stop that happening to them' (interview with Sir Peter Fahy).

Nevertheless, that this function of identification would extend beyond traditional security actors, such as the police, was always a part of the plan. From the beginning, it is clear that Channel was envisaged as a way of mobilising society more broadly to be able to identify and refer those at risk. According to Tony McNulty, one of the early origins for this form of intervention was the realisation that radicalisation could occur fairly quickly, and perhaps that people might be self-starters (interview with Tony McNulty). Thus, in response, Channel seeks to ensure that people who may be present at these crucial moments of change have the knowledge to identify potential to radicalisation, and then to flag this information up to a Channel practitioner. You had to work with everyone. As was evident from chapter 1, getting this taken seriously in other departments and institutions was not easy, but over time this has been achieved. The enacting of Prevent as a statutory duty in 2015 did much to ensure that specified authorities (such as the education, healthcare and social work sectors) were aware of, and committed to, their counter-radicalisation responsibilities.[3]

Whichever way an individual comes to the attention of a Channel panel, if they are deemed to be vulnerable to radicalisation, this potential is mediated through a series of pastoral interventions, geared towards the particular needs of the individual concerned. The guidance suggests that for someone in the 'early stages' of radicalisation, a 'diversionary activity' may be sufficient, whereas someone who was 'already radicalised' might require a 'more focused and structured one-on-one mentoring pro-gramme' (Home Office, 2012: 20). These interventions could take many forms, and might include: life skills, mentoring support, cognitive/behav-ioural contact, education skills, family support, health awareness, and drugs and alcohol awareness (Home Office, 2012: 21). The package could be delivered by a statutory partner or by community partners. In the case of the latter, and in accordance with concerns around non-violent extremism explicitly articulated in the 2011 iteration, the 2012 guidance is clear that these partners' 'reliability, suitability to work with vulnerable people and commitment to shared values needs to be established' (Home Office, 2012: 21). Perhaps the most important tool available to Channel interventions is that of one-on-one mentoring. These mentors are held on a national pool by the OSCT and must be security cleared (interview with Senior Council Official with responsibility for Prevent delivery). Progress is reviewed at least every three months, and the intervention is considered to have achieved its aims when the panel is satisfied that the risks have been successfully reduced or managed. Cases are then reviewed six and twelve months after they leave the Channel process. If the panel is not satisfied there has been progress, alternative strategies may be put in place, or, if the risk of terrorism-based criminality has increased, the case may be escalated through existing police mechanisms and potentially taken outside of Channel (Home Office, 2012: 22).

Data on the number and details of referrals to the Channel programme has, for many years, been limited. The situation has, however, markedly improved with the Home Office publishing detailed figures for the 2015–16 (Home Office, 2017) and 2016–17 (Home Office, 2018b) reporting years. Combined with the data previously released by the NPCC (n.d.), the following trends can be observed (see Table 1).

Table 1 Channel referral numbers

Year	Total number of referrals	Total number of cases discussed at a Channel panel	Percentage of referrals discussed at a Channel panel	Total number of cases that received Channel support	Percentage of referrals resulting in Channel support
2006–7	5	N/A	N/A	N/A	N/A
2007–8	75	N/A	N/A	N/A	N/A
2008–9	179	N/A	N/A	N/A	N/A
2009–10	467	N/A	N/A	N/A	N/A
2010–11	599	N/A	N/A	N/A	N/A
2011–12	580	N/A	N/A	N/A	N/A
2012–13	748	238	31.82%	159	21.26%
2013–14	1,281	314	24.51%	169	13.19%
2014–15	N/A	484	N/A	283	N/A
2015–16	7,631	1,071	14.03%	380	4.98%
2016–17	6,093	1,146	18.81%	332	5.45%

Additionally, of the 3,934 cases referred from the start of the programme up until 31 March 2014, 777 (or 19.75 per cent) were assessed to be vulnerable to being attracted towards terrorism and thus taken into Prevent (NPCC, n.d.). While many original referrals come from the police, many now come from specified authorities. The 2015–16 and 2016–17 data provides figures on this. The police refer 31/32 per cent respectively, with the largest number of referrals coming from schools (33/32 per cent) followed by local authorities (11/12 per cent) and the health sector (6/8 per cent). Channel has been a part of the working life of these institutions since it began. However, enacting it as a statutory duty was, in part, in an effort to get these institutions to take it seriously. This effort to 'mainstream' the Prevent duty into the day-to-day working life of these professionals could thus be considered a success, with such professionals increasingly active in making referrals.

However, these figures do suggest there is a significant over-reporting of perceived vulnerability to radicalisation. In 2015–16, only 14.03 per cent of referrals were discussed at Panel, and only 4.98 per cent were considered suitable for intervention. In 2016–17, the numbers are slightly increased, with 18.81 per cent per cent of referrals being discussed at Panel and 5.45 per cent resulting in an intervention. This represents a high number of false positives. Moreover, it seems a reasonable assumption that such over-reporting is, at least in part, a product of the mainstreaming of Prevent. Until March 2014, the number of referrals which triggered an intervention were just under 20 per cent, now reduced to around 5 per cent. The slight increase in the most recent figures suggest that this potential over-reporting is being reduced, but not to a significant extent.

What is clear from the data is that, in actual terms, the numbers of referrals have, for many years, been on the rise – although the most recent reporting year does signify a drop, contradicting this trend. Time will tell whether this is an aberration or a sign of a levelling out of referral numbers. Further, the number of individuals who are both discussed at a Channel panel and are deemed suitable for a Channel intervention have also, for the most part, increased year on year. This question of over-reporting will be returned to later. Suffice to say at this point, though, that Prevent represents a significant and an increasingly important security instrument, which affects, in some capacity, the lives of thousands of individuals per year.

Channel's pre-criminal space

As demonstrated in chapter 3, the temporal ambition of Prevent is to intervene prior to the actualisation of violence; to 'stop people *becoming* terrorists' (Home Office, 2011a: 6, emphasis added). The Channel process thus seeks to act before the subjects of its interventions have *themselves* seriously considered the possibility of committing an act of terrorism. If they had, the matter would no longer be within the pre-criminal space of the Channel intervention. Key to understanding the Channel process is therefore its relation to potential illegality. Charles Farr, in his evidence to the House of Commons Communities and Local Government Committee, to clarify this point, stated that:

> Clearly if someone is involved in activity which suggests they are being drawn into the world of violent extremism [...] if that activity stops short of something which is illegal under the Terrorism Acts, notably TACT 2006, that is the sort of person we would expect to get referred to Channel, not to criminalise them but precisely to *avoid them criminalising themselves*. (Communities and Local Government Committee, 2010: 16, emphasis added)

Asked to clarify the relation between the Channel process and an individual's potential surveillance by the security services, he assured the committee that this would never knowingly occur:

> We would never get ourselves into a situation [...] where someone was put forward and agreed and nominated on to a Prevent programme whilst they were being subject to surveillance by the security authorities [...] We need, and this happens at the Channel referral process, to understand the individuals being referred. If it is clear that they are engaged in activity which is right on the edge of legality, i.e. are associated with people who may be engaged in terrorist activity, then it would be wrong to put them on any sort of Prevent programme. (Communities and Local Government Committee, 2010: 16)

Further, it is specifically stated in Channel guidance that the process is not appropriate for those already in custody, and moreover, that Channel may not be appropriate for those involved in a different statutory support mechanism such as child protection arrangements (Home Office, 2010: 13).

The temporality of the Channel subject is thus one of identifiable potential future illegality, but, importantly, not yet actualisable illegality. It pushes the boundaries of counter-terrorism work as it seeks to identify those who are at a 'pre-cursor stage' (interview with John Wright). If there were evidence of an imminent transgression of the law, this would place them within the remit of the security services, and an intervention that would result in judicial proceedings. Here, as Charles Farr points out, the point is to mediate their potential before they can criminalise themselves. This is not a question of looking to arrest people, 'the aim is to get far enough upstream that we try and avoid that' (interview with Sir Peter Fahy). The interventions are thus a process that mediates individuals understood to be vulnerable to violent extremism before potentials are manifested – before the individual has even perhaps considered the act that would take them over the threshold of illegality.

This relation to the future therefore differs from that of the pre-emptive power mobilised within community cohesion, and the focus on problem environments within Prevent's assemblage. In the previous chapter, it was argued that cohesion seeks to locate the conditions out of which threat may emerge, wherein threat is made knowable through understanding the circulations of identity. Power is then mobilised at the level of these flows, seeking to direct them in such a way that environments are rendered secure and securing. While rooted in the same problematic, the epistemology and interventions mobilised through the Channel project differ from that of cohesion. In identifying individuals deemed vulnerable to radicalisation, a precautionary future is invoked. Again, following Anderson (2010a), a precautionary logic seeks out a determinate threat. Rather than aim for the (re)generation and normalisation of conditions of life, precautionary interventions emphasise continuity and the need to intervene in order to preserve the current order (Anderson, 2010a). This is evident in the historical origins of the term that Anderson repurposes. Enshrined as the 'precautionary principle', this approach was developed in the 1970s in response to the threat of anthropocentric climate change (see also Commission of the European Communities, 2000; Aradau and van Munster, 2007). The object of precaution in this regard is scientifically uncertain, but the form, the specific actuality the threat will take, is known. Moreover, it is understood that if left unchecked, the effects could be catastrophic. The impetus is thus to act before the threat reaches a state of irreversibility. The question to be asked is one of proportionality – whether the risk of the potential catastrophe is worth the cost of acting within conditions of uncertainty in the present (Anderson, 2010a). The central temporal question within Channel is thus how one can bring to light and intelligibility these potentials.

The Channel process thus seeks to identify individuals who are deemed potentially problematic. If the referral is accepted, then it is judged that the risk of that individual is high enough that action is justified on precautionary grounds – that the risk of inaction is too great. Central then is the question of how this risk is judged. The idea at the heart of Channel is that, with the right knowledge and training, it is possibly to make visible and identify the signs of potential future violence. At its heart is thus an epistemology of the clue, wherein conjectural knowledge is brought to bear in deciphering the potential future becomings of those who may be at risk of becoming violent (Aradau and van Munster, 2011). How this truth is accessed, and how one might come to mediate it, are thus central concerns. What is posited by Prevent is that these signs of vulnerability to radicalisation can be made visible and legible. That, in reading them correctly, the potential future threat of an individual can be disclosed. This problematic accounts for the need to have a wide range of voices feeding in to the referral process. Channel is an act of 'triage' (interview with Lord Carlile of Berriew). It may well be that a flag is raised by one service provider that in isolation may be lost or misinterpreted, but, had it been shared, would have been a piece of the puzzle that allowed for an accurate picture of an individual to be drawn. The Channel process is thus one in which the clues of an individual's potential future path are brought together, related to one another, and out of this process a picture is developed that may necessitate intervention on account of the risk that is seen. The argument of this chapter is that these signs, these indicators of vulnerability, constitute the central means through which the temporal gap of Prevent's Channel interventions are traversed. In so doing, they deploy and develop a pastoral power, and, as will be made clear, the signs of future threat mobilised within this power carry with them a crucial identity politics, ordering the secure 'British' internal and its potentially threatening exterior.

Signs of vulnerability

Key to understanding the concrete identity politics of Prevent is therefore the means through which these subjects of potential future violence are made knowable. The central mechanism through which Prevent enables the identification of individuals who are deemed vulnerable to radicalisation is the 'vulnerability indicator'. Vulnerability is defined within the strategy as 'the condition of being capable of being injured; difficult to defend; open to moral or ideological attack. Within Prevent, the word describes factors and characteristics associated with being susceptible to radicalisation' (Home Office, 2011a: 108). The claim of this section is that through ascribing and then acting on vulnerability, certain identities are produced as risky. Through an analysis of the particular vulnerability indicators that the guidance gives to professionals responsible for maintaining a duty of care, and through the concrete examples of their application, it becomes clear that their application is invested with meaning, structuring the threat of the future in politically contained ways. The argument put forward is that through reading the vulnerability indicators, there are two important claims to be made as to the politics they invoke: first, they render this process as primarily one of psycho-social wellbeing, to the exclusion of an antagonistic and relational politics; and second, they frame the problem as one of identity, wherein certain (British) identities are produced as secure and securing, and other (extreme) ascriptions of identity are produced as risky.

The most conclusive list of vulnerabilities is that found in the Channel Guide. Published in 2012, this iteration lists twenty-two 'vulnerability indicators' under the subheadings of engagement, intent and capability. Taken as a whole, it is understood that their assessment will provide a rounded view of an individual's vulnerability, informing the decision over whether an individual needs support, and, through continued assessment, they can be used to track an individual's progress (Home Office, 2012: 11–12). The following examples are all given within the document. Engagement can thus be seen in:

- 'spending increasing time in the company of other suspected extremists'
- 'changing their style of dress'
- 'loss of interest in other friends and activities'
- 'possession of material or symbols associated with an extremist cause'.

Intention is identified through:

- 'using insulting or derogatory names or labels for another group'
- 'condoning or supporting violence or harm towards others'
- 'plotting or conspiring with others'.

And capability can be seen in the suspect:

- 'having a history of violence'
- 'having occupational skills that can enable acts of terrorism' (all of these are taken from Home Office, 2012: 12; the full list can also be found at that citation).

These thus contain a series of behaviours, skills and political or theological utterances that, while in themselves legal, become identifiable, check-listable indicators of an inner truth that requires mediation due to its perceived potential.

The behaviours with which Channel is concerned are even clearer in the guidance given to those pastoral organisations with specific responsibilities. The most useful documents in this regard are those issued by ACPO and the Department for Children, Schools and Families (DCSF; since transformed into the DfE) to schools, colleges and universities. While these particular guidances, dating from 2008–12, are from the early Channel rollout, the intersection they established between safeguarding and questions of radicalisation was crucial, informing Channel practice and training to this day (see, for example, the WRAP (Workshop to Raise Awareness of Prevent) training (Home Office, 2014)). These provide examples of real-life occurrences that are seen by policymakers to be indicative of potential future violence, and are thus important for practitioners to be aware of. They therefore enable an understanding of the *particular* performances and identifications which are, by nature of their perceived threatening potential, in need of mediation. That they are selected by those implementing policy guidance as exemplary implicitly positions these behaviours as important for professionals to be aware of, and as signs that mediation must, at the very least, be considered.

ACPO's guidance to schools includes a list of 'vulnerable behaviour identified in schools'. It includes:

- '[o]penly anti-Christian, anti-Muslim and anti-Semitic words and behaviour'
- '[s]tudents glorifying acts of violent extremism'
- '[a] religious convert who had also joined a street gang, using inappropriate language in school'
- '[e]xpression of far right racist views'
- '[g]raffiti in school books supporting violent extremism'
- '[p]ossession of a video on a mobile phone, showing a beheading'
- '[a]ggressive behaviour towards fellow students and disrespectful behaviour to staff particularly towards female members of staff'
- '[d]rug use by a school pupil who was a religious convert and had insecure family relationships'
- '[a] student with mental health issues who associated with others who held extremist views'
- '[a] strong desire to possess guns and knives and be part of a gang'. (ACPO, 2009: 34)

Similarly, DCSF guidance also provides 'recent examples' that have arisen in schools. These include:

- pupils bringing 'far-right literature encouraging violence towards a local ethnic community' into school
- 'a primary age pupil in the playground starts talking about the "duty of all true Muslims to prepare for jihad war as we grow up" and talks of the "7/7 martyrs" with admiration'
- 'a supply teacher leaving a book in the school library which stated "that seeking to be killed and pursuing martyrdom are legitimate and praiseworthy acts"'. (DCSF, 2008a: 35)

Lastly, the following three examples are given as 'concerns' that have arisen recently in colleges:

- the 'college is approached by a group of students who find that the local mosques do not provide enough scope for them to discuss and debate particular topical issues that relate to religious ideology and how they can apply their understanding of their faith within the modern world. They want to set up a society where they can do this'
- 'an individual has been seeking to access an Arabic website that is not on the agreed list'

- 'a report that a student is upsetting other students by challenging their clothing as un-Islamic and encouraging them not to mix with non-Muslims'. (DCSF, 2008b: 28)

The first effect of these examples and indicators is to affirm that these vulnerabilities *existed*. Put another way, the *signs* of potential (violent) extremism were available, but were not made visible, or at least, not interpreted correctly. One of Prevent's central tasks is thus *to make* visible; to ensure the generic and specific signs of vulnerability are seen, enabling intervention. It is thus crucial that the knowledges of these vulnerabilities are passed on to the professions, such that they are in a position to see properly. One of the examples that recurs, and was quoted earlier, is that of a young adult writing extremist graffiti in an exercise book. Its appearance as an example across these guidance documents is likely due to the case of Hasib Hussain, one of the 7/7 bombers. Described by Norman Bettison as a 'model student' who had never come to the police's attention prior to the attacks, it was found that his school exercise books were full of supportive references to al-Qaeda. As Norman Bettison goes on to state in his evidence to the Communities and Local Government Committee:

> To write in one's exercise book is not criminal and would not come on the radar of the police, but the whole ethos, the heart of *Prevent* is the question for me of whether someone in society might have thought it appropriate to intervene. What do I mean by intervention? I do not mean kicking his door down at 6 o'clock in the morning and hauling him before the magistrates. I mean should someone have challenged that? They are the sorts of cases that get referred through the *Channel* scheme. (Communities and Local Government Committee, 2010: 17)

Yet there are consequences in portraying threat in this way. Making such acts and utterances visible is not neutral, and enacts an economy of fears and suspicion that focus the pastoral gaze on particular identities and their associated politics and religiosities. These vulnerability indicators, while aiming to identify signs of potential, also serve to produce and constitute their own economies of intelligibility. They serve to render certain spaces, performances and identities visible, and cast others into shadow. These indicators thus attain a luminosity that directs the gaze to a range of legal performances, identifications and identities that now must be read as potentially constituting the signs of future violence, and, thus, themselves require pastoral mediation. Two important consequences of these vulnerability indicators can be identified. First, Channel produces these mediations as pastoral interventions of care, mobilising a pastoral power. Second, this power then takes effect through an identity politics, producing those performances of identity deemed threatening.

The politics of care within Channel

It is pastoral agencies that are at the forefront of identifying vulnerable individuals who might benefit from a Channel intervention, a process which has been achieved over time through the mainstreaming of Channel and its integration into broader safeguarding concerns. This has allowed existing practices to be transferred and existing pastoral expertise to be mobilised; Channel work represents important continuities and extensions, 'a lot of it is based on tried and tested practice, whether it's in law enforcement or other areas' (interview with John Wright). Preventing the vulnerable from the risks posed by extremist thought is understood to work within the same parameters as protecting the vulnerable from drug or alcohol dependency, or from engaging in criminality or gang-based violence (interview with Sir Peter Fahy).

While police services have historically led the way on Channel, the specialist knowledges and visibilities of radicalisation, developed by researchers and policy officials in the DCLG, the Home Office and the academy, is understood to be transferrable. Since the Counter-Terrorism and Security Act 2015, specified authorities now have a statutory duty to engage in this Prevent work, where failure to do so could lead to interventions by central government. Thus, professionals working in healthcare, education, social work and prison and probation services must maintain vigilance towards potential threats, referring those they deem to be of concern to Channel agencies.[4] This has been the object of much academic concern, with an emergent literature arguing that this amounts to the securitisation of social policy, embedding security at the heart of everyday social relations (see Heath-Kelly, 2017; Ragazzi, 2017; Heath-Kelly and Strausz, 2018; Martin, 2018). These vulnerabilities are generalised to the extent that existing expertise and institutional approaches can be mobilised towards questions of violent extremism, yet such particular vulnerabilities also carry their own challenges and specificities. To this end, training such as WRAP and ACT NOW have been developed alongside the sector-specific guidance cited above. WRAP, in particular, has been delivered across the public sector, providing the primary training for many of those with duties of care under Prevent (see Home Office, 2014).

This mainstreaming of the Prevent duty, building it into the work of a range of pastoral professionals, allows Prevent to occupy the precautionary, pre-criminal space, emerging alongside the threat it then attempts to mediate. The assemblage of Channel seeks to be as fluid and mobile as the threat it seeks to prevent. It maintains vigilance for the emergence of threats through being integrated into the day-to-day workings of pastoral professionals who are in regular contact with those who might display signs of vulnerability. It represents an institutional space whose composition can change to match the case in question. Through possessing the requisite expertise, and the knowledge of indicators that would suggest vulnerability to radicalisation, the signs of an individual potentially becoming violent can be seen early and an intervention put in place. Yet, this mainstreaming of the Prevent duty also goes beyond the mere proximity of these professionals, attaching importance to the pastoral duties of care that they already possess in regards to those who are at risk.

Through the inscription of Channel's concerns into a safeguarding regime, it is clear that the 'problem' of radicalisation is positioned as one which, in its correspondence, can utilise duties of care that are already held by various professionals. Prevent thus becomes implicated within the wider safeguarding regime, maintaining an equivalency with other risks and the processes used to mediate them. In ACPO's guidance regarding colleges, it states that:

> it can be useful to consider Prevent alongside these aims:
>
> • Be Safe
> • Be Healthy
> • Enjoy and Achieve
> • Make a positive contribution
> • Achieve Economic wellbeing
>
> Colleges will view Prevent within their safeguarding responsibilities, as well as fitting with their wider educational role, promoting community cohesion and teaching young people to respect others. (ACPO, 2012a: 11)

Consistently, in guidance to statutory partners, their role within Prevent is invoked in terms of a generic caring responsibility, alongside which Prevent becomes another risk to manage. ACPO guidance states:

> Just as they can help to educate young people about risk, colleges offer opportunities to help learners understand the risks associated with extremism and help develop the knowledge and skills to be able to challenge terrorist ideologies. (ACPO, 2012a: 4)

In locating Channel within this framework, professionals with existing duties of care come to occupy a central role in the implementation of the project.

The pastoral power at work within Prevent

Prevent has therefore been thoroughly integrated into the professional duties of many pastoral agents. While it has only been a legal obligation since February 2015, this represents the culmination of a long process of integration through the safeguarding framework. The role of pastoral professions is therefore key in the conceptualisation of Prevent work and, it will now be argued, for an understanding of how Prevent mobilises and enacts an individualising pastoral power. Read as a power of care, concerned for the wellbeing of its subjects, it is worth relating such operations of power to Foucault's analysis of the development of the pastorate. Doing so allows links to be drawn between contemporary and past manifestations of this operation of power. It highlights the contemporary differences that can be brought to light through analysis of the Channel project and, finally, allows important conclusions to be drawn regarding how Channel mobilises pastoral professions in order to both produce and then police the boundaries of 'British' identity.

Targeting individuals at risk, it deploys a language of care, seeking to act on the vulnerable lest they be led astray by the seductive narratives of violent extremism. Such operations of power re-invoke the power of care that is central to the pastor–flock relation. In this tradition, one does not govern a territory or political structure but people, both as individuals and as a collective (Foucault, 2007: 122). It is understood as a 'power of care. It looks after the flock, it sees to it that the sheep do not suffer, it goes in search of those who have strayed off course, and it treats those that are injured' (Foucault, 2007: 127). It is a power that is individualising and directional, seeking the salvation of those it tends. Foucault identifies three broad themes that, combined, distinguish the emergence of the Christian pastorate and, it will be argued, have a continued relevance for understanding the operations of power at work within the Channel programme: the concern for salvation, the concern for the law and the concern for the truth.

First, the concern of the pastor is with the salvation of the flock. Paradoxically, for the pastor, the collective and the individual are ascribed equal weight within this demand, and thus, equal concern must be given to each individual as much as the whole. This entails a series of practical dilemmas that confronted the pastor; if the individual threatens the flock, but is of equal importance, then how should one act? (Foucault, 2007: 169). The pastor is thus enmeshed in a 'subtle economy of merit and fault', taking responsibility for the conduct of self and flock, towards the goal of salvation, upon which ultimately God decides (Foucault, 2007: 173). Second, in regards to the law, conduct within the pastorate is one of pure obedience to the conductor, as opposed to previous relations of authority predicated on the power of rhetoric. The pastoral relation is thus one of complete servitude of one to another, even when one is asked the absurd, the illegal, indeed, *especially* when one is tasked such (Foucault, 2007: 173–180). Lastly, the pastoral form gives rise to a new relationship of the subject to the self, and specifically, to the truth of the self. It is a power that brings into being, and is exercised through, the hidden truth of the individual, a truth that through a series of techniques of investigation and self-examination can come to be known by the pastor and individual. This focused individualisation of the subject, this self-possessed inner truth, allows for the direction of one's daily conduct, in relation to both the temporal and the spiritual. This inner truth is thus intimately concerned with one's spiritual direction, but, unlike in previous forms such as that of the ancient Greeks, it is an involuntary and permanent relation, directed at improved subordination, not self-mastery (Foucault, 2007: 180–182).

Foucault goes on to trace the development of pastorship through the emergence of governmentality as a function of rule within the modern state in Western Europe. Crucially, the objective of pastoral governance comes to be located in this world not the next; salvation is no longer concerned with the sanctity of the spirit but with health, wellbeing and security. This entails the agents of pastoral power multiply, leading to the creation of the police in the eighteenth century and the development of public institutions such as hospitals. This multiplication of the aims and agents of pastoral power will lead in two directions. The first concerns the quantification of the population, the second will retain an analytics of the truth of the individual (Foucault, 1982: 784).[5] Prevent's focus on problematic environments, as was demonstrated, carries with it a governmental focus on the population. Within the Channel project, it is the individual that is highlighted. Such individuals can be understood as existing at the boundaries of the population. They attain a visibility through the concept of radicalisation, being rendered legible as a potentially threatening identity due to the signs of vulnerability they display. It is an operation of pastoral power that allows for an individualising gaze, making intelligible potentially threatening subjects through ordering identities in the present as secure or risky. This intelligibility can be seen in the politics of identity that emerges within the vulnerability indicators.

The politics of identity within Channel

This ordering of threat, through constituting certain performances of identity as risky, is demonstrable through the vulnerability indicators. Thus, in addition to constituting Prevent as a power of care, the vulnerability indicators at work within Channel traverse the temporal gap through producing certain identities and behaviours as vulnerable and therefore threatening. In many of the examples given in this chapter, vulnerability indicators are represented as merely an expression, perhaps verbal, perhaps communicated in images, of a politics or religiosity that may well be distasteful to the mainstream of 'British society'. These are the concrete instantiations of the 'extreme', constituting that which cannot be contained within a normalised British identity.

The constitution of the utterances, behaviours and identities that, through their riskiness, are produced as outside of a normalised Britishness, can be seen within the vulnerability indicators previously discussed. This is the context for indicators concerned with anti-Christian, anti-Semitic or anti-Muslim words and behaviour, expressing racist views, wearing more religious clothing, being a religious convert, writing graffiti, acting out in class or sharing inappropriate videos. It is also the framing for concerns around a group of Muslim students wishing to debate politics and theology outside of their local mosque. These political and theological expressions are now an intimate security concern. Moreover, it clearly raises questions over who judges 'extremism', and where the line is drawn. For instance, there is the example of a supply teacher bringing extremist material into college, which the police aim to help with by assessing its legality and then taking protective actions (ACPO, 2012a: 23). On the one hand, this demands an extra layer of mediating, with colleagues having to judge whether the material might be extreme, thus warranting further police guidance. On the other, it brings in questions of expertise and judgement over the constitution of the boundary of that which is, or is not, 'extreme'. Crucially, it serves to demarcate, order and police those identities seen to be containable within 'Britishness', and those which signify its dangerous exterior.

This identity politics is further demonstrable with reference to the concrete interventions and investigations carried out under Channel auspices. CAGE (2015), a campaigning organisation, has published examples of the reasons behind why individuals have been referred, investigated and targeted by Channel. In one example, a woman working in the health sector was seemingly investigated by Prevent officers as, upon returning to work after a one-year break, she had now decided to wear a hijab. Another case demonstrates that a student was referred by his school to Prevent as he refused to take part in music lessons, which the student believed would be in contravention of his Islamic faith (CAGE, 2015). Other notable cases that have gained media attention include a fourteen-year-old Muslim student, who was questioned by Prevent officers for raising the concept of 'eco-terrorism' in a French class (Dodd, 2015). In another case, a postgraduate Muslim student studying for a master's degree in terrorism studies was investigated, by his own university, for displaying too many red flags, after one of its officials engaged in a conversation with the student after seeing him reading an academic text on terrorism. In this discussion, the member of staff had asked the student questions concerning his views on Islamist terrorism, faith and homosexuality (Ramesh and Halliday, 2015). Lastly, a student was questioned by a Prevent officer after showing support in school for

Palestine. The activities that raised concern included possessing a 'Free Palestine' badge and handing out leaflets in school advocating a boycott of Israeli goods. According to the student, the police officer informed him that these could be interpreted as 'radical', 'terrorist-like' beliefs (Hooper, 2015).

Moreover, in positioning Channel within a safeguarding regime, existing risks, such as drug use or criminality, are reinterpreted. These indicators are not necessarily seen as factors in and of themselves, but are frequently linked to particular 'extreme' identities or behaviours. In so doing, generic issues of welfare become religiously, politically and culturally inscribed. Returning to some of the examples and indicators listed earlier, drug use and insecure family ties may require care and support of some nature, but it would seem that the reason for this being a vulnerability that demands a counter-radicalisation framing is that the individual is a religious convert. Likewise, an example is given of someone with mental health issues, who is associating with others who are deemed to hold extremist views. Lastly, an example is given of a religious convert, who had also joined a street gang, using inappropriate language in school. It is reasonable to assume that problematic language has been a concern at schools prior to Prevent guidance. Yet here, alongside religiosity, it is presented as a threat indicator that teachers should be aware of, specifically in terms of a potentially latent propensity to violent extremism. As such, existing vulnerabilities are placed as indicative of a vulnerability to radicalisation that reads them – when conjoined with particular questions of identity or behaviour – as potential signs of future violence. In such a way, questions of generic welfare are being inscribed with an identity politics (see Martin, 2018). When it is Muslim politics and religiosity that is concretely produced as vulnerable, it is likely that Muslims displaying these other vulnerabilities will be interpreted through this lens.

The role of these indicators in guiding and interpreting ascriptions of 'vulnerability' can be seen within the breakdown of referrals by category of 'extremism' risk. When the data is analysed by type of concern, a clearer picture of the over-reporting noted earlier emerges. Full data is only available for the past two reporting years (Home Office, 2017, 2018b), but it nevertheless tells an interesting story (see Tables 2 and 3).

Additionally, of those referred between April 2012 and the end of March 2014, 56 per cent were recorded as being of Muslim faith, other religions accounted for 11 per cent and the other 33 per cent were recorded as not known (NPCC, n.d.). The Home Office claims around 15 per cent of referrals from the 2015 calendar year were for far-right extremism, with 70 per cent being for 'Islamist-related' extremism (Home Office, 2016: 16).

Table 2 Channel referral numbers by type of concern (2015–16)

Type of concern	Number of referrals	Number of cases discussed at a Channel panel	Percentage of referrals discussed at a Channel panel	Number of cases that received Channel support	Percentage of referrals resulting in Channel support
Islamist	4,997 (65.48% of total)	819 (76.47% of total)	16.39%	264 (69.74% of total)	5.28%
Extreme right wing	759 (9.95% of total)	188 (17.55% of total)	24.77%	98 (25.79% of total)	12.91%
Other	702 (9.20% of total)	64 (5.98% of total)	9.12%	18 (4.74% of total)	2.56%
Unspecified	1,173 (15.37% of total)	N/A	N/A	N/A	N/A
Total	7,631	1,071	14.03%	380	4.98%

Table 3 Channel referral numbers by type of concern (2016–17)

Type of concern	Number of referrals	Number of cases discussed at a Channel panel	Percentage of referrals discussed at a Channel panel	Number of cases that received Channel support	Percentage of referrals resulting in Channel support
Islamist	3,704 (60.79% of total)	760 (66.32% of total)	20.52%	184 (55.42% of total)	4.97%
Extreme right wing	968 (15.89% of total)	271 (23.65% of total)	27.99%	124 (37.35% of total)	12.81%
Other	725 (11.9% of total)	115 (10.03% of total)	15.86%	24 (7.23% of total)	3.31%
Unspecified	696 (11.42% of total)	N/A	N/A	N/A	N/A
Total	6,093	1,146	18.81%	332	5.45%

In absolute terms, the majority of referrals are for concerns regarding 'Islamist extremism'. Thus, there is a clear focus – at least at the reporting level – on those seen to be vulnerable to this particular form. Nevertheless, recent data does suggest that referrals for 'right-wing' extremism may be on the rise. Moreover, in absolute terms, 'right-wing' referrals are more likely to result in an intervention. Thus, while the number of referrals across different types of extremism differ markedly, the gap between the number of interventions for different types is narrowing, with the most recent data showing 55.42 per cent of interventions were for 'Islamist' concerns, and 37.35 per cent for 'right-wing' concerns. Government claims that it is taking 'right-wing' terrorism more seriously should not be discounted.

Of interest though, assuming the 'unspecified' referrals noted above do not distort the data significantly, 'right-wing' referrals are more accurate (at least, in terms of that which Channel panel members deem to be requiring intervention) than referrals for 'Islamist' extremism. Some 12.91/12.81 per cent of right-wing referrals go on to receive a Channel intervention compared with 5.28/4.97 per cent for the 2015–16 and 2016–17 reporting years respectively. Thus, while the accuracy of referrals is low, over-reporting is most significant for 'Islamist' extremism. This indicates that the surveillant net cast over those who are identified as Muslim is important, with significantly higher referrals per intervention than those for right-wing extremism.

What is being instilled through these vulnerability indicators, and what is evident in the concrete instantiations of Channel, is that the expression of certain identities has become considered problematic. Certain religious and political expressions are rendered as potential signs of vulnerability to radicalisation and violent extremism. Through reading these signs, clues as to an individual's trajectory of becoming can be made knowable, and if these clues signify a becoming dangerous, then intervention may be required. In its temporal ambition, precautionary interventions are taken not on the basis of illegality, but on the basis of the potential which certain expressions of identity are seen to contain. One conclusion that can be drawn is that the manifestation of the identity politics of the vulnerability indicator may well be found in the high number of false positives found in the reporting of 'Islamist' extremism.

Traversing the temporal gap in this way has consequences, positioning radicalisation as a question of care and wellbeing. Kundnani (2014), drawing on the analysis of the academic literature around radicalisation, argues that one of the key components of the radicalisation framework is the privileging of psychological phenomena. Thus, he reads in much of the literature the centrality of cognitive openings, of socio-psychological traumas that allow extremist ideas to take hold. In representing these interventions within a framework of pastoral support, Channel is an institutional framework that reinforces this reading of radicalisation. By locating Channel within a pastoral duty of care, the expressly political possibility of radicalisation is downplayed. Following Kundnani (2014; see also Brighton, 2007; Richards, 2011), what is being effaced from processes of becoming violent is an idea that such decisions might be taken out of a conception of oneself as a political actor, consciously engaging within a strategic and adversarial relationship with, for instance, the British state. Thus, even when political articulation might be read as a sign of vulnerability, rather than understand this within a framework of political contestation, Channel engages with political violence through questions around wellbeing and interventions of care. Political expression signifies a risk factor that requires pastoral management.

Most fundamentally though, the effect of these vulnerability indicators is, in service to these demands of preclusive mediation, to implicitly disallow the politics or religiosity that is seen to signify a risk. Or, put another way, to display an 'extreme' or overt political or religious position, that is understood to be indicative of a potential vulnerability to radicalisation, is to already position oneself as demanding precautionary mediation. In essence, it is the views expressed that become intolerable; and thus, a whole range of legal political or religious expressions become subject to the pastoral security gaze. Through these indicators, the identities they highlight are produced as external to a normalised Britishness. Rather than the boundaries of the law, Channel, through its particular economy of intelligibility, inscribes its own boundaries of those identities and performances seen to be secure and those deemed threatening. Such ascriptions will now come to play a key role in judging – and crucially securing – these perceived risks.

What is mobilised is thus a pastoral power that acts through the ordering of identities. It serves to illuminate the subject of vulnerability to radicalisation through identifying potentially problematic performances and identifications. First, it positions this as a question of care, demanding and facilitating Channel processes as pastoral interventions. Second, it produces it as a question of identity, producing those concrete expressions and performances that are seen to be alienated from a normalised Britishness. Together, it entails that the vulnerable subject of Prevent is produced and constituted as a specific object of knowledge. It is a subject that represents the unstable boundary as to which life is deemed secure and which is deemed risky. It mandates the professions engage with their pastoral work through this securing lens; such work now has questions of identity, 'Britishness' and extremism at its core.

Transforming the pastoral power of care

In so doing, Channel serves to transform the pastoral power identified by Foucault. In acting within the temporal ambition of Prevent,
the power deployed goes beyond that of the pastor and his flock. First,
now that salvation is a temporal affair, it is in this world that one must
seek fulfilment. Salvation retains a direction, but the 'good' life comes to
be defined in terms of one's coherence with a normalised British identity that signifies a secure identity. Through locating the possession of
extreme views as indicative of a vulnerability towards radicalisation,
pastoral professions have been mobilised towards vigilance concerning
such identities. Directionality is thus established towards a space of
normalised Britishness. The economy of merits and faults is redrawn,
identities become discernible as either secure or risky. For those of concern, their telos is to be found in the salvation of 'shared British values'.

Second, the pastoral relation to law is no longer one of generalised
obedience. Authority becomes pluralised and modulated, existing not
within a field of obedience but one of manifold agents. Freedom is
assumed, but stepping outside of a normalised Britishness will invest
oneself within the process of pastoral care.[6] Channel has generated a permanent and continuous capacity for identifying vulnerable individuals
by reading the signs of potential they are seen to display, encompassing
many of the institutions of society. Vulnerability to radicalisation now
exists as a life process against which society as a whole must maintain
vigilance. While this is certainly not to deny that the burden of suspicion
falls on Muslim communities, it is also to claim that it is a grid of visibility and intelligibility that covers the whole of society. It is a grid that
is thus modulated, maintaining vigilance across society as a whole, albeit
attuned to particular sites and subjects.

Lastly, the problem of a hidden truth is retained. However, the
techniques of self-examination and confession will not work here – the
subject may not be aware of their latent potentials. This is not the mod-
ernist subject with a potential for self-knowledge. Rather, what is at stake
here is a subject rendered threatening and produced as disassociated
from a normalised Britishness, often through racialisation or on account
of their perceived Muslimness, of whom it is judged knowledge of their
innermost desires must be produced. What is now required are pastoral
expertises that allow for the identification of dangerous becoming. What
is needed is the production of a knowledge that enables the identification of the subject's hidden truth, whether the trajectory and potential
for their becoming is dangerous or benign. Through Channel, the pastoral gaze is thus mobilised towards a newly problematised site of vulnerability to radicalisation. In this process, the pastoral power at work
is reformulated. Within Prevent's temporal ambition to consciously

act within conditions of uncertainty, rather than discover one's truth together, the power that is deployed actively produces the truth of the individuals with which it is concerned.

The problems of the pastorate are thus retained yet radically transformed. What is at stake in Prevent is a power that locates its subjects through a grid of intelligibility, based on an understanding of secure and risky processes of becoming, rooted in conceptions of 'Britishness'. The problems of identification, the law and the truth of the subject will all work towards this end. What is therefore at stake within the Channel project, and Prevent more broadly, is the establishment of the pastoral boundary, one that is not coterminous with the juridical and the boundaries of the law, and is constitutive of its own inside and outside.

Conclusion

These iterative examples of 'vulnerability' should thus be read as acting as the collective institutional imaginary against which the broader themes of cohesion and 'Britishness', and the attendant focus on belonging and securing, play out. This entails a recognition that, while deploying a language of care, what is at stake within Channel's interventions is a productive power that seeks to mediate performances of identity that are deemed indicative of future threat. The temporal gap is traversed in such a way that particular utterances, identifications and behaviours come to demand regulation and amendment on account of the potential they are seen to contain. The clues of the future are read in performances that are intelligible in the present. If such clues are seen to lead to radicalisation, then a precautionary logic is invoked, wherein intervention is mandated on account of the risk such individuals might pose if left unmediated. The pastoral gaze is mobilised and redirected to questions of identity and belonging, and as such, a series of professional bodies are being trained to articulate, and constitute as visible, radicalisation knowledges in their daily work. In crossing the temporal gap in this way, the promise of future violence is structured in politically contained ways. In positioning radicalisation as intimately connected to questions of wellbeing, any understanding of political antagonism is disavowed; in ordering these processes in terms of 'extremism', 'vulnerability' and questions of identity, the professions are mobilised to produce and then police the boundary of a secured 'Britishness'.

When these suspicions are brought within the Channel process, what is demanded is the mediation of these potentially dangerous traits. Ultimately, the individuals undergoing Channel procedures must consent to their realignment in line with a perceived 'secure' identity or be judged dangerous, and most likely subjected to surveillance, always aware that their conduct is suspect. This may well be preferable – even for the mediated individual – than the future that is played out within the alternative history of Prevent's non-interventions. One wherein the individual of Prevent's catastrophic imaginary does decide to take up arms in a violent struggle, and where the result is their potential imprisonment or even death, and perhaps the deaths of others too. Yet, the problem is that this knowledge is impossible; at the moment of mediation, that future is denied its chance of becoming. What remains is the effective silencing of a series of legal identifications, utterances and behaviours, and a series of securing interventions into those that are seen to display them.

Many of those interviewed for the book, when challenged on this point, were quick to agree that this was a concern for those involved in implementing Channel work. That those involved were aware of the potential for circumscribing spaces of Muslim politics. As Lord Carlile stated, the 'Channel project is only entitled to work if it goes beyond the expression of political opinions; it works when fears arise about something that legitimately causes a fear of danger to the public' (interview with Lord Carlile of Berriew). Yet, the argument of this chapter has been that to discuss and institutionalise vulnerability in this way is itself constitutive of a grid of intelligibility that situates threat within expressions of particular ideas and identities. On the one hand, Prevent thus identifies as potentially indicative of threat a range of ideas and expressions that are now the subject of the pastoral gaze. On the other, it is a much broader identity politics at work. The argument of this book is that Prevent has served to produce and mobilise a diagram of power; the diagram of counter-radicalisation. These past two chapters have brought to the fore the two constituent movements within the assemblage of Prevent. Chapter 5 analysed Prevent as concerned with environments within which (potentially dangerous) becoming occurs. This chapter has analysed Prevent as a means of rendering those individuals who are vulnerable to radicalisation as visible. The next chapter brings these movements together, articulating the diagram of counter-radicalisation as a coherent whole, and a crucial site for re-ordering the boundaries of contemporary 'Britishness'.

Notes

1 The standard and problematic narrative of Prevent is that the focus on so-called 'homegrown' terrorism – and its attendant focus on individuals becoming radicalised domestically – is a development in reaction to the attacks of 7/7. This is not the case. It is clear, as shown in chapter 2, that this was a concern for intelligence services and the Cabinet Office from the beginning, and that a Channel-like instrument was always considered as a key part of response.

2 These specified authorities pertain to local government, criminal justice, education and child care, health and social care and the police.
3 It should be noted that this process has been the subject of challenge by some of these now mandated professions. For example, the National Union of Teachers and the Royal College of Psychiatrists have been deeply critical of the duties members of their professions are expected to enact (Adams, 2016; Royal College of Psychiatrists, 2016).
4 This dispersed set of responsibilities raises questions similar to that of Butler's (2006) work regarding petty sovereigns, wherein diffuse bureaucrats have the power to direct, decide and intervene into those deemed to represent a threat, and raises similar issues of expertise, legitimacy and responsibility.
5 This analysis therefore invokes pastoral power specifically in its individualising function, as opposed to Gutkowski's (2011) usage that locates multiple Prevent practices within a conception of the pastorate. Nevertheless, both share a concern with how caring is utilised as a productive power over particular segments of the population.
6 One can refuse a Channel intervention, but in such a scenario, the refusal would itself be taken as a further sign of concern (interview with Sir Peter Fahy).

7

The identity politics of Prevent

Q: What is the difference between a Paris terrorist, a Portsmouth-Syria jihadist and a Right Wing Extremist?

A: Nothing. They all lack a tolerant, integrated national identity. This is not a joke. (Knowles, 2015)[1]

This anti-joke, written by a former police lead on Prevent, cuts to the heart of the problematic detailed in this book, and the power that the assemblage of counter-radicalisation mobilises in response. Those who enact violent extremism, encompassing *all* forms of extremism, are produced as a threat due to being positioned outside of a normalised Britishness. As the previous two chapters have shown, the assemblage that has emerged in response to this problem seeks to make these identities knowable and actionable, securing them through bringing them into line with this 'integrated national identity'. Concretely, this has historically been mobilised in order to make visible those Muslim identities that are seen to be on a path of radicalisation, or at an environmental level, conducive to such radicalisation. Yet, as an abstract, diagrammatic reading of this power will make clear, the function of power produced and mobilised in Prevent goes beyond these bounds. Rather, it will be argued, it constitutes a novel approach to managing threats. It represents the production of a newly realised social space, that of individuals who may become violent, and is a problematic capable of encompassing all who may engage in political violence. This chapter then analyses the political consequences of such a power. It argues that, due to Prevent's temporal ambition to intervene early, the expression of certain identities becomes problematic, read as signs of potential violence, and therefore demanding mediation.

Combining the analysis of Prevent's problematic and assemblage, this chapter starts by outlining the diagram of counter-radicalisation produced and mobilised by Prevent. It will be shown that this is a power that functions to produce, and then act upon, identities, securing the threat of violence in the future by ordering and governing identities in the present. This power, the book argues, contains important and intrinsic consequences for the possibility of political expression in the UK. These consequences will be examined, showing how they radicalise the relation of security and identity, extending the scope of those who are subject to security intervention and those who must maintain vigilance for signs of threat. This reading of Prevent therefore situates the policy as enacting an important logic, a way of thinking about the relationship between security and identity, that occupies a central role in contemporary British identity politics, and foresees its continued, increasing importance.

The diagram of counter-radicalisation

This book has sought to demonstrate that at the heart of Prevent lies an important development in how the state seeks to govern the possibility of future violence. Going beyond previous counter-terrorism strategies, as shown in chapter 3, Prevent contains a temporal ambition to intervene early: to intervene prior to any demonstrable intent of illegality. Taking vulnerability to radicalisation as its problematic, it seeks to identify vulnerable individuals and the environments that might produce them. This assemblage, that Prevent has produced to respond to this problematised threat, has therefore mobilised and deployed particular forms of power in order to mediate identities in the present, such that they are no longer threatening for the future. Chapter 5 showed that Prevent, in seeking to manage environments that might produce radicalisation, has enacted pre-emptive interventions into communities and problem institutions. Mobilising a governmental power, these interventions seek to produce 'British values', while minimising extremist identities, directing the circulations of ideas and identity away from those produced as threatening. Chapter 6 showed that Prevent, in identifying individuals at risk, deployed a precautionary approach in order to mediate this risk. Through mobilising a pastoral power and existing duties of care, Prevent seeks to identify those who may stray, to produce their inner truth through the clues of their life, such that mediative intervention can be taken. While taking effect in two separate ways, the intent in the following section is to show how they combine to produce a singular diagram of counter-radicalisation. A diagram of power that has produced a crucial new role for the state.

First, the diagram of counter-radicalisation orders identities in the UK as either secure or threatening. Imagine a 2D space with a circle in the centre, this circle represents a container within which is those identities produced through Prevent as secure; the 'normalised Britishness', identified in chapter 4, that Prevent renders secure and securing. Outside the circle lies those identities that cannot be contained within a normalised Britishness. Those identities that, in their exteriority, alienation and disassociation, pose a potential threat of becoming radicalised. The boundary of the circle does not therefore represent the law, or that of the territoriality of the state. It is rather a boundary drawn on the basis of potential, and this potential is produced through performances of identity in the present. Outside this space lies another circle. Beyond this line lies those who are already committed to violent extremism. It represents the ideas and identities that justify and enact violence. There therefore exists an inner space of secure identities, then those that are potentially threatening in their insecurity, and lastly those that represent a concrete threat, justifying violent extremism in some form. With the right expert knowledge and training, it becomes possible for the trained cartographer to identify the locations of individuals upon this map, and thus to see within them the threat that they do, or do not, pose.

Second, within these tiered circles, and perhaps cutting across them, exist other shapes that represent communities or institutional spaces that possess their own identities. These spaces, the subject of chapter 5, can be abstracted in this way as they represent a certain intensity of circulation. These environments may be, in some sense, physically enclosed, as is the case in the Trojan Horse schools. They may be more abstract, for instance, representing a particular ethnic or religious community. Yet they matter, as they represent the physical or conceptual space within which ideas and identities circulate with greater intensity, and thus impact upon individuals who are within them. Many of these will be produced as existing solely within the inner circle of a normalised Britishness. But there are also those that straddle the lines between a secure 'Britishness' and its outside. These may also go beyond, encompassing the line of violent extremism. Concretely, a Muslim community in the UK might be represented as a large space that cuts across all three tiers, containing ideas and identities that are secure, potentially threatening and that condone and promote violent extremism. Within this space, there may also be smaller recognisable environments that skew towards one end or the other.

Due to the circulation within these environments, they act as a milieu which effects those who are within them, and renders them more likely to cohere with the ideas and identities prominent in that environment. They therefore entrench certain identities; they render those who inhabit them more likely to become coherent with the predominant identity of the space. Yet, as evident in the discursive analysis of 'Britishness' and extremism in chapter 4, these environments are not static and are capable of being transformed. Through opening them to circulations of secure identities, or by increasing the circulation of more secure ideas, their location within the map can shift. One intention of counter-radicalisation is therefore to expand the conceptual space occupied by the inner core of normalised Britishness. Evident in the governmental power of cohesion identified in chapter 5, by extending this inner circle into other, closed, potentially threatening circulations, the increased flow of secure identities can transform and secure these environments.

Third, individuals, while locatable in this map, are also capable of movement across it. Through knowledge of radicalisation, as discussed in chapter 3, this potential for movement can be identified. Individuals at risk can, thus, be made visible as lines of potential becoming, perhaps extending away from a secure identity. These are therefore temporal lines, representing the possible futures of an individual. This movement exists as a possibility both towards and away from a secure identity. What matters is therefore not only the current location within the map, but also the momentum; the direction of travel taken (towards or away from a secured identity) and the speed of that travel. Interacting with the previous point, when these trajectories intersect with environments, these circulations can act as an accelerant, providing momentum to a particular trajectory. As discussed in chapter 6, by identifying the signs an individual displays, this movement in time can be tracked and predicted. With the correct knowledge, it is possible to produce a map of this potential movement for a given subject. Based on signs in the present, it is possible for the able cartographer to see and make visible these temporal continua.

Fourth, these movements in time, once identified, can be acted upon. Movement in itself is not a problem, but rather a natural occurrence, an occurrence that is capable of being influenced. Negative movement is a consequence of exposure to problematic ideas and identities. It may be that the environments an individual exists within move them towards a risky identity. Prevent, through the identification of problematic spaces and movement, therefore manifests as a series of interventions into this movement across time. As discussed, this involves changing the environments within which movement occurs. It also involves intervening into individuals at particular risk of problematic movement. Channel, as discussed in chapter 6, seeks to intervene within the context of these processes of becoming. Through tailor-made support packages, the direction and momentum of travel can be altered. This may include removing an individual from problematic environments and providing diversionary activities. It often includes specialised mentoring, asking subjects of intervention to critically reflect on their political and religious ideas, opening their world to other viewpoints. Success can be judged and visibly assessed through the same signs that indicate the location and direction of travel of individuals. They are able to leave the process once it is judged their vulnerabilities have been managed, and they are travelling towards a space of normalised Britishness.

Fifth, reacting to these problematic temporal lines is envisaged as co-emergent with the threat. Responsibility for identifying signs of potentially problematic movement is dispersed throughout society. As is evident in the need to mainstream Prevent provision, when signs of a threat emerge, it is necessary to have individuals trained to spot such signs in close proximity. By training the pastoral professions to be able to identify signs of vulnerability to radicalisation, they are then able to start the process of intervention as soon as such signs manifest. The Channel process of referral, assessments and then intervention is produced to emerge in tandem with the first signs of radicalisation displayed by an individual, containing and managing the threat.

In the introduction, the methodological argument was put forward that a diagram of power coheres around a particular function, an abstract way of thinking about how power may be mobilised to produce particular outcomes. In bringing together the analysis of the book so far, the function of counter-radicalisation can be identified. Prevent functions as a power that works to produce secure identities. It orders identities in the present as secure or risky (which at the same time is a productive practice) and then mediates those deemed risky. It produces a means of mapping identities, communally and individually, on account of their coherence, or not, with a normalised British identity. Those identities that are produced as outside of, or alienated from, this 'British' core are rendered potentially threatening. The movement of individuals within this space is produced as knowable on account of signs displayed in the present. Combined, the future becomes actionable on account of performances of identity in the present, wherein certain performances are now rendered as potentially indicative of a future threat. The radical temporal ambition of Prevent – to intervene early, to prevent political violence before it has a chance to develop into political violence – is made possible. The temporal gap is traversed through an analysis of identity in the present. Intervention then occurs at the level of identity. The future is secured through bringing these environments and individuals back into coherence with a secure, 'British' identity. Prevent produces, and polices, 'British' identity.

Yet, as was argued in chapter 3, when securing threats, that which is being secured remains categorically uncertain. There exists a space of uncertainty into which the security act is deployed. In the case of Prevent, this has been achieved through ordering (and therefore producing) identities in the present as risky or secure. While the policy would not express its operations of power in this way, it is nevertheless explicit that it seeks to intervene prior to an individual becoming violent, or, in other words, within conditions of uncertainty. The argument made in chapter 3 was that, when acting within conditions of uncertainty, security actors must necessarily constitute and traverse a temporal gap. As such, they structure and act upon the promise of future threats in politically contained ways. By producing certain identities as threatening on account of their alienation from a normalised Britishness, it demands the mediation of such identities on account of their potential. As has been stated previously, this therefore enacts a boundary that is not coterminous with either the territory of the British state or the law; Prevent is constitutive of its own terrain. This political geography has ramifications. In effect, it is to enact a security demand to transform certain identities on account of the potential they are seen to contain. Such a power is therefore political, with consequences for the expression of the identities deemed potentially threatening. The final section of this book seeks to explore these political consequences, arguing that an intrinsic consequence of the power deployed by Prevent is to deny the political expression of those deemed risky. In so doing, it is a diagram that denies the possibility that these identities, which are produced as external, can make claims on the transformation of the British state.

The political implications of the diagram of counter-radicalisation

In providing this interpretation of Prevent, the intent of the book, following the Foucauldian methodology set out in the introduction, has been to illuminate and expose the power Prevent produces. Doing so brings to the fore the contingency of such a power, and the political decisions that are made in producing and securing the threat of radicalisation. Rather than an objective site for the identification of extant vulnerabilities, this analysis has instead shown how the diagram of counter-radicalisation produces the threat to which it then takes aim, ordering identities as risky or secure in the present, in order to make future violence knowable and actionable. In response to Prevent's novel temporal ambition – of intervention into those who may, potentially, come to engage in political violence – an assemblage has been formed around these sites of vulnerability, in order to mediate the threat they are seen to contain. In mobilising the diagram of counter-radicalisation, a power is deployed that seeks to act on, and transform, these identities now rendered threatening due to their potential.

It is to the consequences of this power that the book now turns. Here, the book argues that this diagram of counter-radicalisation functions as a power that makes the expression of certain ideas and identities problematic. It is a function that represents an extension of the ways in which identities are produced and secured at the expense of political expression. It is a power that acts to remove from political participation those identities that it presumes are, in their potential becoming, risky. In seeking to identify such potentials, it is a function that has extended the task and production of security across society as a whole. In conclusion, it can therefore be shown that Prevent has played an important role in the contemporary identity politics of the UK, producing and policing a boundary as to who, in their secureness, coheres and belongs, and who, in their riskiness, is produced as in need of mediation.

Making expression problematic: politics and the political

Prevent, and the power it produces and deploys, functions through rendering the expression of certain identities as risky, reading into them the possibility of future violence. It is these expressions that, therefore, become the object of mediation, targeted by pre-emptive and precautionary interventions in order to deny the potential threat of the future. In effect, it is the expression of these identities that is rendered problematic. Drawing on a distinction made between 'politics' and 'the political' by Jenny Edkins (1999), two different facets of Prevent's consequences for political expression can be identified. 'Politics' refers to the relatively common-sense idea of what politics is: elections, the arguments of political parties, the workings and doings of government. 'The political', in contrast, refers to the constitution of this space. More specifically, 'politics' is a particular, formalised domain of the social, while moments of 'the political' are those within which the founding principles of the social order are in abeyance (Edkins, 1999: 125–126). Moments of the political represent times and spaces whereby the principles of social order are in the process of becoming: the subjects, spaces and contestable topics that will form the basis of 'politics' are open to ordering. This goes beyond an account that would position a domain of politics as natural and pre-given. Instead, it insists that the spaces of politics, who may contest them, and who may, and may not, speak and act within them, are necessarily contingent. The question of identity thus cannot be divorced from the constitution of a particular social order. Power does not represent relations between pre-existing identities, but rather is constitutive of the identities themselves (Mouffe, 2000: 13–14; see also Campbell, 1998b; Laclau and Mouffe, 2001).

In terms of politics, it is clear through the functioning of Prevent that certain expressions of identity are now considered risky and therefore require mediation. Clear examples, evident within the 'vulnerability indicators' discussed in chapter 6, are the expression of a political position that is understood to be extremist, or becoming more overtly religious, such as through wearing the hijab or growing a beard. Concretely, as the examples given in chapter 6 demonstrate, it is expressions of a politics or religiosity associated with Islam that have come to signify a potential indicator of vulnerability. The result being that articulations and performances of an Islamic identity are understood as a threat.

Academic research is emerging that demonstrates the consequences of this representation of threat. Mythen *et al.* (2012) provide interview evidence from young British Muslims of self-censorship in response to British counter-terrorism policies. They provide qualitative data, showing how their Muslim respondents are very much aware of the practices that are seen to signify risk. Interviewees articulate how they try not to appear overtly Muslim in certain spaces, via, for instance, concealing their beards. They talk of the need to modify how they present their religious and political beliefs out of a fear that, while such statements may be legal, they might be misinterpreted and could lead to investigation and even arrest (Mythen *et al.*, 2012: 393). This is further corroborated by research undertaken by Brown and Saeed (2015; see also McGlynn and McDaid, 2016). Through a qualitative study of Muslim students in higher education, their work raises similar evidence of the self-censorship of expressions of Muslim politics or religiosity. Their respondents are clearly aware of Prevent and its implications, claiming they feel unable to display their political and theological convictions, out of a fear they would be seen as engaged within, or vulnerable to, radicalisation (Brown and Saeed, 2015). Ultimately, Prevent, in producing and policing certain identities as risky, can be read as leading to a 'trend of quietism arising from the desire of many Muslims to avoid being seen as "dangerous" or "critical"' (Breen-Smyth, 2014: 237).

In terms of the political, the diagram of counter-radicalisation has ramifications for how the political is reproduced, and who within this political order is allowed to make a claim on, and seek to perhaps transform, state identities. This is most visible in regards to the discussion of cohesion undertaken by the book, but underpins the entirety of the diagram. Some commentators have sought to understand community cohesion as a rebalancing of multiculturalism, wherein the recognition of minority communities through multiculturalism is maintained, yet a need to also focus on emphasising a shared commonality is accepted. This is a position held by Meer and Modood (2009; see also Cantle, 2005; Thomas, 2012), who argue the recognition of a meta-membership of 'Britishness' could itself sustain diversity, and what is required is that multiculturalism be tied to an inclusive national identity; civic inclusion is premised upon *all* being able to make claims on and reformulating this core national identity. In Modood's words, to be 'a citizen, no less than to have just become a citizen, is to have a right to not just be recognized but *to debate the terms of recognition*' (Modood, 2010: 161, emphasis added). Yet this interpretation fails to recognise the role played by the diagram of counter-radicalisation, and the effects of cohesion within it. As shown in chapter 5, these spaces of dialogue, and of the mixing and circulation of identities, are already constrained. To partake, a community, or an individual, must already demonstrate an upholding of the shared,

'British values', and a coherence with a normalised Britishness, which is then framed as the object of contestation within the discourse of cohesion. The analysis of Meer and Modood thus fails to recognise how cohesion and Prevent come together to produce certain ideas and identities as *already* excluded, preclusively denied a claim upon that which is shared or held in common, due to the potential threat they represent.

A diagrammatic analysis of Prevent therefore allows a further, and more fundamental, claim to be made. Prevent can be understood as a function of power that, in producing 'Britishness' and its outside, and then rendering this outside as potentially threatening and therefore in need of mediation, produces that which is alienated as unable to make a claim on that which *is* 'Britishness'. It is therefore a power that carries the capacity to designate those identities which, due to their potential, are denied a claim upon the reproduction of the social order. The resulting security of Prevent is one that removes from active political participation those subjects and spaces deemed threatening. The power Prevent produces is one that designates those identities that may become a threat, denying them an ability to contribute to the reproduction of that which is shared, common and 'British'.

In this regard, the diagram of counter-radicalisation can be understood as a mode of power that actively reproduces and secures the existing order. In producing a normalised British identity at the centre of its topography of secure and securing identities, disassociation from this centre becomes policed. The book has shown how this takes effect both through ensuring environments generate secure life and through the policing of individualised identities. The effect of such security actions is to deny these disassociations the possibility of politically contesting the production of these boundaries; the boundaries that produce certain identities as secure and others as threatening. In taking life processes of becoming as an explicit means of securing the future, the political is then iteratively reproduced through the exclusion of that which may, it is thought, become dangerous. When security takes as its object processes of becoming, it thus takes as its object the constitution of the political itself. Within this pre-criminal space, the expression of certain identities – at communal, institutional and individual levels of analysis – become intolerable due to the potential that is seen to reside within them.

In traversing the future, Prevent has drawn a relation between security and identity, and produced a power that has important ramifications for contemporary British identity politics. Within the scope of this preclusive security – when intervention is sought prior to the manifestation of the threat it seeks to secure – the extent of that which then becomes an object of security is radicalised. The above discussion has sought to highlight the concrete consequences of this power for political expression. Now, the book analyses this power as an abstract function, highlighting the broader consequence that this way of thinking about threat has for the UK. The book argues that this power – this preclusive security – extends both the scope of who is subject to security interventions and who is responsible for their enactment.

Extending who is secured

This form of power defines its own boundary. Not coterminous with the territory of the state or the law, it enacts its own political geography of who belongs and who, in their riskiness, must be brought into coherence with a normalised Britishness. In designating identities which are temporally prior to illegality as risky and therefore requiring transformation, it denies equal citizens of the UK the ability to freely express themselves and make claims upon the identity of the state. A denial that is based upon potential that is ascribed to them. A potential that, even on Prevent's own terms, may never manifest. It therefore establishes strata of belonging that determine the possibility of political participation. Those identities that are read as contained within a normalised Britishness are allowed free expression. Those that are produced as alienated are curtailed. Expression, and the possibility of transforming the British state, becomes contingent on demonstrating coherence within a normalised conception of 'Britishness' and 'British values' (and even then, it is state security practices that carry a discursive power to produce the boundaries of the 'British' and the alienated).

While all acts of security involve the traversal of a temporal gap (as was argued in chapter 3), Prevent represents a contemporary ambition to explicitly and self-consciously act within these conditions of uncertainty. This ambition, and the particular ways through which Prevent seeks to traverse the temporal gap, renders intelligible individuals as always in the process of becoming. With the right knowledge, the trajectories and possibilities of this becoming can be read, and that which is becoming dangerous can be secured. When certain identities are rendered as objects of security because of the dangerous becoming they are seen to potentially contain, what is produced is a preclusive denial of these identities to engage in politics and political transformation. The expression of certain political positions, which break no law, and may never do so, is made problematic, subject to a security gaze and possible intervention. The environments that engender this becoming can be interpreted as positive or problematic. Individuals, and their potential movement in time towards identities, can be charted.

Through Prevent, there emerges a vision of security in which all life that may become dangerous can be rendered the subject of mediation, purely on account of the potential that it is seen to contain. If part of the human condition is change over time – of becoming – then the promise held by Prevent is that, with the right training, becoming that is becoming dangerous can be made visible in the present, can be identified, and, ultimately, can be mediated before such danger manifests. It is life as a process of becoming that is the site of security. All life thus becomes the subject of this gaze, such that any dangerous becoming can be identified. Prevent thus extends a security imperative into all life processes, demanding vigilance of any performance, no matter how slight, that would indicate a risk.

Extending who secures

When processes of becoming are envisaged as an object of security, then all spaces in which becoming takes place are encapsulated within this security demand. The diagram of counter-radicalisation is therefore one that extends a demand to enact security throughout society. As the book has shown, throughout the operations of Prevent, the role of traditional 'security' actors only accounts for part of Prevent's work. While the police are certainly involved, they are not the main actors within Prevent, and their role is being increasingly minimised. Instead, through Channel, it is teachers, social workers, healthcare practitioners, local authorities and community organisations who are expected to maintain vigilance for signs of vulnerability. Moreover, with regards to the broader security of cohesion work, it is again local and voluntary organisations that are expected to be at the forefront of ensuring this coherence, supported by local authorities and communities themselves. This is not to suggest that Prevent represents the first time security imperatives have been enacted beyond traditional security actors. Yet it is to highlight a vision of security within which all life must be watched, on account of the signs of becoming violent that life may display; therefore, a central imperative of this diagram is to extend the security gaze into all facets of social existence.

In turn, the multitude of actors who now enact Prevent work are transformed into agents of security. What is produced as a site of pastoral care within Channel has thus integrated millions of public sector workers into an ethos of securing vulnerability. When securing processes of becoming, all such spaces within which becoming takes place must be open to the gaze of this security imperative. Those who thus exert responsibility require training, enabling them to spot and interpret signs correctly. The power produced by Prevent envisages a security in which the whole of society is vigilant, attuned to spotting signs of potential threat. When this threat takes identity as its intelligibility, it is then a security gaze that plays an active role in ordering and producing identities as risky

or secure. It is a power that sees society as mobilised towards the reproduction, and policing, of the boundary of Prevent.

Extendable to any identity that may become threatening

Lastly, it is a power that is capable of extension beyond its genesis.
Prevent has, for the most part, been targeted at Muslims living within
the UK. Yet, this diagrammatic and abstracted reading of the power
Prevent produces and deploys, allows this book to make a broader claim
regarding the diagram of counter-radicalisation. Prevent's practices of
political bordering, with its attendant problematisation of threat, and
the assemblage that then seeks to manage this threat, can be deployed
towards other performances of identity that are read as signifying potential violence. It is a function of power that thus represents a capacity to
enact a border between those identities that are rendered secure, and
those that are deemed risky in their potential. An analysis of the diagram
of power drawn by Prevent shows how the policy exceeds its localised
formation. What is at stake within the diagram of counter-radicalisation
is a way of making sense of life as a process of (potentially) becoming
(violent), and a series of mechanisms for making such processes visible,
intelligible and actionable. It is a response to a novel problematisation of
threat, which establishes vulnerability to becoming violent as an object
of thought. Then it is the constitution of an assemblage that responds
to this potential becoming violent. It is a power of mediation, in that
it envisages such spaces and subjects can be transformed directionally
towards a more secure identity. It is a grid of intelligibility that has been
installed, both conceptually and practically, across society as a whole.
While focused on certain ideas, identities and performances, it is not
reducible to them. If all life is in a process of becoming, it is a diagram
that maps these processes in their potential.

The Prevent approach is already applied to cases of white supremacist
radicalisation. While the policy has been critiqued for its predominant
focus on Muslim communities, this ambition to apply to all forms of political violence should not be underestimated. Hazel Blears, a key architect
of the policy and an early advocate of a broad approach, focused on values
and identities, argued that Prevent can and should apply 'to kind of any
narrative that seeks to exploit people's vulnerabilities because they lack a
sense of identity about who they are, what their place in the world is and
what their future holds for them' (interview with Hazel Blears). The analysis
of this book affirms and troubles this intent. As a diagrammatic function of
power, it agrees that what Prevent achieves is to put in place a framework
that can apply to any identity practices deemed indicative of potential violence. Yet it troubles a view that positions such vulnerabilities and identities

as, in and of themselves, threatening due to this lack and alienation. Rather, through Prevent, such boundaries are produced, demarcating the secure interior of 'British values' and those who are rendered alienated, external, threatening and thus in need of transformation.

In so doing, this is an analysis that goes beyond much of the critical and supportive literatures that view Prevent as a question of responding to a specific Muslim threat. It is clear that Prevent develops in a specific time and place. Prevent, as a way of thinking through how to respond to terrorism, emerges in the wake of the attacks of 9/11. Radicalisation, as discussed in chapter 3, takes a prominent conceptual role, in part, as a response to ideas around 'New Terrorism' that privilege religious motivations of violence. Moreover, cohesion comes to the fore due to questions of belonging and alienation directed at Muslim communities, which, as chapter 5 discussed, both prefigure and develop within the Prevent regime. Much of the literature discussed in chapter 2 has, for good reason, focused on the Muslim community as a direct target of the Prevent policy. Counter-insurgency approaches frame CONTEST as an attempt by the British state to target and silence British Muslim communities who are understood to be an internal enemy. The suspect community literature, similarly, sees Prevent as concerned with Muslims, focusing on the way police practices and security discourses produce Muslimness as suspect. This suspicion then results in Muslims being targeted unjustly by security actors, through, for instance, stop and search measures. Yet, and while not trying to minimise the burden that has fallen on Muslim communities in the UK, this reading of Prevent positions the policy as central to the development of a broader, diagrammatic approach to questions of political violence.

Prevent can instead be located as a particular means of thinking about threat, wherein early intervention is made possible through the identification of those individuals who may become violent, and the environments within which such becoming is impelled. The knowledge practices developed within Prevent, and the institutional capacities for intervention it has put in place, are translatable. It is an abstract vision of politics, in which any set of identifications that can be understood as potentially indicative of violence, can be mediated. In effect, it is to deny the potential futures that such identities, and their political and theological expressions, might produce – futures that might break no law, nor can be demonstrably said to cause harm, but which are now subject to restriction.

Conclusion

Prevent is not merely a blunt instrument with which to target and spy upon Muslims, who are now, de facto, considered the problem. Nor is it an enlightened, liberal means through which care can be utilised towards vulnerable populations in order to prevent violence. Rather, in the name of that care, it is the identification of a series of signs through which it is deemed future threat can be read. Yet this future is by necessity partial, and readings of threat are coloured: coloured by race, by religion, by politics. A series of non-illegal and non-harmful performances become intolerable based upon the threat they are seen to carry. Prevent has thus sought to shape an environment such that these performances are pre-emptively mitigated, stopping their emergence. It has then sought to enable their location, such that when they come to light, a whole network of actors is deployed, such that they can be identified and brought back to a secure identity. It is constitutive of its own boundaries; boundaries that are not sanctioned by law nor cohere with British territoriality, and are the responsibility of a vast range of professionals to police and enforce.

In demonstrating that Prevent is constitutive of a diagram of power that enacts a logic that combines security, identity and temporality, this analysis enables a reading of such power beyond its particular and often focused gaze on Muslim communities in the UK. While this is not to diminish or in any way play down the hardships that have faced Muslim communities through Prevent, in taking this approach, it brings to the fore a means of enacting government that is transferable and translatable. It sees within Prevent the problematisation of a newly understood phenomena of radicalisation. This has resulted in the generation of a new set of knowledges and practices that seek to make knowable a newly realised social space: that of individuals becoming violent. The preclusive security of Prevent, and its ambition of early intervention, thus radicalises the relation of security and identity. It temporally extends the identities deemed threatening from the harm such identities might cause, and in doing so, it extends responsibility for identifying these signs of potential future violence through society.

Prevent, through this reading, can thus be understood to have played an important role in contemporary British identity politics. It represents a central means of ordering identities as secure or risky, at the same time, producing these identities as coherent with a normalised Britishness or alienated from it. Through this ordering, it has acted to transform those identities deemed threatening, making their political expression problematic, always aware that they are liable to security interventions. In mobilising community cohesion discourses, it is a power that has transformed thought regarding the problems of communities in the UK. Ordering environments as risky, or rendering them secure and securing, it has developed into a range of mechanisms that seek to ensure 'British values' are circulated and promoted, while those identities deemed threatening are minimised. This thinking is also clear in the approach to institutions. Many are now subject to statutory duties to ensure Prevent work is carried out, constituting them as environments that promote 'British values', circulate 'British' identities, and maintain vigilance for those in their charge who might stray. It is a power that has demarcated that which, on the basis of its potential, cannot be contained within a 'British' identity, signifying its risky exterior. It is an assemblage that then intervenes into and polices these boundaries, making the expression of these threatening identities problematic.

Prevent thus functions to reproduce and police British identity, itera- tively fixing the boundaries of the political while maintaining a vigilant eye on performances of identity that may, potentially, cross it. Temporally, it fixes the threat of the future, seeking to unearth the indicators of that which may come to be a danger such that its threat can be mediated in the present. On the basis of such judgements, movement in time is prevented and halted, privileging and stabilising the current order. Spatially, it fixes the geographical and imaginative mappings of identity through the pro- duction, iteration and policing of that which is rendered external to 'Britishness'. Through such ascriptions and interventions, those identities deemed risky through the UK's security policies and practices can be identified, and the boundary that is produced articulated. This boundary is then policed. These practices produce their own economy of intelligi- bility that illuminates subjects and spaces that are ascribed vulnerability. It thus unites identity and temporality, in that it inscribes in space and time the modulated gaze of the security actor; it fixes the gaze, and as such, determines who may safely perform their identity and who may not, for to do so would be deemed risky, inviting intervention.

Note

1 David Knowles led the Hampshire Constabulary Prevent Team from 2013–16. He previously held a national Prevent role within ACPO, specialising in edu- cation and writing ACPO guidance for the education sector.

8

Conclusion

Moving full circle, it is now possible to see how the Trojan Horse scandal encapsulates the core, diagrammatic function of counter-radicalisation mobilised through Prevent. The immediate and localisable problem of the Trojan Horse allegations was not that children were being taught violent creeds, nor that any child was being actively radicalised into committing an act of violence. No evidence was found of staff engaged in radicalisation, nor adhering to violent extremism. There was no question of imminent transgression. Yet, in the conservative, Islamic space that was deemed to be being created, these school environments were seen to be set apart from a core, normalised Britishness, cutting themselves off from wider flows of identity and thus failing to prepare children for life in modern Britain. As the Clarke Report concluded, this alienation from a mainstream 'Britishness', and this promotion of a 'hardline strand of Sunni Islam raises concerns about their vulnerability to radicalisation in the future' (Clarke, 2014: 13). Existing within institutional circulations that promoted problematic identities, and minimised secure and securing 'British' ones, these children were being put at risk of being made vulnerable to radicalisation. As Nicky Morgan, then Minister for Education concluded, the response must be to tackle 'the dangers posed by extremism well before it becomes violent' (Morgan, 2014).

This enclosure thus left the children in a state of increased potential towards becoming vulnerable, and, therefore, more likely to engage with extremist, maybe even violent, ideas. Positioned at the edges of, if not beyond, a normalised Britishness, their potential for further movement, and to amass momentum, was problematic and threatening. In this way, majority Muslim schools were framed as a security risk of national import. The analysis of this book allows this reading of the Trojan Horse scandal, and, moreover, shows it to be a key example of the novel power that Prevent has constituted. These identities are produced as threatening on account of the perceived potential they are seen to contain, and, therefore, this potential must be mediated. The power this book has sought to articulate pushes the boundaries of how security and identity come to be related within the UK. When identity comes to be the preclusive object of intervention, on the basis of the potential it might contain, life, in its continual becoming, and the spaces and institutions in which this takes place, are necessarily brought within a security framework that seeks to monitor and govern this becoming.

In analysing Prevent as a specific assemblage, responding to a novel problematisation of threat, it becomes possible to situate the policy as one that is integral to understanding the terrain of the UK's contemporary identity politics. As the book has shown, this has resulted in two sets of practices, that, although they mobilise different forms of power, find coherence as a function that seeks to secure the future through transforming those identities deemed risky. The first set of practices emerge as a means of governing environments. Bringing forward an analysis of community tensions and extremism, this mobilises a policy of cohesion in order to generate communities that are more secure and securing. This same power can also be seen in its application to institutions. Both seek to manage the flows of identity within these spaces as circulations that can be intervened into. The second set of practices seek to identify those individuals at risk of radicalisation – those whose performances of identity signify a trajectory towards violent extremism – and then intervene in order to manage this risk. Both order identities in the present as secure or risky on account of their coherency with a normalised British identity, and then demand the transformation of those deemed risky. While these performances of identity break no law, they nevertheless are positioned as demanding some form of securing, in order to govern and minimise the risk of radicalisation they are seen to contain.

In identifying this power, the book has contested the reading of Prevent that is given by the policy documents, and that came through in many of the interviews carried out for this research. These political debates and their limitations form the basis of the first substantive claim of the book. Chapter 1 outlined the history of Prevent as that of a contestation within government. These debates concern the extent to which targeted interventions into processes of radicalisation, and wider questions of identity and values, should be linked. Must government focus on the former? Or should it also tackle the latter? If both, then how should they be institutionally related? The history of Prevent, as told by policymakers and the policy documents, is, therefore, one in which these security and identity strands of Prevent can, and perhaps should, be separated. The different iterations of Prevent, and the changes they have enacted in the strategy's institutional location and delivery, were read as different answers to these questions. Chapter 2 then showed that this analysis of the relation between security and identity within Prevent is reproduced by much of the academic literature. Even when ostensibly critical readings of Prevent were given, these still adhere to a reading of the 'problem' of Prevent as being that of the relation between these two strands. Critical of Prevent's wider focus, the literature has often situated the 'solution' to be the separation of the two. Chapters 1 and 2 thus outlined the dominant narrative that informs how Prevent has been understood: a narrative that problematically represents Prevent as having historically contained two, separable approaches, the first focusing on communities and the ideas and values they hold, the second focused on individuals at risk.

The second claim developed by the book was that this reading of the policy is inadequate. Rather, through providing a second reading of Prevent that outlined its problematic – that of vulnerability to radicalisation and violent extremism – a different analysis was given in chapters 3 and 4. First, it was argued that Prevent represents a novel temporal ambition, seeking, unlike previous approaches to political violence in the UK, to intervene into processes of *becoming* violent. Or, in other words, to act prior to an individual engaging in any form of illegality, or even considering such acts. Through a reading of the emerging literature on temporality and security, the term 'preclusive security' was introduced, signifying that, when securing within conditions of uncertainty, the act of the problematisation of threat is one that produces this potential harm as knowable and actionable in the present. Within the context of Prevent, it is the concept of radicalisation that structures the relation with the future, seeing life to be in the process of becoming, such that this process can then be rendered intelligible and made an object of intervention.

Chapter 4, through a discursive analysis of vulnerability and extremism, showed that Prevent traverses this temporal gap – the space between the present and the future violence one seeks to avoid – through an articulation of certain identities as threatening, rendering them intelligible as signs of potential future violence. It is those identities that are understood to be alienated or distanced from 'Britishness' and 'British values' that are positioned as vulnerable, and thus at risk of going down a pathway that may lead to violent extremism. In doing so, the uncertainty of the future is mediated in the present, allowing security to be enacted and produced by governing these identities. In illuminating this problematisation at the heart of Prevent, it demonstrates that to separate security and identity within Prevent is illusory, and that the intervention of both stem from a shared problematic. These identities may be individuals who are vulnerable, or they may be communal or institutional environments that engender vulnerabilities to radicalisation, both represent the same understanding of threat. In both, the future is secured through intervening into identities in the present.

However, read through a post-structuralist framework that emphasises the act of problematisation, these ascriptions of threat, it was argued, do not represent an objective reading of the world. Rather, they represent a set of productive practices that are constitutive of those identities deemed alienated, and thus at risk and threatening. Those identities that are produced as threatening are therefore also produced as the outside of 'Britishness' and 'British values'. Once produced as threatening due to being outside of this 'Britishness', these identities are then acted upon through Prevent, in order to bring them more in line with a secure, 'British' identity. In this process, the account of 'Britishness' within Prevent is normalised; it is produced as secure and securing. Prevent, therefore, establishes its own boundary that then requires policing and securing, enacting a diagrammatic geography that separates those identities deemed secure, and those that, in their exteriority, are rendered as potentially threatening. Prevent is thus productive of a preclusive identity politics.

On the basis of this analysis, the third claim the book made was that Prevent responds to this problematisation of threat through the production of an assemblage that enacts a diagram of counter-radicalisation. The specific modes of power, the forces Prevent deploys, were detailed in chapters 5 and 6, before the diagram as a whole was articulated in the first section of chapter 7. The argument was made that this diagram functions to produce and inscribe certain identities as alienated, and thus outside of a normalised Britishness. It is these security acts of Prevent, therefore, that serve to produce this interior and exterior, those who are deemed secure and those who must be deemed threatening in their potential. Prevent then polices this line. Not through the criminal justice system, but through mobilising the circulations of ideas and identities within communities and institutions, and the pastoral duties of care held by professionals, in order to act on these risky identifications.

Chapter 5 argued that the analysis of communities developed within conceptions of cohesion is carried through into Prevent, uniting the two policies, and providing a means for Prevent to govern communal environments that are understood to be generative of extremism, and, therefore, potentially violence. It is a theorisation of environments that allows for their transformation through a governmental focus on the circulations of ideas and identities within them. Therefore, through managing these circulations, the identities within these spaces can be effected and brought further in line with a normalised Britishness. Yet, and going beyond a purely governmental focus on naturalising circulations, that these identities contain a directionality entails that there is a need to promote 'British' identities, and negate and block access to extremist ones. These mobilisations of power were demonstrated through outlining some of the key Prevent projects that have taken as their object, and thus produced, Muslim communities in the UK as the spaces that need to be brought into line with this normalised Britishness. This analysis of problem spaces can also be seen in Prevent's approach to institutions considered to be risky. This aspect of Prevent has been in place since it began, but comes to the fore in the 2011 iteration. Spaces such as prisons, schools and universities are seen to be at risk, potentially containing, in part or in whole, closed spaces in which secure, 'British' identities are unable to circulate. Efforts have, therefore, been made to open up these spaces, and ensure that secure identities are being circulated and promoted. The Trojan Horse scandal is a key example of this focus.

Chapter 6 showed how the diagram of counter-radicalisation is mobilised in regards to individuals understood to be vulnerable to radicalisation. It provided a detailed analysis of the history and processes of the Channel project, an institutional capacity generated within Prevent in order to identify those at risk of radicalisation. Channel, it was argued, invokes a pastoral logic that works through producing the truth of the individual, and thus that which they may become. In reading the signs of an individual in the present, the vulnerability indicators they display, it becomes possible for a range of pastoral professionals to render intelligible those lives that may be on a trajectory towards violence. These indicators render certain performances of identity, such as religiosity or politics, to be of concern, potentially requiring action in the present in order to manage the threat they are seen to pose. Concretely, it was shown, the subjects of Channel's concern can be read as a series of performances of Muslimness, evident in both the vulnerability indicators that require vigilance and the documented cases of Channel interventions.

Combined, this analysis allows the book to make its core contribution, providing a detailed analysis of the diagram of counter-radicalisation, or, in other words, the power that Prevent has produced and deployed. It is a diagram that orders identities as in the process of becoming, wherein the centre exists as a secure and normalised Britishness, yet lines of becoming exist between this centre and the threatening exterior. These lines of becoming can, however, be identified through reading into these processes of becoming the clues left in the present. Moreover, environments can impel or hinder such movement, and thus are also the object of the security gaze. Within this spatiality and temporal becoming of identity, intervention is made possible through mediating these spaces and becomings, seeking to instil a secure 'Britishness' within those at risk. Identity is thus rendered as an intelligibility that discloses the future. The responsibility for identifying these spaces and subjects of problematic becoming is enmeshed throughout society, both within communities and, increasingly, within the daily work of many professions. It is a power that, therefore, generates security in the present by producing certain identities as threatening for the future, and then acting to transform these identities in the present. In so doing, it establishes its own political geography of the inside and outside, rendering certain performances of identity as risky, and, therefore, in need of preclusive mediation. In sum, what is at stake within Prevent is the production of a novel role for the state. While it is certainly the case that the state has previously sought to intervene into the identity politics of its subjects, what emerges in Prevent is the need for the state to take an active role, across a number of domains of social relations, in the *preclusive management of identity*, in order to minimise risks of extremism, violent extremism and radicalisation. A new analytic of threat has led to a new assemblage of practices which invoke a novel power; a power that mobilises society as a whole to produce and police a newly realised border between the secure internal, and those that, it is deemed, occupy the risky exterior. The book thus situates Prevent as having played a key role in producing and policing contemporary identities in the UK.

This challenges the existing literature on Prevent, urging it to go beyond an analysis that sees its interventions of security and identity as separable, and, instead, finds within Prevent a power that responds to a problematisation of threat that acts on identities, in order to produce security. Going beyond approaches that argue Muslims in the UK have been rendered as suspect or an internal enemy to be pacified, this book instead reads Prevent as the problematisation of a novel conceptualisation of threat. In constituting vulnerability to radicalisation as an object of thought, it has enabled the generation of knowledges and practices that seek to make these processes of becoming knowable and actionable. This mediation then takes racialised forms in how it has tackled Islamic radicalisation, but it is not reducible to them.

Through outlining this diagram of power, a fourth claim is made, which is that this preclusive mediation of threat has intrinsic consequences for political expression. In targeting vulnerability to radicalisation, Prevent targets the potential that life may develop into; it does not target illegality, but the spaces that may produce violent extremism, and the individuals who may become terrorists. The result is that identities that are deemed threatening are then precluded from political expression. On the one hand, to represent publicly these problematic identities, such as through Muslim politics or religiosity, is to signify a threat and thus possible intervention. On the other, it precludes such identities from engaging in the reproduction of the political order, contributing to the production of that which is a 'shared', 'core', 'British' identity. Thus, these identities, both communally and individually, that are produced as vulnerable are those that cannot be allowed on the basis of the potential threat they are seen to contain. It is a power that, therefore, has important ramifications for British identity politics. It is a power that orders identities in the UK as risky or secure, demarcating those who belong, and those whose belonging is rendered problematic because of the potential threats they may give rise to. This particular security, in taking processes of becoming as its object of intervention, thus targets the constitution of the political itself. It is a power that produces and polices its own boundary as to who is, and who is not, allowed expression and belonging within the UK.

Temporality, security, identity

This book has analysed Prevent as a diagram of power. In so doing, it has provided a discursive and textual reading of the articulations of Prevent, in order to come to an understanding of how policymakers within the UK conceptualise the contemporary threat of domestic terrorism, and how this can be averted. This reading has allowed the book to make broad claims regarding the modality of power that Prevent invokes. Yet, in abstracting the analysis to the diagram of power produced by policy articulations, there are facets of Prevent that it does not address.

First, it does not engage with Prevent as a situated, embodied, material set of practices. In affirming that discourse matters, it thus stands at odds with an approach that argues it is in the process of actualisation and translation that security is produced (Bigo, 2002; Huysmans and Buonfino, 2008; Huysmans, 2011). The security acts made visible through focusing on practices may differ radically from that which is articulated in policy. Bureaucratic politics, institutional cultures, and the specific techniques and tools utilised, might all reconfigure the security under consideration (Bigo et al., 2010; Bonelli and Ragazzi, 2014). It might well be the case that the practices of Prevent differ from, and may even exist in a perverse relation to, the policy intent. It is also the case that Prevent provision has, at times, differed markedly from one local authority to the next (interview with Senior Council Official with responsibility for Prevent delivery; Innes et al., 2011; Thomas, 2012, 2017; O'Toole et al., 2016). When, in the early years of Prevent, local authorities were responsible for allocating funds, this led to substantial regional variation in regards to what exactly Prevent did (interview with Senior Council Official with responsibility for Prevent delivery). In arguing that it is the *conceptualisation* of Prevent that matters, disclosing novel ways of thinking about the role of the state, the book does not capture or engage with the granularity of implementation, and the potential ramifications for the understanding of Prevent that such engagement might allow.

Second, in analysing Prevent as a diagram of power, the book minimises a critical race analysis that would locate Prevent as embedded within specific histories of Islamophobic and racist state practices of policing and security. Neither does it engage with the lived experiences of those affected by Prevent, who are predominantly of Muslim faith or heritage, an approach that might well situate Prevent as a series of integrally racialised practices. This book does locate the production of Prevent in relation to these histories. British Muslim communities are recognised as the key site of problematisation. But in reading Prevent as the productive operation of a diagram of power, it could be argued that the book reduces the role of Muslimness in Prevent to a contingency rather than an integral function of Prevent work. Questions of race and religiosity are therefore important to the history of Prevent, but ultimately are not considered an essential component of the power Prevent produces. The strength of this approach is that it allows the book to make a wider claim about the translatability and malleability of the modality of power organised within Prevent. However, it does so at the cost of minimising the specific, racialised histories of the policing of minority ethnic communities in the UK and broader questions of Islamophobia. It is hoped that in so doing, this reading illuminates more than it obscures. Yet for some readers, this will be a marginalisation too far, discounting the very real violences against the Muslim community within British counter-terrorism policy, in favour of this broader, abstracted account.

However, in articulating the Prevent policy as a coherent diagram of counter-radicalisation that brings together security, identity and temporality in important and novel ways, it is hoped that the book has said something meaningful about the conceptual and practical relationships between temporality, security and identity, and the politics that these linkages produce.

First, the book has sought to clarify the theoretical relation between security and temporality, contributing to the emerging literature on preclusive security. As shown in chapter 3, it is a literature that has often located acting within conditions of uncertainty to be a particularly modern problem. Yet, the argument made here is that all acts of securing threat rely upon the production of an uncertain future that, nevertheless, requires action in the present. In so doing, this future space is then itself produced through the security act. The literature has drawn important attention to contemporary security practices that self-consciously seek to act within conditions of uncertainty. Yet, it was demonstrated that this should not be ontologised as a juncture in history, but, rather, requires an analysis that privileges how security actors constitute threat. The effect of this is to shift analysis from an account of ontological shifts in contemporary security to an account that privileges the question of epistemology, and the processes through which future threats are produced.

This approach to temporality enables the book to emphasise the politics of the production of threat within conditions of uncertainty. It centres analysis on how problematisations of security traverse the temporal gap. This in turn opens up a space for political analysis, wherein the structuring of the temporal relation, and the knowledge produced to make objects of threat intelligible in the present, can be analysed and potentially contested. In demonstrating the productivity at the heart of the relation between security and temporality, the contingency of the security acts they inform can, therefore, be brought to the fore. It is to ask how certain futures become constituted as threatening and how their mediation in the present becomes possible. Thus, while there are contemporary shifts towards a focus on preclusive security, these should not be read as an ontological shift in the nature of modern threat, and, therefore, the responses to it. Rather, they represent shifting problematisations that open up demands, and also the possibilities, for early intervention into that which might, if left unmediated, become threatening. This production is, therefore, a political process, one that is informed and limited by cultural and sociological assumptions. In constituting and traversing the temporal gap, security actors structure the promise of future threats, and the possibility of action in the present.

This approach to security epistemologies thus meshes with a methodological approach of problematisation, shifting the analytical gaze to security actors and policymakers, and their discursive production of threat. Moreover, the book provides an in-depth case study of how such an analysis can be applied empirically: articulating the relation to the future established within the problematic before showing how future threats are produced as intelligible, and therefore actionable, in the present. Within Prevent, the concept of radicalisation structures the relation to the future as one in which people are in the process of becoming, and that, through an understanding of these processes, certain forms of intervention become possible. On the one hand, the environments within which becoming takes place can be pre-emptively altered. On the other, the signs of someone becoming radicalised can be made knowable. It then demonstrated that these particular methods of traversal contain an intrinsic politics, precluding the political expression of that deemed threatening. It is hoped that, in demonstrating the methodological utility of this approach, the book can impel further scholarship that attends to the temporal problematisations of threat within security practices.

Second, the book enables a reading of Prevent that situates it at the forefront of a conscious ambition by state actors to act within conditions of uncertainty. While all security within conditions of uncertainty necessarily has to traverse a temporal gap, it was also emphasised in chapter 3 that there are a series of contemporary security practices that seek to self-consciously intervene into threats before they emerge. Within the temporal ambition of Prevent, there is a clear demand from policymakers to intervene early: to manage the risk of radicalisation prior to its occurrence. As this analysis has shown, Prevent therefore enacts this temporal ambition by identifying certain identities as potentially problematic, and thus in need of mediation. In so doing, this analysis shows how Prevent radicalises the contemporary relation between security and identity, and thus contributes to a post-structuralist literature that locates the identity of the self as one that is produced through the ascription of threat to otherness and alterity. When life, as framed within Prevent, is understood as always in the process of becoming, not only is there a spatiality of the inside/outside, but there is also a temporality of the life that may become outside and the life that, it is presumed, will not. In emphasising the importance of Prevent's temporal ambition to intervene prior to the emergence of threat, the book therefore troubles an analysis of security and identity that serves to merely demarcate the self and alterity.

Moreover, this reading allows for a clear understanding of the political implications of Prevent, and opens up a window onto the contemporary security ambitions of state actors. In shifting the security gaze to early intervention, it is identities in their potential that require attention and, potentially, mediation. This therefore redefines and extends the scope of both those who must maintain vigilance for signs of threat, and those subject to these security interventions. As the diagram of counter-radicalisation showed, Prevent has produced a topology within which those identities that have broken no law, and may never go on to represent a threat on Prevent's own terms, may now be considered risky due to the potential they are seen to contain. The environment within which people move, and the signs that might indicate the trajectory their life is taking, are now intimate security concerns. This analysis, therefore, pushes scholarship to consider the ways in which threats are produced as knowable and actionable in the present. In regard to identity, this entails that it is not merely the other who must be mediated, but those who are seen to exhibit potentials for becoming other, and the environments seen to be conducive to such movement.

Further, as is evident though the mainstreaming of Prevent work, the duty to keep watch for signs of radicalisation has been extended into the day-to-day work of a number of pastoral professions. Possessing the required expertise to analyse and judge performances of identity that might indicate a risk is now a core responsibility within the daily work of millions who have duties of care towards those they work with. While produced as a power of care, these duties and interventions are, nevertheless, those of security, creating those who must engage with them as key actors in policing the boundaries of British identity. When all life is in the process of becoming, the relation between security and identity becomes embedded within a temporality that demands life processes in their entirety be rendered intelligible to the security gaze. In so doing, life, and the spaces within which it becomes, become the intimate objects of security, such that response can co-emerge with the threat.

What thus emerges in this reading of Prevent is a vision of security that, working through the whole of society, seeks to make visible and knowable signs of future threat prior to their emergence, such that this risk can be preclusively managed. In this regard, the reading given here goes beyond the bounds of the UK's Prevent strategy. First, it invites comparative reading and explanation of other counter-radicalisation strategies. While the UK can be considered as a trailblazer of the policy, the last decade has seen Prevent or Prevent-like instruments adopted across the world. Policies are now in place across North America, Western and Northern Europe, Australasia, the Middle East and the European Union. The reading provided here situates a 'normalised Britishness' as central to understanding the operations of power in the UK context. Comparator policies in other countries differ in their specifics, but, the broad approach outlined in this book, charting the mechanisms through which counter-radicalisation both produces and then enables preclusive intervention, would enable a clearer understanding of the power they produce. Further research would seek to map differences and continuities, charting the genealogy of the diagram identified in this book, and its translation and application in other countries and contexts.

Second, this reading allows Prevent to be situated at the forefront of a number of state security policies which, in seeking to consciously act within conditions of uncertainty, can be considered operations of preclusive security. From the utilisation of big data in order to predict the future, and those who may harm it (see Amoore and de Goede, 2008b; Amoore, 2009), to transformation in the policing of protest, and the use of precautionary arrests and banning orders, the UK (and other states) have developed security numerous mechanisms that seek to act on potential future harms in explicit contexts of uncertainty. The future of security, it would seem, is increasingly preclusive. The questions posed by this analysis, are what sort of threats are thus being produced in the anxieties of security actors? Who and what is made visible as risky? What assemblages are being mobilised in order to preclusively act on such risks? And what politics is at stake in such security mechanisms?

The answer to those questions in regards to Prevent are worrying. This analysis has troubled and contested a security analysis which would see Prevent as an objective response to the threat of radicalisation, but instead, shows how Prevent represents a productive site, ordering, and seeking to transform, identities in the present such that it can manage the threats it envisages for the future. In doing so, Prevent has carved out an important role for the state, enacting a function that preclusively manages identities in order to produce and promote those considered to be both secure and securing, and minimise those deemed to be risky.

This function has spread and extended across many facets of social relations. The logic that Prevent has enacted is increasingly important, governing many aspects of British life. It informs social work decisions on whether parents are putting children at risk due to espoused ideologies;

it informs schooling in the UK, demanding a pedagogical focus on 'British values'; it governs who is and is not allowed to speak on university campuses, and who can only speak with appropriate challenge; it is a part of the decision-making progress concerning visa applications to the UK; and it guides regulation on online content and what we do, or do not, see when accessing the internet. It takes effect as a both a governmental, pre-emptive approach to the management of circulations of identity across communities and institutional spaces, and it takes effect as precautionary, pastoral interventions into those deemed to be at risk. Moreover, it is a function with a temporal ambition that is extendable, pushing ever-further temporally away from the enactment of the violence that is being precluded. Within the Counter-Extremism strategy, what is at stake are a series of legal and non-legal instruments that continue to extend the problem of extremism ever-temporally further from the act of terrorism: that the genesis of the act can be traced ever further back into the political or theological articulations from which it is deemed a potential, yet nevertheless causal, result.

In situating Prevent at the intersection of security, identity and temporality, this book has thus articulated a reading of Prevent that situates it as central to the identity politics of the UK, ordering and normalising that life deemed coherent and secure, and producing, excluding and seeking to transform that deemed alienated and risky. Prevent has played a key role in producing the boundaries of the 'British' interior. Prevent's significance, to date, has been underestimated. It is, as this book has explored and brought to the fore, a novel way of thinking about threat. It demands security of that which, on its own terms, may never represent a danger. It is a power that temporally extends who must be secured, reading expressions of identity in the present as a potential risk for the future. It thus expands who must enact this security. Security as a life process demands vigilance of all life, and in all the spaces life inhabits. Already, these temporal ambitions are being extended, further divorcing the threat being managed from the signs in the present that render it knowable and actionable. It is a seductive power, promising to preclude the possibility of future violence through early intervention, utilising soft policing, community engagement and mentoring. Yet, as this book has shown, this is not without consequence. It enacts a boundary of who can securely express their identity, and who, in being deemed alienated, cannot, due to the threat such identity is seen to potentially contain. The book shows that Prevent has played a crucial role in producing and policing the boundaries of contemporary British identity. It is a power that has had profound consequences for life in the UK; it is a power that shows no sign of abating.

References

Abbas, M. (2018), 'Producing "internal suspect bodies": Divisive effects of UK counter-terrorism measures on Muslim communities in Leeds and Bradford' *The British Journal of Sociology* [online first], DOI: 10.1111/1468–4446.12366.

ACPO (Association of Chief Police Officers) (2009), *Prevent, Police and Schools: Guidance for Police Officers and Police Staff to Help Schools Contribute to the Prevention of Violent Extremism*, London: ACPO.

ACPO (Association of Chief Police Officers) (2012a), *Prevent, Police and Colleges: Guidance for Police Officers & Police Staff to Help Colleges Contribute to the Prevention of Terrorism* [online]. Available at: www.npcc.police.uk/documents/TAM/2012/201205TAMPreventPandCollGui.pdf (accessed on 26 January 2016).

ACPO (Association of Chief Police Officers) (2012b), *Prevent, Police and Universities: Guidance for Police Officers and Police Staff to Help Higher Education Institutions Contribute to the Prevention of Terrorism* [online]. Available at: www.acpo.police.uk/documents/TAM/2012/201205TAMPrevent PandUniGui.pdf (accessed on 28 June 2012).

Adams, R. (2014), 'Is the Trojan Horse row just a witch hunt triggered by a hoax?', *Guardian*, 8 June [online]. Available at: www.theguardian.com/education/2014/jun/08/trojan-horse-extremism-political-storm-michael-gove-ofsted (accessed on 25 January 2016).

Adams, R. (2016), 'Teachers back motion calling for Prevent strategy to be scrapped', *Guardian*, 28 March [online]. Available at: www.theguardian.com/politics/2016/mar/28/teachers-nut-back-motion-calling-prevent-strategy-radicalisation-scrapped (accessed on 9 February 2018).

Ali, N. (2014), 'Mapping the Muslim community: The politics of counter-radicalisation in Britain' in C. Baker-Beall, C. Heath-Kelly and L. Jarvis (eds), *Counter-Radicalisation: Critical Perspectives*, Abingdon and New York: Routledge, 139–155.

Amin, A. (2002), 'Ethnicity and the multicultural city: Living with diversity' *Environment and Planning A*, 43, 959–980.

Amoore, L. (2009), 'Algorithmic war: Everyday geographies of the war on terror' *Antipode*, 41 (1), 49–69.

Amoore, L. and M. de Goede (eds) (2008a), *Risk and the War on Terror*, New York and Abingdon: Routledge.

Amoore, L. and M. de Goede (2008b), 'Transactions after 9/11: The banal face of preemptive strike' *Transactions of the Institute of British Geographers*, 33 (2), 173–185.

Anderson, B. (2010a), 'Pre-emption, precaution, preparedness: Anticipatory action and future geographies' *Progress in Human Geography*, 34 (6), 777–798.

Anderson, B. (2010b), 'Security and the future: Anticipating the event of terror' *Geoforum*, 41, 227–235.

Anderson, B. and P. Adey (2012), 'Governing events and life: "Emergency" in UK civil contingencies' *Political Geography*, 31, 24–33.

Aradau, C. and R. van Munster (2007), 'Governing terrorism through risk: Taking precautions (un)knowing the future' *European Journal of International Relations*, 13(1), 89–115.

Aradau, C. and R. van Munster (2008), 'Taming the future: The *dispositif* of risk in the war on terror' in L. Amoore and M. de Goede (eds), *Risk and the War on Terror*, London and New York: Routledge, 23–40.

Aradau, C. and R. van Munster (2011), *Politics of Catastrophe: Genealogies of the Unknown*, London and New York: Routledge.

Ashley, R. K. (1988), 'Untying the sovereign state: A double reading of the anarchy problematique' *Millennium: Journal of International Studies*, 17 (2), 227–262.

Awan, I. (2012), '"I am a Muslim not an extremist": How the Prevent strategy has constructed a "suspect" community' *Politics & Policy*, 40 (6), 1158–1185.

Bartelson, J. (1995), *A Genealogy of Sovereignty*, Cambridge: Cambridge University Press.

Bartlett, J., J. Birdwell and M. King (2010), *The Edge of Violence*, Demos [online]. Available at: www.demos.co.uk/files/Edge_of_Violence_-_full_-_web.pdf?1291806916 (accessed on 21 January 2013).

BBC News (2005), 'Blair vows hard line on fanatics', *BBC News*, 5 August [online]. Available at: http://news.bbc.co.uk/1/hi/uk/4747573.stm (accessed on 25 January 2016).

BBC News (2007), 'Five get life over UK bomb plot', *BBC News*, 30 April [online]. Available at: http://news.bbc.co.uk/1/hi/uk/6195914.stm (accessed on 25 January 2016).

Beck, U. (2002), 'The terrorist threat: World risk society revisited' *Theory, Culture & Society*, 19 (4), 39–55.

Beck, U. (2003), 'The silence of words: On terror and war' *Security Dialogue*, 34 (3), 255–267.

Benjamin, D. and S. Simon (2002), *The Age of Sacred Terror*, New York: Random House.

Bettison, N. (2009), 'Preventing violent extremism: A police response' *Policing*, 3 (2), 129–138.

Bigo, D. (2002), 'Security and immigration: Toward a critique of the governmentality of unease' *Alternatives*, 27, 63–92.

Bigo, D., P. Bonditti and C. Olson (2010), 'Mapping the European field of security professionals', in D. Bigo, S. Carrera, E. Guild and R. B. J. Walker (eds), *Europe's 21st Century Security Challenge: Delivering Liberty*, Farnham: Ashgate, 49–64.

Birt, Y. (2009), 'Preventing virulent envy: Reconsidering the UK's terrorist prevention strategy' *RUSI Journal*, 154 (4), 52–58.

Blair, T. (2003), 'Tony Blair's speech to the US Congress', 18 July [online]. Available at: www.theguardian.com/politics/2003/jul/18/iraq.speeches (accessed on 19 September 2016).

Bleich, E. (2009), 'State responses to "Muslim" violence: A comparison of six West European countries' *Journal of Ethnic and Migration Studies*, 35 (3), 361–379.

Bleich, E. (2010), 'Faith and state: British policy responses to "Islamist" extremism', in R. Eatwell and M. Goodwin (eds), *The 'New' Extremism in Twenty-First-Century Britain*, Abingdon: Routledge, 67–84.

Bonelli, L. and F. Ragazzi (2014), 'Low-tech security: Files, notes, and memos as technologies of anticipation' *Security Dialogue*, 45 (5), 476–493.

The Bradford District Race Review Panel (2001), *Community Pride not Prejudice: Making Diversity Work in Bradford* (chaired by Sir Herman Ouseley) [online]. Available at: http://resources.cohesioninstitute.org.uk/Publications/Documents/Document/DownloadDocumentsFile.aspx?recordId=98&file=PDFversion (accessed on 26 January 2016).

Breen-Smyth, M. (2014), 'Theorising the "suspect community": Counterterrorism, security practices and the public imagination' *Critical Studies on Terrorism*, 7 (2), 223–240.

Briggs, R. (2010), 'Community engagement for counterterrorism: Lessons from the UK' *International Affairs*, 86 (4), 971–981.

Briggs, R., C. Fieschi and H. Lownsborough (2006), *Bringing It Home: Community-Based Approaches to Counter-Terrorism*, London: Demos.

Brighton, S. (2007), 'British Muslims, multiculturalism and UK foreign policy: "Integration" and "cohesion" in and beyond the state' *International Affairs*, 83 (1), 1–17.

Brown, K. E. and T. Saeed (2015), 'Radicalization and counter-radicalization at British universities: Muslim encounters and alternatives' *Ethnic and Racial Studies*, 38 (11), 1952–1968.

Burnley Task Force (2001), *Burnley Speaks, Who Listens?* (chaired by Tony Clarke) [online]. Available at: http://resources.cohesioninstitute.org.uk/Publications/Documents/Document/DownloadDocumentsFile.aspx?recordId=95&file=PDFversion (accessed on 26 January 2016).

Butler, J. (2006), *Precarious Life: The Powers of Mourning and Violence*, London and New York: Verso.

Cabinet Office (2010), *Securing Britain in an Age of Uncertainty: The Strategic Defence and Security Review*, London: Her Majesty's Stationery Office.

Cabinet Office (2013), *Tackling Extremism in the UK: Report from the Prime Minister's Task Force on Tackling Radicalisation and Extremism*, London: Cabinet Office.

CAGE (2015), *Failing Our Communities: A Case Study Approach to Understanding Prevent*, London: CAGE Advocacy UK Ltd.

Cameron, D. (2011), *PM's Speech at Munich Security Conference*, 5 February [online]. Available at: www.gov.uk/government/speeches/pms-speech-at-munich-security-conference (accessed on 26 January, 2016).

Campbell, D. (1998a), *Writing Security: United States Foreign Policy and the Politics of Identity*, revised edition, Manchester: Manchester University Press.

Campbell, D. (1998b), 'Why fight: Humanitarianism, principles and post-structuralism' *Millennium – Journal of International Studies*, 27 (3), 497–521.

Cantle, T. (2005), *Community Cohesion: A New Framework for Race and Diversity*, Basingstoke and New York: Palgrave Macmillan.

Casciani, D. (2005), 'Analysis: Segregated Britain?', *BBC News*, 22 September [online]. Available at: http://news.bbc.co.uk/1/hi/technology/4270010.stm (accessed on 26 January 2016).

Casciani, D. (2006), 'Minister backs new Muslim group', *BBC News*, 19 July [online]. Available at: http://news.bbc.co.uk/1/hi/uk/5193402.stm (accessed on 25 January 2016).

Casey, L. (2016), *The Casey Review: A Review into Opportunity and Integration*, commissioned by the Department for Communities and Local Government [online]. Available at: https://assets.publishing.service.gov.uk/government/uploads/system/uploads/attachment_data/file/575973/The_Casey_Review_Report.pdf (accessed on 28 May 2018).

Clarke, P. (2014), *Report into Allegations Concerning Birmingham Schools Arising from the 'Trojan Horse' Letter*, London: Her Majesty's Stationery Office.

Collier, S. J. and A. Lakoff (2008), 'Distributed preparedness: The spatial logic of domestic security in the United States' *Environment and Planning D: Society and Space*, 26 (1), 7–28.

Collier, S. J. and A. Lakoff (2009), *On Vital Systems Security*, International Affairs Working Paper 2009–01.

Commission of the European Communities (2000), *Communication from the Commission on the Precautionary Principle* [online]. Available at: http://ec.europa.eu/dgs/health_consumer/library/pub/pub07_en.pdf (accessed on 29 May 2013).

Communities and Local Government Committee (2010), *Preventing Violent Extremism*, HC 65, Sixth Report of Session 2009–2010.

Connolly, W. E. (1991), *Identity/Difference: Democratic Negotiations of Political Paradox*, Ithaca: Cornell University Press.

Dalgaard-Nielsen, A. (2010), 'Violent radicalization in Europe: What we know and what we do not know' *Studies in Conflict & Terrorism*, 33 (9), 797–814.

Davies, L. (2016), 'Security, extremism and education: Safeguarding or surveillance?' *British Journal of Educational Studies*, 64 (1), 1–19.

DCLG (Department for Communities and Local Government) (2007), *Preventing Violent Extremism: Winning Hearts and Minds*, Wetherby: Communities and Local Government Publications.

DCLG (Department for Communities and Local Government) (2008a), *Preventing Violent Extremism Pathfinder Fund: Mapping of Project Activities 2007/2008*, Wetherby: Communities and Local Government Publications.

DCLG (Department for Communities and Local Government) (2008b), *Empowering Muslim Women: Case Studies*, Wetherby: Communities and Local Government Publications.

DCLG (Department for Communities and Local Government) (2008c), *Preventing Violent Extremism: Next Steps for Communities*, Wetherby: Communities and Local Government Publications.

DCLG (Department for Communities and Local Government) (2012), *Creating the Conditions for Integration* [online]. Available at: www.gov.uk/government/uploads/system/uploads/attachment_data/file/7504/2092103.pdf   (accessed on 26 January 2016).

DCSF (Department for Children, Schools and Families) (2008a), *Learning Together to be Safe: A Toolkit to Help Schools Contribute to the Prevention of Violent Extremism* [online]. Available at: www.education.gov.uk/publications/eOrderingDownload/00804–2008BKT-EN.pdf (accessed on 28 June 2012).

DCSF (Department for Children, Schools and Families) (2008b), *Learning Together to be Safe: A Toolkit to Help Colleges Contribute to the Prevention of Violent Extremism* [online]. Available at: www.education.gov.uk/consultations/downloadableDocs/17132_DIUS_Learning_Be_Safe.pdf (accessed on 27 January 2016).

de Goede, M. (2008), 'Beyond risk: Premediation and the post-9/11 security imagination' *Security Dialogue*, 39 (2–3), 155–176.

de Goede, M. and S. Simon (2013), 'Governing future radicals in Europe' *Antipode*, 45 (2), 315–335.

de Goede, M., S. Simon and M. Hoijtink (2014), 'Performing preemption' *Security Dialogue*, 45 (5), 411–422.

Deacon, R. (2000), 'Theory as practice: Foucault's concept of problematization' *Telos*, Winter, 118, 127–142.

Dean, M. (2010), *Governmentality: Power and Rule in Modern Society*, 2nd edition, London: Sage Publications.

Deleuze, G. (1986), *Nietzsche and Philosophy*, trans. Hugh Tomlinson, London and New York: Continuum.

Deleuze, G. (2006), *Foucault*, London, New Delhi, New York and Sydney: Bloomsbury.

Deleuze, G. and F. Guattari (1987) [2002], *A Thousand Plateaus: Capitalism and Schizophrenia*, trans. Brian Massumi, London and New York: Continuum.

Department of Health (2011), *Building Partnerships, Staying Safe: The Health Sector Contribution to HM Government's Prevent Strategy: Guidance for Healthcare Workers* [online]. Available at: www.nhserewash.com/safeguarding/dh_131912%20prevent.pdf (accessed on 28 June 2012).

DfE (Department for Education) (2014), *Promoting Fundamental British Values as Part of SMSC in Schools: Departmental Advice for Maintained Schools* [online]. Available at: www.gov.uk/government/uploads/system/uploads/attachment_data/file/380595/SMSC_Guidance_Maintained_Schools.pdf (accessed on 27 January 2016).

DfE (Department for Education) (2015), *The Prevent Duty: Departmental Advice for School and Childcare Providers* [online]. Available at: https://assets.publishing.service.gov.uk/government/uploads/system/uploads/attachment_data/file/439598/prevent-duty-departmental-advice-v6.pdf (accessed on 28 May 2018).

Dodd, V. (2015), 'School questioned Muslim pupil about Isis after discussion on eco-activism', *Guardian*, 22 September [online]. Available at: www.theguardian.com/education/2015/sep/22/school-questioned-muslim-pupil-about-isis-after-discussion-on-eco-activism (accessed on 19 September 2016).

Durodié, B. (2016), 'Securitising education to prevent terrorism or losing direction?' *British Journal of Educational Studies*, 64 (1), 21–35.

Edkins, J. (1999), *Poststructuralism and International Relations: Bringing the Political Back In*, Boulder and London: Lynne Rienner.

Education Committee (2014), *Oral Evidence: Extremism in Schools*, 9 July [online]. Available at: http://data.parliament.uk/writtenevidence/committeeevidence. svc/evidencedocument/education-committee/extremism-in-schools/oral/ 11342.html (accessed on 25 January 2016).

Fortier, A. (2010), 'Proximity by design? Affective citizenship and the management of unease' *Citizenship Studies*, 14 (1), 17–30.

Foucault, M. (1978), *The History of Sexuality. Volume 1: An Introduction*, trans. Robert Hurley, New York: Pantheon Books.

Foucault, M. (1982), 'The subject and power' *Critical Inquiry*, 8 (4), 777–795.

Foucault, M. (1990), 'The concern for truth' in Lawrence Kritzman (ed.), *Politics, Philosophy, Culture: Interviews and Other Writings 1977–1984*, London and New York: Routledge, 255–270.

Foucault, M. (1991a), 'Truth and power' in P. Rabinow (ed.), *The Foucault Reader: An Introduction to Foucault's Thought*, St. Ives: Penguin Books, 51–75.

Foucualt, M. (1991b), 'Nietzsche, genealogy, history' in P. Rabinow (ed.), *The Foucault Reader: An Introduction to Foucault's Thought*, St. Ives: Penguin Books, 76–100.

Foucault, M. (1995), *Discipline and Punish: The Birth of the Prison*, trans. Alan Sheridan, 2nd edition, New York: Vintage Books.

Foucault, M. (2000), 'Polemics, politics and problematizations' in P. Rabinow (ed.), *Essential Works of Foucault: Vol. 1 Ethics*, Chippenham: Penguin, 111–119.

Foucault, M. (2007), *Security, Territory, Population: Lectures at the Collège de France, 1977–78*, trans. Graham Burchell and ed. Michel Senellart, Chippenham: Palgrave Macmillan.

Ghannoushi, S. (2008), 'The Blears fallacy', *Guardian*, 25 July [online]. Available at: www.theguardian.com/commentisfree/2008/jul/25/islam.religion (accessed on 27 January 2016).

Gilligan, A. (2014), 'Trojan Horse: How the *Guardian* ignored and misrepresented evidence of Islamism in schools', *Telegraph*, 9 June [online]. Available at: http:// blogs.telegraph.co.uk/news/andrewgilligan/100275346/trojan-horse-how-the-guardian-ignored-and-misrepresented-evidence-of-islamism-in-schools/ ?utm_source=dlvr.it&utm_medium=twitter (accessed on 25 January 2016).

Githens-Mazer, J. (2010), 'Mobilization, recruitment, violence and the street: Radical violent takfiri Islamism in early Twenty-First-Century-Britain' in R. Eatwell and M. Goodwin (eds), *The 'New' Extremism in Twenty-First-Century Britain*, Abingdon: Routledge, 47–66.

Githens-Mazer, J. and R. Lambert (2010), 'Why conventional wisdom on radicalization fails: The persistence on a failed discourse' *International Affairs*, 86 (4), 889–901.

Goldberg, D., S. Jadhav and T. Younis (2017), 'Prevent: What is pre-criminal space?' *British Journal of Psychiatry Bulletin*, 41, 208–211.

Grusin, R. (2004), 'Premediation' *Criticism*, 46 (1), 17–39.

Guardian (2001), 'Full text of David Blunkett's speech' [online]. Available at: www. guardian.co.uk/politics/2001/dec/11/immigrationpolicy.race (accessed on 2 July 2012).

Guardian (2014), 'Ofsted credibility at stake over "Trojan Horse" schools enquiry', 3 June [online]. Available at: www.theguardian.com/education/2014/jun/03/ ofsted-credibility-at-stake-trojan-horse (accessed on 25 January 2016).

Gutkowski, S. (2011), 'Secularism and the politics of risk: Britain's Prevent agenda, 2005–9' *International Relations*, 25 (3), 346–362.

Hastings, C. (2006), 'Revealed: How the BBC used MI5 to vet thousands of staff', *Telegraph*, 2 July [online]. Available at: www.telegraph.co.uk/news/uknews/ 1522875/Revealed-how-the-BBC-used-MI5-to-vet-thousands-of-staff.html (accessed on 16 September 2016).

HC Deb 14 November (2007), cc. 669–670, 'National security'.

HC Deb 9 November (2010), c. WS13, 'Prevent review/new independent reviewer of terrorism legislation'.

Heath-Kelly, C. (2012), 'Reinventing prevention or exposing the gap? False positives in UK terrorism governance and the quest for pre-emption' *Critical Studies on Terrorism*, 5 (1), 67–85.

Heath-Kelly, C. (2013), 'Counter-terrorism and the counterfactual: Producing the "radicalisation" discourse and the UK PREVENT strategy' *The British Journal of Politics and International Relations*, 15 (3), 394–415.

Heath-Kelly, C. (2017), 'Algorithmic autoimmunity in the NHS: Radicalisation and the clinic' *Security Dialogue*, 48 (1), 29–45.

Heath-Kelly, C. and E. Strausz (2018), *Counter-Terrorism in the NHS: Evaluating Prevent Duty Safeguarding in the NHS* [online]. Available at: https://warwick. ac.uk/fac/soc/pais/research/researchcentres/irs/counterterrorisminthenhs/ project_report_60pp.pdf (accessed on 28 May 2018).

Hewitt, S. (2008), *The British War on Terror: Terrorism and Counter-Terrorism on the Home Front Since 9/11*, Trowbridge: Continuum.

Hill, R. (2017), 'Counter-extremism in British schools: Ensuring respect for parents' rights over their children's religious upbringing' *British Journal of Educational Studies*, DOI: 10.1080/00071005.2017.1417540.

Hillyard, P. (1993), *Suspect Community: People's Experience of the Prevention of Terrorism Acts in Britain*, London: Pluto Press.

Hoffman, B. (2006), *Inside Terrorism*, revised and expanded edition, New York: Columbia University Press.

Holmwood, J. and T. O'Toole (2018), *Countering Extremism in British Schools? The Truth about the Birmingham Trojan Horse Affair*, Poole: Policy Press.

Home Affairs Committee (2005), *Terrorism and Community Relations*, HC 165-I, Sixth Report of Session 2004–05, Volume 1.

Home Affairs Committee (2012), *Roots of Radicalisation*, HC 1446, Nineteenth Report of Session 2010–12, Volume 1.

Home Office (2001a), *Community Cohesion: A Report of the Independent Review Team* (chaired by Ted Cantle), London: The Home Office.

Home Office (2001b), *Building Cohesive Communities: A Report of the Ministerial Group on Public Order and Community Cohesion* (chaired by John Denham), London: The Home Office.

Home Office (2004), *The End of Parallel Lives? The Report on the Community Cohesion Panel*, London: Her Majesty's Stationery Office.

Home Office (2005a), *Improving Opportunity, Strengthening Society: The Government's Strategy to Increase Race Equality and Community Cohesion* [online]. Available at: http://resources.cohesioninstitute.org.uk/Publications/Documents/Document/DownloadDocumentsFile.aspx?recordId=83&file=PDFversion (accessed on 3 June 2016).

Home Office (2005b), *Terrorism and Community Relations: The Government Reply to the Sixth Report from the Home Affairs Committee Session 2004–05*, London: The Stationery Office.

Home Office (2005c), *'Preventing Extremism Together' Working Groups: August-October 2005* [online]. Available at: http://webarchive.nationalarchives.gov.uk/20120919132719/http://www.communities.gov.uk/documents/communities/pdf/152164.pdf (accessed on 12 April 2013).

Home Office (2005d), *Preventing Extremism Together: Response to Working Group Reports* [online]. Available at: http://webarchive.nationalarchives.gov.uk/20120919132719/http://www.communities.gov.uk/documents/communities/pdf/151978.pdf (accessed on 12 April 2013).

Home Office (2006), *Countering International Terrorism: The United Kingdom's Strategy*, London: Her Majesty's Stationery Office.

Home Office (2009a), *The United Kingdom's Strategy for Countering International Terrorism*, London: Her Majesty's Stationery Office.

Home Office (2009b), *Memorandum Submitted by the Home Office* [online]. Available at: www.publications.parliament.uk/pa/cm200809/cmselect/cmhaff/212/212we13.htm (accessed on 12 April 2013).

Home Office (2009c), *Delivering the Prevent Strategy: An Updated Guide for Local Partners* [online]. Available at: http://webarchive.nationalarchives.gov.uk/20120919132719/www.communities.gov.uk/publications/deliveringpreventguideupdate (accessed on 27 January 2016).

Home Office (2010), *Channel: Supporting Individuals Vulnerable to Recruitment by Violent Extremists. A Guide for Local Partnerships*, London: Home Office.

Home Office (2011a), *Prevent Strategy*, London: Her Majesty's Stationery Office.

Home Office (2011b), *CONTEST: The United Kingdom's Strategy for Countering Terrorism*, London: Her Majesty's Stationery Office.

Home Office (2012), *Channel: Protecting Vulnerable People from Being Drawn into Terrorism – A Guide for Local Partners* [online]. Available at: www.gov.uk/government/uploads/system/uploads/attachment_data/file/118194/channel-guidance.pdf (accessed on 12 April 2013).

Home Office (2013), *CONTEST: The United Kingdom's Strategy for Countering Terrorism Annual Report*, London: Her Majesty's Stationery Office.

Home Office (2014), *Workshop to Raise Awareness of Prevent: Full Workshop Script*, London: Home Office.

Home Office (2015a), *Counter-Extremism Strategy*, London: Her Majesty's Stationery Office.

Home Office (2015b), *Prevent Duty Guidance: For Further Education Institutions in England and Wales* [online]. Available at: https://assets.publishing.service.gov.uk/government/uploads/system/uploads/attachment_data/file/445915/Prevent_Duty_Guidance_For_Further_Education__England__Wales_-Interactive.pdf (accessed on 28 May 2018).

Home Office (2015c), *Prevent Duty Guidance: For Higher Education Institutions in England and Wales* [online]. Available at: https://assets.publishing.service. gov.uk/government/uploads/system/uploads/attachment_data/file/445916/ Prevent_Duty_Guidance_For_Higher_Education__England__Wales_.pdf (accessed on 28 May 2018).

Home Office (2016), *CONTEST: The United Kingdom's Strategy for Countering Terrorism: Annual Report for 2015*, London: Her Majesty's Stationery Office.

Home Office (2017), *Individuals Referred to and Supported Through the Prevent Programme, April 2015 to March 2016* [online]. Available at: www.gov.uk/government/uploads/system/uploads/attachment_data/file/662824/individuals-referred-supported-prevent-programme-apr2015-mar2016.pdf (accessed on 23 December 2017).

Home Office (2018a), 'Charter for the commission for countering extremism', Home Office [online]. Available at: www.gov.uk/government/publications/charter-for-the-commission-for-countering-extremism/charter-for-the-commission-for-countering-extremism (accessed on 28 May 2018).

Home Office (2018b), *Individuals Referred to and Supported through the Prevent Programme, April 2016 to March 2017* [online]. Available at: https://assets. publishing.service.gov.uk/government/uploads/system/uploads/attachment_ data/file/694002/individuals-referred-supported-prevent-programme-apr2016-mar2017.pdf (accessed on 28 May 2017).

Home Office (2018c), *CONTEST: The United Kingdom's Strategy for Countering Terrorism*, London: Her Majesty's Stationery Office.

Hooper, S. (2015), 'Stifling freedom of expression in UK schools', *Al Jazeera*, 23 July [online]. Available at: www.aljazeera.com/indepth/features/2015/07/ stifling-freedom-expression-uk-schools-150721080612049.html (accessed on 19 September 2016).

Horgan, J. (2008), 'From profiles to pathways and roots to routes: Perspectives from psychology on radicalization into terrorism' *Annals of the American Academy of Political and Social Science*, 618, 80–94.

Huysmans, J. (2011), 'What's in an act? On security speech acts and little security nothings' *Security Dialogue*, 42 (4–5), 371–383.

Huysmans, J. and A. Buonfino (2008), 'Politics of exception and unease: Immigration, asylum and terrorism in parliamentary debates in the UK' *Political Studies*, 56, 766–788.

Innes, M., C. Roberts and H. Innes (2011), *Assessing the Effects of Prevent Policing* [online]. Available at: www.npcc.police.uk/documents/TAM/2011/ PREVENT%20Innes%200311%20Final%20send%202.pdf (accessed on 27 January 2016).

Intelligence and Security Committee (2006), *Report into the London Terrorist Attacks on 7 July 2005* (chaired by Paul Murphy), London: The Stationery Office Ltd.

The Iraq Inquiry (2011), *Evidence of the Rt. Hon. Tony Blair*, The Iraq Inquiry [online]. Available at: www.iraqinquiry.org.uk/media/50865/20110121-Blair. pdf (accessed on 14 April 2012).

Jackson, W. (2013), 'Securitisation as depoliticisation: Depoliticisation as pacification' *Socialist Studies*, 9 (2), 146–166.

Kassimeris, G. and L. Jackson (2012), 'British Muslims and the discourses of dysfunction: Community cohesion and counterterrorism in the West Midlands' *Critical Studies on Terrorism*, 5 (2), 179–196.

Kepel, G. (2004), *The War for Muslim Minds: Islam and the West*, trans. Pascale Ghazaleh, Cambridge, MA and London: The Belknap Press of Harvard University Press.

Kepel, G. (2008), *Beyond Terrorism and Martyrdom: The Future of the Middle East*, Cambridge, MA and London: The Belknap Press of Harvard University Press.

King, M. and M. D. Taylor (2011), 'The radicalization of homegrown jihadists: A review of the theoretical models and social psychological evidence' *Terrorism and Political Violence*, 23, 602–622.

Knowles, D. (2015), '"Prevent" in education within Hampshire', *openDemocracy*, 15 January [online]. Available at: www.opendemocracy.net/david-knowles/ %E2%80%98prevent%E2%80%99-in-education-within-hampshire (accessed on 29 January 2016).

Kundnani, A. (2001), 'From Oldham to Bradford: The violence of the violated', Institute of Race Relations [online]. Available at: www.irr.org.uk/news/from-oldham-to-bradford-the-violence-of-the-violated/ (accessed on 19 September 2016).

Kundnani, A. (2007), *The End of Tolerance: Racism in 21st Century Britain*, London and Ann Arbor: Pluto Press.

Kundnani, A. (2009), *Spooked: How Not to Prevent Violent Extremism*, London: Institute of Race Relations.

Kundnani, A. (2012), 'Radicalisation: The journey of a concept' *Race & Class*, 54 (2), 3–25.

Kundnani, A. (2014), *The Muslims are Coming: Islamophobia, Extremism and the Domestic War on Terror*, London and Brooklyn: Verso.

Kymlicka, W. (1995), *Multicultural Citizenship: A Liberal Theory of Minority Rights*, Clarendon: Oxford University Press.

Laclau, E. and C. Mouffe (2001), *Hegemony and Socialist Strategy: Towards a Radical Democratic Politics*, 2nd edition, London and New York: Verso.

Laqueur, W. (1999), *The New Terrorism: Fanaticism and the Arms of Mass Destruction*, New York: Oxford University Press.

Lentin, A. and G. Titley (2011), *The Crisis of Multiculturalism: Racism in a Neoliberal Age*, London and New York: Zed Books.

Local Government Association (2002), *Guidance on Community Cohesion*, London: Local Government Association.

Local Government Association (2008), *Leading the Preventing Violent Extremism Agenda: A Role Made for Councillors*, London: Local Government Association.

Mackinlay, J. (2009), *The Insurgent Archipelago: From Mao to Bin Laden*, London: Hurst and Company.

Maguire, T. J. (2015), 'Counter-subversion in early Cold War Britain: The official Committee on Communism (Home), the Information Research Department, and "state-private networks"' *Intelligence and National Security*, 30 (5), 637–666.

Maher, S. and M. Frampton (2009), *Choosing Our Friends Wisely: Criteria for Engagement with Muslim Groups*, London: Policy Exchange.

Maniglier, P. (2012), 'What is a problematic?' *Radical Philosophy*, May/June [online]. Available at: www.radicalphilosophy.com/wp-content/files_mf/rp173_article2_maniglier_whatisaproblematic.pdf (accessed on 26 January 2016).

Martin, T. (2018), 'Identifying potential terrorists: Visuality, security and the Channel project' *Security Dialogue*, 49 (4), 254–271.

Massumi, B. (2007), 'Potential politics and the primacy of preemption' *Theory & Event*, 10 (2) [online]. Available at: http://muse.jhu.edu/journals/theory_and_event/v010/10.2massumi.html (accessed on 26 January 2016).

Massumi, B. (2013), 'The remains of the day' in *On Violence Volume 1: 2013–14*, 13–49.

May, T. (2014), *Theresa May: Speech to Conservative Party Conference 2014*, 30 September [online]. Available at: http://press.conservatives.com/post/98799073410/theresa-may-speech-to-conservative-party (accessed on 30 October 2014).

May, T. (2015), *Home Secretary Speech at Summit on Countering Extremism*, 19 February [online]. Available at: www.gov.uk/government/speeches/white-house-summit-on-countering-violent-extremism (accessed on 16 September 2016).

McCulloch, J. and S. Pickering (2009), 'Pre-crime and counter-terrorism' *The British Journal of Criminology*, 49 (5), 628–645.

McGhee, D. (2003), 'Moving to "our" common ground: A critical examination of community cohesion discourse in twenty-first century Britain' *The Sociological Review*, 51 (3), 376–404.

McGhee, D. (2008), *The End of Multiculturalism? Terrorism, Integration and Human Rights*, Glasgow: Oxford University Press.

McGlynn, C. and S. McDaid (2016), 'Radicalisation and higher education: Students' understanding and experiences' *Terrorism and Political Violence*, DOI: 10.1080/09546553.2016.1258637

Meer, N. and T. Modood (2009), 'The multicultural state we're in: Muslims, "multiculture" and the "civic re-balancing of British multiculturalism"' *Political Studies*, 57, 473–497.

MHCLG (Ministry of Housing, Communities and Local Government) (2018), *Integrated Communities Strategy Green Paper: Building Stronger, More United Communities* [online]. Available at: https://assets.publishing.service.gov.uk/government/uploads/system/uploads/attachment_data/file/696993/Integrated_Communities_Strategy.pdf (accessed on 28 May 2018).

Miah, S. (2017a), 'The Muslim problematic: Muslims, state schools and security' *International Studies in Sociology of Education*, 26 (2), 138–150.

Miah, S. (2017b), *Muslims, Schooling and Security: Trojan Horse, Prevent and Racial Politics*, London: Palgrave Macmillan.

Miller, D. and R. Sabir (2012), 'Counter-terrorism as counterinsurgency in the UK "war on terror"' in S. Poynting and D. Whyte (eds), *Counter-Terrorism and State Political Violence: The 'War on Terror' as Terror*, Abingdon: Routledge, 12–32.

Modood, T. (2010), 'Multicultural citizenship and Muslim identity politics' *Interventions: International Journal of Postcolonial Studies*, 12 (2), 157–170.

Morgan, N. (2014), *Oral Statement by Nicky Morgan on the 'Trojan Horse' Letter*, 22 July [online]. Available at: www.gov.uk/government/speeches/oral-statement-by-nicky-morgan-on-the-trojan-horse-letter (accessed on 25 January 2016).

Mouffe, C. (2000), 'Deliberative democracy or agonistic pluralism' *Political Science Series*, 72 [online]. Available at: www.ihs.ac.at/publications/pol/pw_72.pdf (accessed on 13 June 2016).

Mythen, G., S. Walklate and F. Khan (2009), '"I'm a Muslim. But I'm not a terrorist": Victimization, risky identities and the performance of safety' *The British Journal of Criminology*, 49 (6), 736–754.

Mythen, G., S. Walklate and F. Khan (2012), '"Why should we have to prove we're alright?": Counter-terrorism, risk and partial securities' *Sociology*, 47 (2), 383–398.

National Commission on Terrorist Attacks Upon the United States (2004), *The 9/11 Commission Report* [online]. Available at: www.9–11commission.gov/report/911Report.pdf (accessed on 28 May 2013).

Neocleous, M. (2011), '"A brighter and nicer new life": Security as pacification' *Social & Legal Studies*, 20 (2), 191–208.

NHS England (2017), *Guidance for Mental Health Services in Exercising Duties to Safeguard People from the Risk of Radicalisation* [online]. Available at: www.england.nhs.uk/wp-content/uploads/2017/11/prevent-mental-health-guidance.pdf (accessed on 28 May 2018).

NPCC (National Police Chief's Council) (n.d.), *National Channel Referral Figures* [online]. Available at: www.npcc.police.uk/FreedomofInformation/NationalChannelReferralFigures.aspx (accessed on 27 January 2016).

O'Donnell, A. (2016), 'Securitisation, counterterrorism and the silencing of dissent: The educational implications of Prevent' *British Journal of Educational Studies*, 64 (1), 53–76.

Ofsted (Office for Standards in Education, Children's Services and Skills) (n.d.), *Ofsted Reports Database* [online]. Available at: http://reports.ofsted.gov.uk/ (accessed on 28 January 2016).

Ofsted (Office for Standards in Education, Children's Services and Skills) (2015), *School Inspection Handbook: Handbook For Inspecting Schools in England Under Section 5 of the Education Act 2005* [online]. Available at: www.gov.uk/government/uploads/system/uploads/attachment_data/file/458866/School_inspection_handbook_section_5_from_September_2015.pdf (accessed on 27 January 2016).

Oldham Independent Review Panel (2001), *Oldham Independent Review: One Oldham One Future* (chaired by David Ritchie) [online]. Available at: http://resources.cohesioninstitute.org.uk/Publications/Documents/Document/DownloadDocumentsFile.aspx?recordId=97&file=PDFversion (accessed on 26 January 2016).

Omand, D. (2009), *The National Security Strategy: Implications for the UK Intelligence Community*, Institute for Public Policy Research [online]. Available at: www.ippr.org/files/images/media/files/publication/2011/05/National%20Security%20Strategy_1675.pdf?noredirect=1 (accessed on 3 July 2016).

Omand, D. (2010), *Securing the State*, London: Hurst & Company.

O'Toole, T., N. Meer, D. Nilsson DeHanas, S. H. Jones, and T. Modood (2016), 'Governing through Prevent? Regulation and contested practice in state-Muslim engagement' *Sociology*, 50 (1), 160–177.

Pantazis, C. and S. Pemberton (2009), 'From the "old" to the "new" suspect community: Examining the impacts of recent UK counter-terrorist legislation' *British Journal of Criminology*, 49 (5), 646–666.

Pantucci, R. (2010), 'A contest to democracy? How the UK has responded to the current terrorist threat' *Democratization*, 17 (2), 251–271.

Pickles, E. and T. Ahmad (2015), *Letter to British Mosques* [online]. Available at: www.gov.uk/government/uploads/system/uploads/attachment_data/file/396312/160115_Final_Draft_Letter_to_Mosques_PDF.pdf (accessed on 27 January 2016).

Pisoiu, D. (2013), 'Coming to believe "truths" about Islamist radicalization in Europe' *Terrorism and Political Violence*, 25 (2), 246–263.

Putnam, R. D. (1995), 'Bowling alone: America's declining social capital' *Journal of Democracy*, 6 (1), 65–78.

Ragazzi, F. (2017), 'Countering terrorism and radicalisation: Securitising social policy?' *Critical Social Policy*, 37 (2), 163–179.

Ramesh, R. and J. Halliday (2015), 'Student accused of being a terrorist for reading book on terrorism', *Guardian*, 24 September [online]. Available at: www.theguardian.com/education/2015/sep/24/student-accused-being-terrorist-reading-book-terrorism (accessed on 19 September 2016).

Richards, A. (2011), 'The problem with "radicalization": The remit of "Prevent" and the need to refocus on terrorism in the UK' *International Affairs*, 87 (1), 143–152.

Rizq, R. (2017), '"Pre-crime", Prevent, and the practices of exceptionalism: Psychotherapy and the new norm in the NHS' *Psychodynamic Practice*, 23 (4), 336–356.

Roy, O. (2004), *Globalized Islam: The Search for a New Ummah*, New York: Columbia University Press.

Royal College of Psychiatrists (2016), *Counter-Terrorism and Psychiatry* [online]. Available at: www.rcpsych.ac.uk/pdf/PS04_16.pdf (accessed 9 February 2018).

Saeed, T. and D. Johnson (2016), 'Intelligence, global terrorism and higher education: Neutralising threats or alienating allies?' *British Journal of Educational Studies*, 64, 37–51.

Sabir, R. (2017), 'Blurred lines and false dichotomies: Integrating counter-insurgency into the UK's domestic "war on terror"' *Critical Social Policy*, 37 (2), 202–224.

Sageman, M. (2004), *Understanding Terror Networks*, Philadelphia: University of Pennsylvania Press.

Sageman, M. (2008), *Leaderless Jihad: Terror Networks in the Twenty-First Century*, Philadelphia: University of Pennsylvania Press.

Schmid, A. P. (2013), *Radicalisation, De-Radicalisation, Counter-Radicalisation: A Conceptual Discussion and Literature Review*, The Hague: International Centre for Counter-Terrorism.

Sedgwick, M. (2010), 'The concept of radicalization as a source of confusion' *Terrorism and Political Violence*, 22 (4), 479–494.

Silva, D. M. D. (2018), '"Radicalisation: The journey of a concept", revisited' *Race & Class*, 59 (4), 34–53.

Smith, J. (2009), *Jacqui Smith speaks to the Smith Institute* [online]. Available at: www2.labour.org.uk/home_secretary_jacqui_smiths_speech_to_the_smith (accessed on 29 September 2014).

Sobolewska, M. (2010), 'Religious extremism in Britain and British Muslims: Threatened citizenship and the role of religion' in R. Eatwell and

M. Goodwin (eds), *The 'New' Extremism in Twenty-First-Century Britain*, Abingdon: Routledge, 23–46.

Spalek, B. and R. Lambert (2008), 'Muslim communities, counter-terrorism and counter-radicalisation: A critically reflective approach to engagement' *International Journal of Law, Crime and Justice*, 36, 257–270.

Spalek, B., S. El Awa and L. McDonald (2008), *Police-Muslim Engagement and Partnerships for the Purposes of Counter-Terrorism: An Examination*, Summary Report [online]. Available at: www.religionandsociety.org.uk/uploads/docs/2009_11/1258555474_Spalek_Summary_Report_2008.pdf (accessed on 27 January 2016).

Stanley, T. and S. Guru (2015), 'Childhood radicalisation risk: An emerging practice issue' *Practice*, 27(5), 353–366.

Stanley, T., S. Guru and V. Coppock (2017), 'A risky time for Muslim families: Professionalised counter-radicalisation networks' *Journal of Social Work Practice,* 31 (4), 477–490.

Stevens, D. (2009), 'In extremis: A self-defeating element in the "Preventing Violent Extremism" strategy' *The Political Quarterly*, 80 (4), 517–525.

Taylor, C. (1994), 'The politics of recognition' in A. Gutmann (ed.), *Multiculturalism: Examining the Politics of Recognition*, Princeton: Princeton University Press, 25–74.

Thomas, P. (2009), 'Between two stools? The government's "Preventing Violent Extremism" agenda' *The Political Quarterly*, 80 (2), 282–291.

Thomas, P. (2010), 'Failed and friendless: The UK's "Preventing Violent Extremism" programme' *The British Journal of Politics and International Relations*, 12, 442–458.

Thomas, P. (2012), *Responding to the Threat of Violent Extremism: Failing to Prevent*, London and New York: Bloomsbury Academic.

Thomas, P. (2014), 'Divorced but still co-habiting? Britain's Prevent/community cohesion policy tension' *British Politics*, 9 (4), 472–493.

Thomas, P. (2017), 'Changing experiences of responsibilisation and contestation within counter-terrorism policies: The British Prevent experience' *Policy & Politics*, 45 (3), 305–321.

van Munster, R. and C. Sylvest (2014), 'Reclaiming nuclear politics? Nuclear realism, the H-bomb and globality' *Security Dialogue*, 45 (6), 530–547.

Veyne, Paul (1997), 'Foucault revolutionizes history' in A. I. Davidson (ed.), *Foucault and His Interlocutors*, Chicago and London: University of Chicago Press, 146–182.

Walker, R. B. J. (1993), *Inside/Outside: International Relation as Political Theory*, Cambridge: Cambridge University Press.

Warner, M. (2002), *Publics and Counterpublics*, New York: Zone Books.

Werbner, P. (2005), 'The translocation of culture: "Community cohesion" and the force of multiculturalism in history' *The Sociological Review*, 53 (4), 745–768.

Wiktorowicz, Q. (2005), *Radical Islam Rising: Muslim Extremism in the West*, Lanham, Boulder, Toronto and Oxford: Rowman & Littlefield.

Wilshaw, M. (2014), *Advice Note from Sir Michael Wilshaw, Her Majesty's Chief Inspector, to the Secretary of State for Education*, 14 October [online] Available at: www.gov.uk/government/uploads/system/uploads/attachment_data/file/ 379544/Advice_20note_20on_20the_20first_20monitoring_20visits_20to_ 20academies_20and_20maintained_20schools_20subject_20to_20special_ 20measures_20in_20Birmingham.pdf (accessed on 25 January 2016).

Wintour, P. (2013), 'Cameron vows to "drain the swamp" creating Islamic extremism', *Guardian*, 3 June [online]. Available at: www.theguardian.com/ politics/2013/jun/03/cameron-recommendations-islamic-extremism (accessed on 27 January 2016).

Wintour, P. (2015), 'Muslim Council of Britain objects to Pickles letter to Islamic leaders', *Guardian*, 19 January [online]. Available at: www.theguardian.com/ politics/2015/jan/19/uk-muslim-council-objections-eric-pickles-letter (accessed on 27 January 2016).

Zedner, L. (2007), 'Pre-crime and post-criminology?' *Theoretical Criminology*, 11 (2), 261–281.

Index

Lightning Source UK Ltd.
Milton Keynes UK
UKHW021353091121
393671UK00012B/138